The [illegible] Hostel Guide 2005

Britain and Europe

Edited by Sam Dalley

The Backpackers Press

ISBN 0-9536185-4-4

The Independent Hostel Guide 2005: Britain and Europe

14th Edition

Editor : Sam Dalley
Assistant Editor: June Dalley
Colour Editor: Bob Oldfield

British Library Cataloguing in Publication Data
A Catalogue record for this book is available from the British Library ISBN 0-9536185-4-4

Published by: The Backpackers Press, Speedwell House, Upperwood, Matlock Bath, Derbyshire, DE4 3PE
Tel/Fax: +44 (0) 1629 580427
Email: Sam@BackpackersPress.com

Printed by: Pindar, Preston (01772) 620999
Cover Artwork : mulberry square ltd (01509) 416544
Maps : Contour Design, (01629) 825435

Distributed in the UK by:-
Cordee Books and Maps, 3a De Montfort Street. Leicester, LE1 7HD, Tel: (0116) 2543579

Distributed overseas by:-
Faradawn, South Africa, Tel: 11 885 1847
Wilderness Press, USA, Tel: 510 558 1696
Global Exchange, Australia and New Zealand, Tel: (02) 4929 4688

CONTENTS

This Guide printed on V-Star Silk manufactured from 100% recycled materials

Thanks to all the Hostels who provided photographs for the cover

BACKPACKERS PRESS PUBLICATIONS BY MAIL ORDER

The Backpackers Press,
Speedwell House, Upperwood,
Matlock Bath, Derbyshire, DE4 3PE, UK
Tel/Fax +44 (0) 1629 580427

Sam@BackpackersPress.com

Book	Price	No	Total cost
The Independent Hostel Guide, 2005	£4.95		
The Independent Hostel Guide, 2006 (available Jan 2006)	£4.95		
UK Postage and Packing	£1 first book + 50p for each extra book		
Overseas Postage and Packing	£2 first book + £1 for each extra book		
Total			

Please send the above order to :

I enclose a UK cheque, payable to the Backpackers Press.
OR
Please charge my Mastercard/Visa account (we cannot accept Visa Credit, Visa Electron or Switch) the sum of :- ________

The credit card statement address is the same as that given above and the credit card number is :- ________________

Expiry date ________ Name on card ________________

Signature ________________ Date ________________

ABOUT THIS BOOK

The IHG was first produced in 1985 by Sam Dalley and has been updated annually ever since. At the time of the first edition the number of Independent Hostels was much less than nowadays and most people were unaware of their existence. Sam recognised the need of owners and customers for a publication pulling them together. The very first edition was just a hand stapled print-out of 18 hostels. It has steadily grown and nowadays it is widely regarded as the ultimate reference guide to Independent Hostels in Britain. Recent additions include less extensive sections on Ireland and Continental Europe. The entries in the guide are now routinely entered in the website:

www.IndependentHostelGuide.co.uk

INDEPENDENT HOSTELS

Many of the places in this guide are in wild and beautiful areas and are ideal for those pursuing outdoor activities; others are in towns and cities and are intended for international backpackers; and some fall between the two categories. All the accommodation has shared common areas and most have cooking facilities, some offer private rooms and family apartments, while others may have only dormitories. No membership is required, all the hostels being run by independent individuals. All offer friendly, comfortable and clean accommodation at prices that are hard to beat.

The editors welcome any feedback on the hostels you stay in, as well as information about places that you think should be in next year's edition. We will send a free book in return for useful contributions.

SYMBOLS

Mixed dormitories

Single sex dormitories

Private rooms

Blankets or duvets provided

Sheets required - can be hired

Sheets required

Sleeping bags required

Sleeping bags required - can be hired

Hostel fully heated (including common room)

Common room only heated

Drying room available

Hot water available

Showers available

Cooking facilities available

Shop at hostel

Meals provided at hostel (with notice)

Breakfast only at hostel (with notice)

Meals available locally

Clothes washing facilities available

Public telephone

Facilities for less-able people.

Internet facilities

Nomads Membership Discount of 10%

1m Within 1 mile of a Sustrans cycle route

3m Within 3 miles of a Sustrans cycle route

5m Within 5 miles of a Sustrans cycle route

ABBREVIATIONS

pp	per person
GR	Ordnance Survey grid reference
€	Euros
£	Pounds Sterling
CHF	Swiss Francs
US$	United States Dollars, C$ Canadian Dollars
NOK	Norwegian Kroner

HOSTEL ASSOCIATIONS

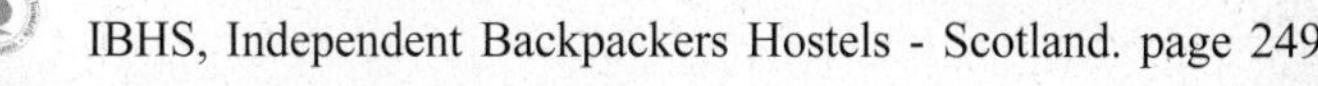

IBHS, Independent Backpackers Hostels - Scotland. page 249

Hostels of Wales. page 173

ABO, Association of Bunkhouse Operators. page 135

IHO, Independent Hostel Owners - Ireland. page 292

IHH, Independent Holiday Hostels Ireland.

Swiss Backpackers.

Gomio

Independently owned hostel affiliated to YHA, page 69

TELEPHONE CODES

Continental Europe:- phone and fax numbers are given with the international code included. **Republic of Ireland:-** phone and fax numbers are given with the local dialling code. To phone from overseas remove the first 0 and replace with +353. **UK :-** phone and fax numbers are given with the local dialling code. To phone from overseas remove the first 0 and replace with +44.

Liverpool
78, 79
80
Manchester
77
Shrewsbury
61
WALES
60
Cheltenham
38
Bristol
39
Minehead
29
30
31
32
37
Bude
22
28
Exeter
26
25
24
27
Newquay
18-21
23
Plymouth
14
13
12
17
Penzance
15,16
0 miles 50
0 kilometres 80

KEY

45 – Hostel page number

45 – Page number of group only accomodation

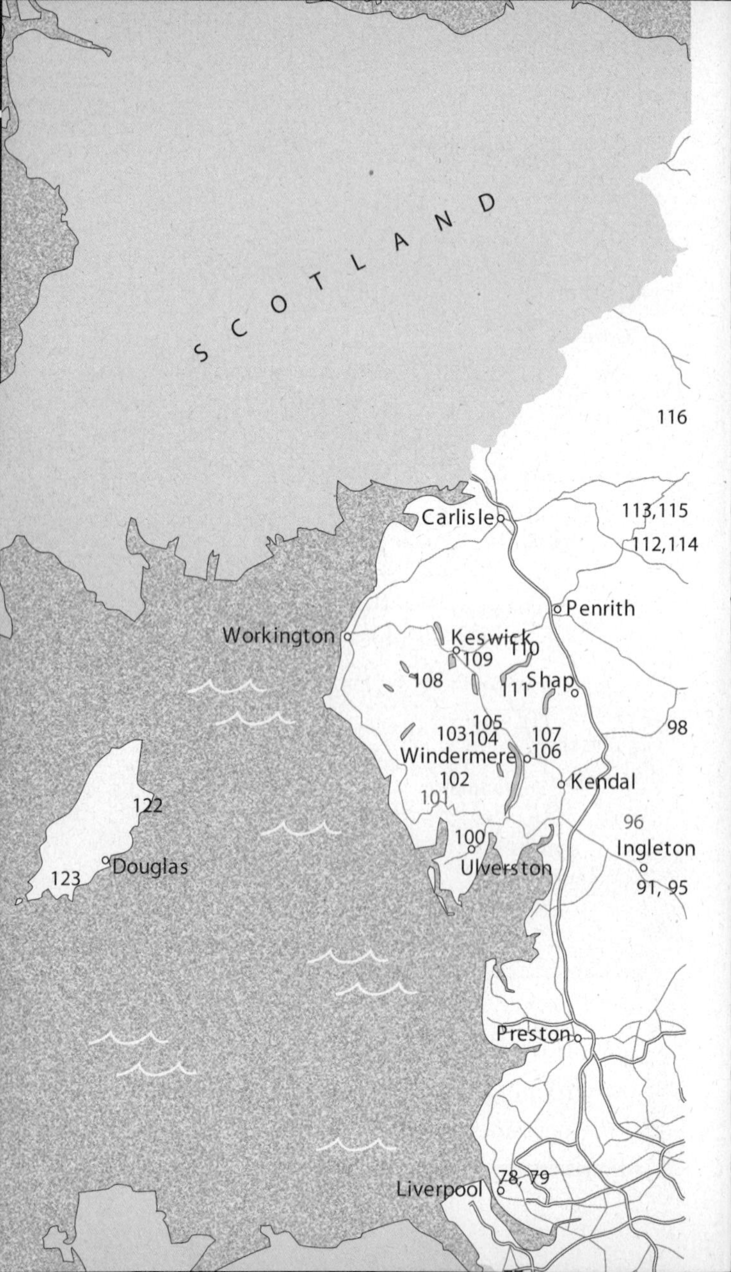

SCOTLAND

116

Carlisle

113,115

112,114

Penrith

Workington

Keswick

110

109

108

111

Shap

105

103

104

107

98

Windermere

106

102

Kendal

101

122

100

96

Ingleton

Douglas

Ulverston

123

91, 95

Preston

78, 79

Liverpool

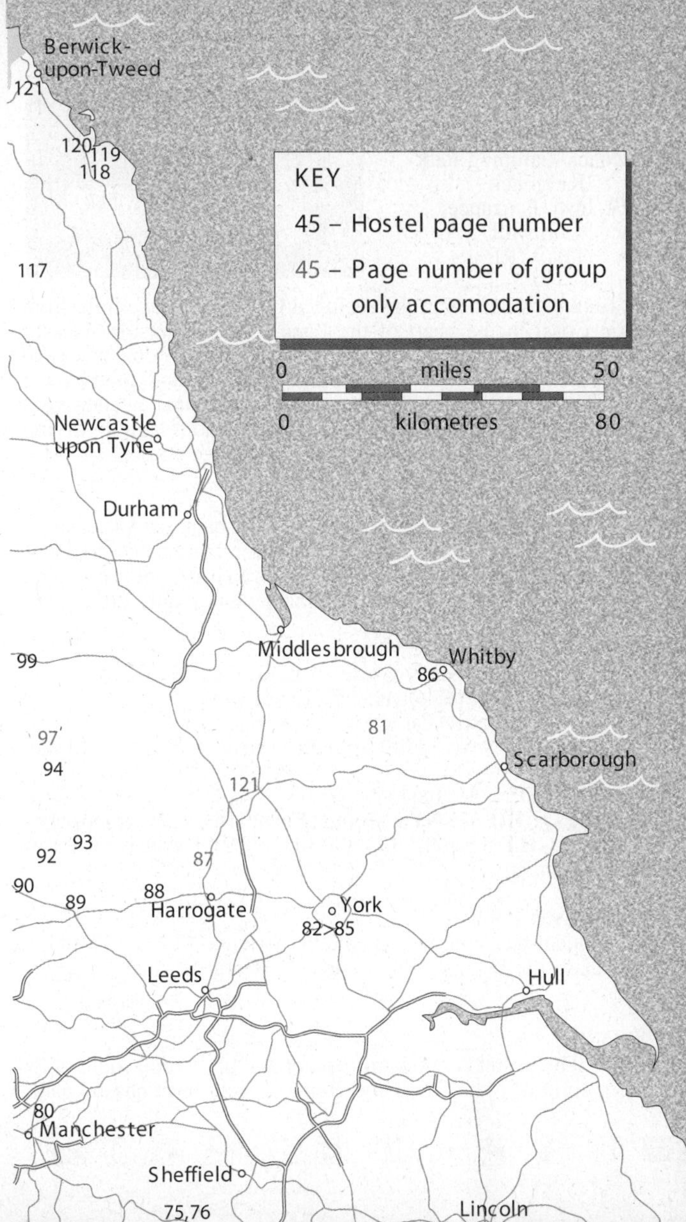

Berwick-upon-Tweed
121
120
119
118
117
KEY
45 – Hostel page number
45 – Page number of group only accomodation
0 miles 50
0 kilometres 80
Newcastle upon Tyne
Durham
Middlesbrough
Whitby
86
99
81
97
94
Scarborough
121
93
92
87
90
88
89
Harrogate
York
82>85
Leeds
Hull
80
Manchester
Sheffield
75,76
73,75
Lincoln

KELYNACK BUNKBARN

Kelynack Camping Park
Kelynack
St Just Penzance
Cornwall
TR19 7RE

Kelynack Bunkbarn nestles in the secluded Cot Valley, one mile from the Atlantic Coast in the heart of the Land's End Peninsula Area of Outstanding Natural Beauty. The Barn has one twin room, one two-bedded and one four-bedded bunkroom. Blankets and pillows are provided. There is a toilet/shower room and communal kitchen with full cooking facilities. Adjacent is the bike store and a laundry/drying room shared with the campers on site. We also have a small shop for essentials.

St Just, a mile away has plenty of food shops, some banks and a selection of pubs and take-aways. Kelynack is ideal for coast and moorland walking, spending time on the beaches, birdwatching, rock climbing and exploring the ancient villages, standing stones and tin mining heritage of unspoilt West Penwith.

CONTACT Francis or Wendy Grose. Tel: (01736) 787633
E-mail: Francis&Wendy@kelynackholidays.co.uk
OPENING SEASON All year
OPENING HOURS Arrive after 2pm and vacate by 10am. All day access during stay.
NUMBER OF BEDS 8: 1 x 4 : 2 x 2.
BOOKING REQUIREMENTS Booking is advised (25% deposit).
PRICE PER NIGHT £8 adult, £4 child (under 12). Exclusive use £50 per night. No meters.

PUBLIC TRANSPORT
There is a frequent bus from Penzance Rail Station to St Just. Hostel is one mile south of St Just. Free transport from St Just by prior arrangement.

DIRECTIONS
GR 373 301. The hostel is 200 yards east of B3306, 1 mile south of St Just, 5 miles north of Land's End and 20 mins' walk from coastal path.

THE OLD CHAPEL BACKPACKERS/CAFE

Zennor
St Ives
Cornwall
TR26 3BY

Zennor is a small picturesque village situated between St Ives and Land's End and is a haven for walkers, bird watchers and anyone who wants a taste of the rural way of life or just simply to relax! The hostel is located very close to the pub and St Ives is nearby for shopping, clubbing, cinemas, restaurants and some of the finest beaches in Cornwall.

The Old Chapel Backpackers has been converted to a very high standard and is perfectly situated for clear views over the sea and moorland. We have four rooms that sleep six people, one room that sleeps four and a family room with double bed. There are washbasins in every room and the hostel is centrally heated throughout. We can offer self-catering and we can provide breakfast, packed lunches and evening meals if required. There is also a café on the premises serving delicious soup, rolls and cakes.

CONTACT Paul or Hetty, Tel: (01736) 798307, Email: zennorbackpackers@btinternet.com
OPENING SEASON All year, winter by prior arrangement.
OPENING HOURS All day
NUMBER OF BEDS 32: 4 x 6 : 1 x 4 : 1 x family room
BOOKING REQUIREMENTS Booking is advisable, 20% deposit.
PRICE PER NIGHT from £10 per person all year

PUBLIC TRANSPORT
There are train stations at St Ives (4 miles) and Penzance (10 miles). Local buses run to/from St Ives every few hours. The taxi fare from St Ives is approximately £5.

DIRECTIONS
Approximately 4 miles from St Ives on Coastal Road heading towards Land's End.

ST IVES BACKPACKERS

Town Centre
St Ives
Cornwall
TR26 1SG

St Ives is the jewel in the crown of the beautiful Cornish Riviera, famous for its artistic community, Tate Gallery, picturesque town, harbour, surf beaches and bay. An ideal location for relaxing, surfing (5 minutes' walk to Porthmeor Beach), climbing, scuba diving, walking the coast path, fishing, great restaurants, shopping or just relaxing in a quaint Cornish seaside town.

St Ives Backpackers was originally a Wesleyan Chapel School built in 1845. The building is based around a central courtyard - ideal for barbecues and socialising. Clean and comfortable surroundings, friendly and informal atmosphere, E-mail and internet facilities. Discounts for local cafes, restaurants and nightclubs. NO CURFEW!!!. Fully equipped kitchen. Bedding included. Surfboard/ wetsuit storage. Regular barbecues. Pool table and football table

www.backpackers.co.uk

CONTACT Reception, Tel: (01636) 799444,
Email: st.ives@backpackers.co.uk
OPENING SEASON All Year
OPENING HOURS 24 Hours
NUMBER OF BEDS 67: 8 x 3, 6 x 3, 5 x 1, 3 x 4, 2 x twin, 2 x double.
BOOKING REQUIREMENTS Advisable, groups require deposit.
PRICE PER NIGHT Sept to April £10.95, May £11.95, June £12.95, July and August £16.95. Extra charges bank holidays/special events.

PUBLIC TRANSPORT
Tour bus: Roadtrip, Bus: National Express, Train: Mon - Sun 12 per day (change at St. Erth). Five minutes' walk from bus and train stations.

DIRECTIONS
Car: Signposted off the A30.

P AM

PENZANCE BACKPACKERS

The Blue Dolphin
Alexandra Road
Penzance TR18 4LZ

Penzance, with its mild climate, its wonderful location looking across to spectacular St Michael's Mount, with all the coach and rail services terminating here, is the ideal base for exploring the far SW of England and the Scilly Isles. Whether you are looking for sandy beaches and sheltered coves; the storm lashed cliffs of Land's End; sub-tropical gardens; internationally acclaimed artists; the remains of ancient cultures; or simply somewhere to relax and take time out, Penzance Backpackers is for you.

We are situated in a lovely tree-lined road close to the sea front, with the town centre, bus station and railway station only a short walk away. Accommodation is mostly in small bunk-bedded rooms with bed-linen, a fully equipped self-catering kitchen, hot showers, comfortable lounge, lots of local information and a warm welcome all included in the price.

www.pzbackpack.com

CONTACT Tel: (01736) 363836. Email: info@pzbackpack.com
OPENING SEASON Open all year
OPENING HOURS 24 hours
NUMBER OF BEDS 33: 2x1 double : 1x1double + 2bunks : 3x6 : 1x7.
BOOKING REQUIREMENTS It's best to phone.
PRICE PER NIGHT From £13 per person. Discount for long stays.

PUBLIC TRANSPORT
Penzance has a train station and National Express service. 15 mins' walk from train/bus station or catch buses 1, 1a, 5a or 6a from Tourist Information/bus/train station. Ask for top of Alexandra Road.

DIRECTIONS
From Tourist Information/bus/train station follow Quay and Promenade to mini-roundabout, turn right up Alexandra Rd, we are a short way up on left; or follow main road through town centre until second mini-roundabout, turn left, Alexandra Rd; we are on the right.

Y M C A CORNWALL (PENZANCE)

International House
The Orchard
Alverton
Penzance
TR18 4TE

West Cornwall is famous for its rugged coastlines, secret coves and long sandy beaches. It offers the chance to relax and unwind, to surf, rock climb, walk, deep sea dive, fish, horse ride and to visit galleries, small harbours and villages. There are many attractions such as the famous Minack open air theatre.

The YMCA is more than just a hostel, we offer sporting facilities as well as an internet café. Our facilities provide the ideal location for school/youth groups of any size, for short weekends or for longer holidays. Sports and conference facilities also available. The YMCA has been serving the community of Penwith since 1893, providing an ideal base for you to discover all the area has to offer.

CONTACT David Smith. Tel: (01736) 365016
Email: Admin@cornwall.ymca.org.uk
OPENING SEASON All Year
OPENING HOURS 8am to 10pm (except by prior arrangement)
NUMBER OF BEDS 51: 3 x 5, 9 x 4
BOOKING REQUIREMENTS, booking not essential but advisable in Summer
PRICE PER NIGHT £13 until 24.03.05 then £14.50, 25.3.05 to 27.09.05
Discount for parties of 15 plus. 10% discount for students.

PUBLIC TRANSPORT
Penzance Train Station 10 min walk. Penzance Bus Station bus service numbers 1A and 1B. Taxi from Penzance centre approx £3.

DIRECTIONS
From the train/bus station, turn left towards the centre of town onto Market Jew Street. Turn left and follow Market Jew Street until it becomes Alverton Road, go straight over the roundabout until you see our sign on the left.

FALMOUTH LODGE BACKPACKERS

9 Gyllyngvase Terrace
Falmouth
Cornwall TR11 4DL

Falmouth's beautiful natural harbour, provides a picturesque background to the main street of charming shops, restaurants, cafés and pubs; good opportunity to sample Cornish cream teas, pasties, local seafood and real ales. Falmouth is renowned for its sandy beaches, Pendennis Castle, exotic gardens, the Falmouth Arts Centre and the Princess Pavilion. Go sightseeing on passenger ferries to St. Mawes, Truro, Flushing and the Helford Passage. On a rainy day visit Ships and Castle leisure pool and the new National Maritime Museum. Take advantage of watersports, fishing trips, sailing, diving, with tuition and equipment hire. Falmouth Lodge Backpackers is conveniently situated next to Princess Pavilion, 100 metres from main beach, coastal footpath and minutes to town, harbour and castle. Relax in a friendly, clean, homely, smoke free atmosphere. Owner managed, by experienced world traveller. Guests have use of well-equipped kitchen, dining room and TV lounge; games, bikes, frisbee, boogie board and stunt kite.

www.falmouthbackpackers.co.uk

CONTACT Charlotte. Tel: (01326) 319996. mobile 07754 438572
Email : charlotte@mitchell999.fsworld.co.uk
OPENING SEASON All year
OPENING HOURS 7am - 12pm and 4pm - 10pm
NUMBER OF BEDS 18: 1 x 2 : 1 x 3 : 2 x 4 : 1 x 5 (some seaviews)
BOOKING REQUIREMENTS Telephone or email in advance.
PRICE PER NIGHT from £14.00pp

PUBLIC TRANSPORT
Train, change Truro for Falmouth station 250 mtrs. Bus, N.Express, "the Moor" Falmouth. Air, London Stansted/Gatwick to Newquay.

DIRECTIONS
By car From M5, A30 over Bodmin Moor to Truro, A39 to Falmouth stay on A39 until Gyllyngvase Road on right, then left into Gyllyngvase Terrace.

P H AM 5m

THE ORIGINAL BACKPACKERS NEWQUAY

Towan Beach, Beachfield Ave
Newquay
Cornwall, TR7 1DR

Overlooking one of Newquay's finest beaches, we offer low cost accommodation in the heart of town for international travellers and surfers. We offer mainly dorm style accommodation, however one twin room is available.

Other facilities include a self-catering kitchen, next to which is a common room, we have hot showers and board/bike storage. There is no curfew just come and go as you please. Being centrally based The Original Backpackers is ideally located for the beaches, the town's many pubs, clubs and other amenities. A relaxed atmosphere is guaranteed.

www.originalbackpackers.co.uk

CONTACT Manager Tel: (01637) 874668.
Email originalbp@hotmail.com
OPENING SEASON All year
OPENING HOURS 24 hours
NUMBER OF BEDS 30: 4 x 6 : 1 x 4 : 1 x 2
BOOKING REQUIREMENTS Booking is recommended for both groups and individual travellers, although individual spaces may be available on arrival.
PRICE PER NIGHT On production of this guide:- off peak £6pp, peak times £12pp.

PUBLIC TRANSPORT
Newquay has a train station and is served by National Express and an airport.

DIRECTIONS
If driving, head towards Fistral Beach, turn right at Tower Garages. Follow this road following outbound traffic, take the second left, signposted Beachfield Ave & The Crescent. Pass in front of The Central, turn right, Beachfield Ave is at the bottom of this road, the hostel is on the right.

1m

MATTS SURF LODGE

110 Mount Wise
Newquay, Cornwall
TR7 1QP

Newquay is about having fun - and the fun starts here! The Lodge has been open for eight years and still offers the same easygoing relaxed atmosphere that has given us our reputation. Newquay is an all year round mecca for surfers, students and travellers, with dramatic cliffs, idyllic beaches and attractions galore. We are situated at the highest point of the town, only five minutes' walk from Central Square with its nightlife and shops. Fistral Beach and the Town beaches are all within ten minutes' walk.

All our rooms are clean and comfortable, many with seaview or ensuite facilities. Our rates include breakfast, tea/coffee all day and unlimited hot showers. There is a fully equipped kitchen and no curfews. Our licensed bar has good music and over 100 videos to choose from, plus a games room with library, games and pool table.

www.surflodge.co.uk

CONTACT Matt, Tel: (01637) 874651
OPENING SEASON All year
OPENING HOURS 24
NUMBER OF BEDS 49: 4 x 6 : 3 x 4 : 1 x 3 : 5 x twin/double
BOOKING REQUIREMENTS Recommended for weekends and peak season, but not essential. First night's fee required as deposit.
PRICE PER NIGHT £8 (£10 for en-suite seaview) £15/£20 July/ August & Bank Holidays. From £45per week mid-season, and from £35 per week during low season.

PUBLIC TRANSPORT
Local train station and bus station. Free pickup when available.

DIRECTIONS
Walking: From train station, turn left onto High St, walk for 2 mins to coach station. Opposite coach station is Tourist Info on Marcus Hill, at the top of this hill is Mount Wise. We are 5 mins' walk on right hand side. **Driving:** A30, Newquay exit, follow Newquay (Porth) signs. After Train Station turn left at lights, leads onto Mount Wise.

P AM 1m

THE ZONE

Fistral Beach
Newquay
Cornwall
TR7 1HN

The Zone Backpackers Hotel and Hostel is one of the South West's largest hostels. It has rooms with sea views and many have their own TV. Double en-suite, twin rooms and multi-bed dorms available. There is a fully licensed public bar, music and games rooms. The hostel overlooks the famous Fistral Beach where the World Surfing Championship is held every year. We have a secure watersport storage area with shower at the front of the building.

The Zone provides budget accommodation with breakfast for surfers and international travellers. Open all year long, ideally located for work, rest and play. Seasonal café on site.

Take a look at the Zone's new website. Have a look at the weather today or the view using our groovy new Webcam. If you would like to book a room, just use the 'Contact' button.

www.backpackers.co.uk

CONTACT Reception, Tel: (01637) 872089,
Email: thezone@backpackers.co.uk
OPENING SEASON All Year
OPENING HOURS 24 Hours
NUMBER OF BEDS 100+
BOOKING REQUIREMENTS Advisable, groups require deposit.
PRICE PER NIGHT Sept to April £9.95, May £10.95, June £11.95, July and August £19.95. Extra charges bank holidays/special events.

PUBLIC TRANSPORT
Check out our website for details of planes, trains and buses. The hostel is five minutes' walk from Newquay train station and national buses.

DIRECTIONS
On the Fistral Beach sea front close to the centre of Newquay.

P AM

NEWQUAY BACKPACKERS

69-73 Tower Road
Newquay
Cornwall
TR7 1LX

Newquay Backpackers is at the heart of the European surfing capital, which is also England's fifth largest holiday resort and the night life capital of the South West. On the beautiful North Cornwall coast, Newquay also has the finest beaches and coastline in Europe.

Newquay Backpackers is for surfers and international travellers with the emphasis on meeting people and making new friends. It offers comfortable surroundings and a friendly informal atmosphere. The hostel has a fully equipped kitchen, vending machines, central heating, video lounge, hot showers, sauna and h&c in each room. Also storage facilities for surfboards and wetsuits and we provide a clothes wash/dry service and barbecues at the hostel.

The hostel is in the best area to enjoy Newquay's beaches and night life and there is no curfew!!! Brochure available on request.

www.backpackers.co.uk

CONTACT Reception, Tel: (01637) 879366, Email: newquay@backpackers.co.uk
OPENING SEASON All Year
OPENING HOURS 24 Hours
NUMBER OF BEDS 70: 3 x 6, 6 x 4, 2 x 3, 3 x twin, 2 x double
BOOKING REQUIREMENTS Advisable, groups require deposit.
PRICE PER NIGHT Sept-April £8.95, May £9.95, June £11.95 , July £15.95, August £15.95. Extra charges for bank holidays and special events.

PUBLIC TRANSPORT
Newquay train station/National coaches 5 minutes' walk from hostel.

DIRECTIONS
From Bristol M5 south to Exeter then the A30 south west. From the A30 take the A392 for Newquay then follow the Fistral Beach/Town Centre signs to Tower Road.

NORTHSHOREBUDE

57 Killerton Road
Bude
Cornwall
EX23 8EW

You can make your stay whatever you want it to be. A relaxed place with a variety of bedrooms, large garden, close to town, beaches and South West Coastal path. An ideal base to see the South West's attractions; The Eden Project, Tintagel Castle, The Tamar Lakes, Dartmoor, Bodmin Moor and South West Coastal Path.

There are competition standard surfing beaches nearby. Families with children aged over 5 welcome. Meet old friends or make new ones, on the deck, in the lounge or around the dining room table after cooking up a storm in the fully fitted kitchen.

www.northshorebude.com

CONTACT Sean or Janine. Tel: (01288) 354256 or 07970 149486
Email: info@northshorebude.com
OPENING SEASON All year except Christmas week
OPENING HOURS 8.30am to 2pm and 4.30pm to 10.30pm
NUMBER OF BEDS 43: 2x6 : 5x4 : 1x3 : 1x2 : 3xDbl
BOOKING REQUIREMENTS Advisable, credit card secures booking. Photo ID at check in.(Groups 6 or more by prior booking)
PRICE PER NIGHT from £12pp dorm rooms £17.50pp double rooms (£5 single supplement)

PUBLIC TRANSPORT
To Bude :From Exeter Via Okehampton X9, From Plymouth X8. From Newquay X10 (changing at Okehampton); From Bideford 85. All buses- First Bus Company. There are train and bus links from London to Exeter.

DIRECTIONS
From A39, head into Bude down Stratton Rd past Safeways on your right, follow the road down past Esso garage. Take the second road on the right, Killerton Road (before the Bencollen Pub). Continue up to the top of the road and "northshorebude" is on the corner on your left, turn into Redwood Grove and parking is the first on the left.

P 1m

GLOBE BACKPACKERS PLYMOUTH

172 Citadel Road
The Hoe, Plymouth
PL1 3BD

Globe Backpackers Plymouth is located just five minutes' walk from the ferry port, where boats leave for Roscoff and Santander. The hostel is close to all amenities and a short stroll to the famous Barbican waterfront, Mayflower Steps and city centre. Also near to the bus and railway stations. Excursions to Dartmoor, canoeing on the Tamar River, local boat trips, sailing and walking the coastal paths can be arranged from Plymouth. The theatre, sports/leisure centre, ice-skating rink and National Aquarium are a short walk from the hostel.

We have 4, 6 and 8 bedded dorms, plus 4 double rooms. Bedding and linen included in the price. Guests can enjoy a fully equipped self-catering kitchen, TV lounge, separate social room and courtyard garden.

CONTACT Tel: (01752) 225158, Fax: (01752) 207847,
Email: plymback@hotmail.com
OPENING SEASON All year
OPENING HOURS Reception open 8am-11pm only.No curfew once checked in
NUMBER OF BEDS 48
BOOKING REQUIREMENTS Phone ahead to secure booking
PRICE PER NIGHT From £12 pp. Weekly deals available

PUBLIC TRANSPORT
National Express, local bus companies and various rail networks.

DIRECTIONS
From train station walk up Salt Ash Road to North Croft roundabout. Turn right along Western Approach to Pavilions on your left. From bus station walk up Exeter Street, across roundabout to Royal Parade. Cross road to Union Street, Pavilions on your left. From Plymouth Pavilions walk towards the Hoe, turn left up Citadel Road, the hostel is in 100 metres on the right hand side.

P 1m

THE PLUME OF FEATHERS INN BUNKHOUSE

Princetown
Yelverton
Devon
PL20 6QQ

The Plume of Feathers Inn is situated in the moorland village of Princetown which is the main village in Dartmoor National Park. The park covers 368 square miles and is famous for its rugged beauty, quaint villages, prehistoric remains, and its many peaks, such as High Willhays (2039ft) and Yes Tor (2030ft).

The Plume is a traditional, family-run Inn dating from 1785, it has log fires, real ale and plenty of atmosphere. The Alpine bunkhouse and New bunkhouse provide comfortable low cost accommodation and the Inn also has B&B accommodation and a 75 tent camping area with toilets and showers. There is a wide range of activities available in the Dartmoor area including: sailing, fishing, riding, abseiling, white water canoeing, climbing, pony trekking and walking.

CONTACT Tel: (01822) 890240, Fax: (01822) 890780
OPENING SEASON All year
OPENING HOURS All day
NUMBER OF BEDS 46: 2 x 10 : 5 x 4 : 1 x 2 : 1 x 4
BOOKING REQUIREMENTS To secure beds, book in advance with 50% deposit. Booking three to four months in advance may be required for weekends.
PRICE PER NIGHT From £5.50 to £7 per person. Campsite from £4.50 per person per night.

PUBLIC TRANSPORT
Nearest train and National Express services are in Plymouth (17 miles) and Exeter (26 miles). The Transmoor Link bus service between Plymouth and Exeter stops at Princetown, bus fare is £4 - £5. Taxi fare from Plymouth approx £18, from Exeter approx £25.

DIRECTIONS
The Plume of Feathers Inn is in Princetown village square, next to the Dartmoor National Park, High Moorland Centre.

See page 210 for colour photo

DARTMOOR EXPEDITION CENTRE

Widecombe-in-the-Moor
Newton Abbot
Devon, TQ13 7TX

Great for walking, climbing, canoeing, caving, archaeology, painting or visiting places of interest nearby. Stay at the Dartmoor Expedition Centre in two 300-year-old barn bunkhouses with their cobbled floors and thick granite walls. Simple but comfortable accommodation with bunk beds and a wood burning stove. Convector heaters (one in each area) and night storage heating (one in each barn). Kitchen area equipped with fridge, gas water heater and electric stoves and kettles. All crockery and pans provided, and there is freezer space available. Electric appliances are coin operated (£1 coins). Improved hot water system for free showers in wash rooms.

The House Barn has the living area downstairs and upstairs sleeps 9 plus 5 in an inner cubicle. The Gate Barn sleeps 11 downstairs and 10 upstairs. There are two upgraded rooms (1 double, 1 twin). Beds are provided with fitted sheet/pillow/pillowcase, sleeping bags needed.

www.dartmoorbase.co.uk

CONTACT John Earle, (01364) 621249. E-mail: earle@clara.co.uk
OPENING SEASON All year
OPENING HOURS 7.30am to 10.30pm
NUMBER OF BEDS 37: 1 x 1 : 1 x 2 : 1 x 8 : 1 x 5 : 1 x 11 : 1 x 10
BOOKING REQUIREMENTS Book as far in advance as possible with 25% deposit.
PRICE PER NIGHT £9.00pp (£10.00 per person in private room).

PUBLIC TRANSPORT
Newton Abbot is the nearest train station. In summer there are buses to Widecombe (1½ miles from hostel). Taxi fare from station £20.

DIRECTIONS
GR 700 764. Come down Widecombe Hill into the village. Turn right 200yds after school and travel up a steep hill past Southcombe onto the open moor. Continue for one mile until you reach crossroads. Turn right and take first left after 400yds. Hostel is 200yds on left.

SPARROWHAWK BACKPACKERS

Vegetarian Hostel, 45 Ford Street
Moretonhampstead
Dartmoor
Devon, TQ13 8LN

This small, friendly, 'green' hostel is located within Dartmoor National Park, in the village of Moretonhampstead, 14 miles west of Exeter. Formerly a farm, visitors are accommodated in a beautifully converted stable. High open moorland is close by for great walking, climbing and cycling country. Magnificent Tors, stone circles and burial sites of ancient civilizations together with wild ponies, buzzards, flora and fauna are all here to be explored. There are year round guided talks and walks organised locally and by the National Park. Mortonhampstead village has a few shops, cafés, pubs, an outdoor heated swimming pool, and footpaths leading to the open moors. We are easily accessible by public transport, on the Dartmoor Way route, and CTC End to End. There is a secure place for your bikes. This hostel aims to be environmentally alert and has a dedicated policy of being vegetarian, recycling waste, and solar heated water. Individuals, families and groups are all welcome.

www.sparrowhawkbackpackers.co.uk

CONTACT Alison or Darran, Tel: (01647) 440318 - 07870 513570.
Email: enquiries@sparrowhawkbackpackers.fsnet.co.uk
OPENING SEASON All Year
OPENING HOURS All Day
NUMBER OF BEDS 18: 1 x 4 : 1 x 14
BOOKING REQUIREMENTS Book ahead if possible
PRICE PER NIGHT Adults £12. Child under 14 £6. Private room £30.

PUBLIC TRANSPORT Direct from Exeter Bus 359 or 82. Direct from Plymouth Bus 82. From Okehampton or Newton Abbot Bus 173 or 179. Devon bus enquiries Tel 0870 6082608.

DIRECTIONS
From Exeter, take the B3212 signposted on the one-way system at Exe Bridges. From Plymouth head towards Yelverton and then B3212. From Oke. or N.Abbot take A382. The hostel is on Ford Street (A382) 100 metres from tourist office.

See page 208 for colour photo

TORQUAY BACKPACKERS INTERNATIONAL HOSTEL

119 Abbey Road, Torquay
Devon , TQ2 5NP

Torquay is on the English Riviera, famous for warm weather and Mediterranean atmosphere. Turquoise sea, red cliffs, long sandy beaches and secret shingle coves combine to create one of the UK's most beautiful coastlines. Torquay is renowned as a watersport mecca with sailing, water-skiing, windsurfing, diving etc and for its nightlife with pubs, clubs and restaurants a mere stagger from the hostel which is in the heart of Torquay.

Hostel activities include beach barbecues, jam nights, international food nights and video evenings. There are also trips to Dartmoor exploring emerald river valleys where pixies dwell and the open tor-dotted moors. Night trips, at full moon can be a ghostly experience! The hostel offers travellers a friendly, almost family atmosphere. Those who find it hard to leave can easily find work.

www.torquaybackpackers.co.uk

CONTACT Jane, Tel: (01803) 299924
Email: jane@torquaybackpackers.co.uk
OPENING SEASON All year
OPENING HOURS 24 hrs. Check in 9-11am and 5-9pm, please phone to arrange arrival time. No curfew.
NUMBER OF BEDS 46: 1 x double : 3 x 4 : 1 x 5 : 2 x 6 : 1 x 7 : 1 x 8.
BOOKING REQUIREMENTS Advised at all times.
PRICE PER NIGHT £8 to £12/night. £56 to £75/week.

PUBLIC TRANSPORT
Torquay can be reached by coach or train from all major towns. From London take a train from Paddington/Waterloo,or a coach from Victoria/ Heathrow. Free pickup on arrival, if pre-arranged.

DIRECTIONS
Drivers: follow signs to sea front. Turn left. At junction with lights and Belgrave Hotel, bear left up Sheddon Hill. Next T junction is Abbey Road. Turn left. Hostel is 200m on right.

GLOBE BACKBACKERS

71 Holloway Street
Exeter
EX2 4JD

Globe Backpackers is situated in a mid-18th-century town house, centrally located, only minutes' walk from the main high street, Cathedral and historic waterfront. We offer dorm-style accommodation and one large double room with a four poster bed. We offer a fully equipped self-catering kitchen, free tea, coffee, sugar, oil and spices, a social/dining area and separate TV/video room. Other facilities include internet access and laundry service wash. Exeter is a University and Cathedral City with a fun relaxed atmosphere. One of the oldest cities in Britain, Exeter was founded almost 2000 years ago. It is also the only city in Britain to open its 14th-century underground waterways to the public. Exeter has a mix of pubs, clubs, live music venues, restaurants and cafés. Just 20 minutes' drive away from either the sandy beach at Exmouth, a great place for all sail sports or to the edge of Dartmoor for activities such as walking, rock climbing, cycling and horse riding. Exeter is an excellent place to find work.

www.exeterbackpackers.co.uk

CONTACT Tel: (01392) 215521, Fax:(01392) 215531,
Email: info@exeterbackpackers.co.uk
OPENING SEASON All year
OPENING HOURS 8am - 11pm only. No curfew once checked in.
NUMBER OF BEDS 58: 1 x 2 : 3 x 6 : 1 x 8 : 3 x 10
BOOKING REQUIREMENTS Phone ahead to secure booking
PRICE PER NIGHT from £12 per person. Weekly rates available

PUBLIC TRANSPORT
National Express, local bus companies and various rail networks.

DIRECTIONS
Bus Station exit near Paris Café, cross road, take side turning Southernhay East. Stay on LH side until Southgate Hotel. We are diagonally opposite on other side of junction. Central rail station down Queen St to High St, turn right and at 1st set of lights, turn left South St, continue to junction at bottom of hill. Cross at lights and you will find us on right. St David's the direct route is down St David's Hill, over Iron Bridge, onto North St, then South St to the junction.

1m

See page 202 for colour photo

OCEAN BACKPACKERS

29 St James Place
Ilfracombe
Devon, EX34 9BJ

Ocean Backpackers is a homely hostel with a laid back atmosphere and no curfew. Situated in a quaint North Devon town built around an ancient fishing harbour, central to the harbour itself, the bus station, high street, pubs, restaurants and many beaches including surfers' favourites, Croyde, Saunton and Woolacombe. If the surf is down, don't despair just try the other activities available; quad biking, paint balling, kayaking, adventure swimming, mountain biking and micro lighting. Adrenalin not your thing? then take a trip to Lundy Island, spot rare birds, seals, basking sharks and dolphins. Wonderful walking country, the coastal path between Woolacombe and Lynton is breathtaking and Exmoor has an abundance of walks through Britain's most spectacular scenery. The Hostel facilities include a communal lounge, self-catering kitchen, surf board storage and a car park. Come eat in our award winning restaurant (seasonal). Ilfracombe has plenty of summer work so why not come and hang out here for a while.

www.oceanbackpackers.co.uk

CONTACT Chris and Abby Tel: (01271) 867835
Email:- info@oceanbackpackers.co.uk
OPENING SEASON Open all year
OPENING HOURS Reception 9.00am to 12noon - 4.30pm to 10pm, other times by arrangement.
NUMBER OF BEDS 36:- 5 x 6 : 1 x double : 1 x double & bunk.
BOOKING REQUIREMENTS Booking advised but not essential.
PRICE PER NIGHT Dorm £10/£12pp. Dbl/twin £32 per room 2 share.

PUBLIC TRANSPORT
Direct coaches from London Victoria/Heathrow/Plymouth/Exeter. By train take the Tarka line to Barnstaple then bus to Ilfracombe.

DIRECTIONS
From M5 take A361. From Cornwall take A39 to Barnstaple then follow the signs to Ilfracombe. Ocean Backpackers is by the harbour opposite the bus station. See Website for more detailed directions.

P H 1m

EXMOOR BASECAMP

Countisbury
Lynton, Devon
EX35 6NE

Exmoor Basecamp is a converted barn giving comfortable, high standard bunkhouse accommodation. There are 2 large dormitories each sleeping 8 in bunkbeds and a 2 bedded leaders' room. There are excellent hot showers, drying room, lounge/eating area, fully equipped kitchen and a barbecue.

The Basecamp is situated at Countisbury on the North Devon coast. The surrounding countryside includes the dramatic Watersmeet Valleys, moors of Exmoor and coastal paths. Lynton and Lynmouth are the nearest villages and the Atlantic surf beaches are within easy reach. The Basecamp is owned and managed by The National Trust. For those wanting an active break a free night's accommodation can be earned for each day's conservation work arranged with the local wardens. Other activities in the area are walking, horse riding, boat trips, fishing and cycling. However you spend your time the basecamp is ideal for your group to 'get away from it all'.

www.nationaltrust.org.uk/basecamps

CONTACT Karen, Tel: (01598) 741101 / 07974 829171,
Email: Karen.elkin@nationaltrust.org.uk
OPENING SEASON All Year
OPENING HOURS 24 Hours
NUMBER OF BEDS 18: 2x8, 1x2
BOOKING REQUIREMENT Booking essential with £40 deposit.
PRICE PER NIGHT £100 winter, £140 summer. 10% off for 4+ nights.

PUBLIC TRANSPORT
The nearest train and coach stations are in Barnstaple (approx. 20 miles), from there take a local bus to Lynton. Buses to Countisbury are very limited and summer only. Taxis from Lynton approx £5.

DIRECTIONS
From Minehead follow A39 to Countisbury. We are on the left after the Sandpiper Inn. From Lynmouth we are first building on right. Car Park is opposite basecamp.

BASE LODGE

16 The Parks
Minehead
Somerset
TA24 8BS

Base lodge is ideally situated for exploring Exmoor, The Quantocks and The North Devon Coast by mountain bike or foot. Excellent off and on road mountain biking for all levels. Guided mountain biking and secure lock up facilities are available.

Exmoor affords excellent scenic moor and coastal views and the 600+ mile-long South West Coastal Path starts here in Minehead. Other activities can be arranged including surfing, wind-surfing, pony-trekking and natural history walks and talks. Base Lodge is clean, comfortable and friendly, providing a shared fully equipped kitchen, dining room and lounge. Local pubs and restaurants are all within walking distance.

www.togooutdoors.com

CONTACT Wendy or Graham, Tel: (01643) 703520 or 07731651536, Email: togooutdoors@hotmail.com
OPENING SEASON All Year
OPENING HOURS All day
NUMBER OF BEDS 25: 1x7: 1x6: 1x5: 1x3: 2x2
BOOKING REQUIREMENTS Not essential but advisable. Deposit and advanced booking required for groups or exclusive use.
PRICE PER NIGHT From £12.50 pp, twin rooms from £25: exclusive use of Base Lodge from £220 per night. Family rates available please enquire.

PUBLIC TRANSPORT
Bus station 5 min walk. Buses from Taunton, Exeter and Tiverton. Train station: Taunton (26 miles). Minibus pick-up available for groups from their home town by prior arrangement.

DIRECTIONS
With the sea behind you, drive/walk up The Parade until you reach Park Street, continue straight on until you reach a fork. Take the right into The Parks (Baptist church on your right). Limited parking only.

CAMPBELL ROOM ACTIVITY CENTRE

Aley, Over Stowey
Bridgwater Somerset
TA5 1HB

Sheltered rural position at mouth of attractive wooded valley leading to heart of **Quantock Hills**, an 'area of outstanding natural beauty'. Many routes for walking, mountain biking or horse-riding with extensive views from moorland tops. Suitable for D of E also ideal for natural history of heath, conifer and oak woodlands. Transport needed for easy access to rocky beaches (pools and fossils) West Somerset Railway (steam and diesel), Cannington Countryside Visitor Centre, Tropicana at Washford. Well placed for exploring Wells (Cathedral), Wookey Hole and Cheddar (caves), Taunton, (county town) Cricket St. Thomas (wildlife park) Dunster, (historic village), Exmoor and Minehead. Indoor swimming ¼ mile away as well as Bridgwater's (fun pool).

Accommodation consists of a main hall with 18 good mattresses, two rooms sleeping 3 each, washrooms and showers, a fully equipped kitchen, and drying room. There is a small grassed area with room for a tent or two and a campfire area.

CONTACT Mrs Briggs Tel: (01278) 662537
Email: campbellroom@tiscali.co.uk
OPENING SEASON All year
OPENING HOURS By arrangement
NUMBER OF BEDS **24**: 1 x 18 : 2 x 3
BOOKING REQUIREMENTS Booking essential, at least 1 month in advance. Deposit required.
PRICE PER NIGHT £3.50 pp (3 leaders free for groups over 12)

PUBLIC TRANSPORT
Train and bus stations Bridgwater, bus No 15/15A to Nether Stowey, (1 mile to Centre).

DIRECTIONS
M5 junction 23 or 24 Bridgwater. A39 west to Nether Stowey, follow signs to Over Stowey. From church follow road 300m east, then 400m south (toward Forest Trail Ramscombe). Centre at T junction.

GLASTONBURY BACKPACKERS

Crown Hotel
Market Place
Glastonbury
Somerset
BA6 9HD

Glastonbury Backpackers is the place for budget accomodation in Glastonbury. Shrouded in legend and myth the burial place of Arthur and Guinevere. Now famous for its religious, cultural and musical events including the Glastonbury Music Festival.

The hostel is a 16th-century coaching inn which has been renovated to provide a unique and lively place to stay. Accommodation is in backpackers' dorms and twin and double rooms, most with en-suite. There is free bed linen, self-catering kitchen, TV and video lounge, and adjacent parking There is a café bar and public bar with happy hours and live music on most Friday nights. The town centre boasts many shops and restaurants, all with the unique style and atmosphere that is Glastonbury.

www.GlastonburyBackpackers.co.uk

CONTACT Tel: (01458) 833353, Fax: (01458) 835988,
Email: info@GlastonburyBackpackers.co.uk
OPENING SEASON All Year
OPENING HOURS 24 Hours
NUMBER OF BEDS 42
BOOKING REQUIREMENTS Phone with credit card.
PRICE PER NIGHT From £12 per person.

PUBLIC TRANSPORT
National Express and the cheaper Bakers Dolphin coaches do daily returns to London Victoria, dropping outside the hostel. Nearest trains stations are Castle Cary and Bristol. From Bristol catch 376 bus from end of station drive to outside of hostel.

DIRECTIONS
At the bottom of Glastonbury High Street, adjacent to the market cross. The hostel is painted bright blue.

BRISTOL BACKPACKERS HOSTEL

17 St Stephen's Street
Old City
The Centre
Bristol
BS1 1EQ

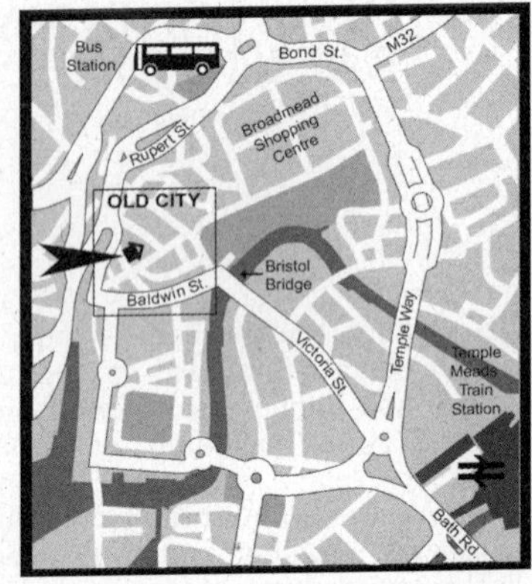

Very central, sociable lounge and bar, brilliant showers 24 hrs, large kitchen, very cheap internet, free coffee/tea/hot chocolate all day, free bed linen, TV area, secure indoor bike storage, safe hire, luggage storeroom, laundry, fantastic city to visit, loads of jobs for a working holiday!

www.bristolbackpackers.co.uk

CONTACT Tel: +44 (0)117 9257900
Email :- info@bristolbackpackers.co.uk
OPENING SEASON All year
OPENING HOURS Reception hours 0900 - 2330 (No curfew)
NUMBER OF BEDS 90: Bunk bed accommodation in private twin, private triple, or six, eight and ten bed dormitories
BOOKING REQUIREMENTS most cards, phone or walk in.
PRICE PER NIGHT £14pp. Private rooms from £35. See website for discounts

PUBLIC TRANSPORT
City Centre location therefore ideal for Temple Meads Rail station (15 min walk) Marlborough Bus/Coach station (10 min walk) and Bristol International Airport for Easyjet, bmi, Ryanair, British Airways.

DIRECTIONS
See website or map above.

1m

BATH BACKPACKERS HOSTEL

13 Pierrepont Street
Bath
BA1 1LA

The closest hostel to Bath's railway and bus station. Centrally located to all amenities and shops and close to all historic sites. During the week, there are organised walking tours around the area, taking in the River Avon and town centre.

Bath Backpackers is in an historic Georgian building that is over 200 years old. It is the only independent hostel in Bath with a self-catering kitchen, social room, smoking den, and sound system throughout the hostel and shower rooms.

Bath Backpackers is a totally fun packed place to stay for international travellers. No curfews. Discounts given when booking ahead to Oxford Backpackers (01865) 721761.

www.hostels.co.uk

CONTACT Manager Tel: (01225) 446787
Email: bath@hostels.co.uk
OPENING SEASON All year
OPENING HOURS 24 hr access, service 8am to 12 midnight
NUMBER OF BEDS 54
BOOKING REQUIREMENTS Booking is advised.
PRICE PER NIGHT From £13 per person. Discount for longer stays. Discount when you book ahead to Oxford Backpackers Hostel. Tel (01865) 721761.

PUBLIC TRANSPORT
Both Bus and Train Stations are in the heart of town, close to the Hostel.

DIRECTIONS
From Bath railway station:- walk straight out of the entrance and follow Manvers Street, 200m past bus station, Manvers Street runs into Pierrepont Street. Bath Backpackers hostel is on the left. From bus station, follow route above.

BOURNEMOUTH BACKPACKERS HOSTEL

3 Frances Road
Bournemouth
BH1 3RY

Welcome to Bournemouth one of the UK's leading (sandy) beach resorts. It's a great base to explore the beautiful Dorset/Hampshire countryside and the World Heritage listed, Jurassic Coast. There's also plenty of nightlife and great work opportunities.

This clean and cosy Backpackers is conveniently located on one side of the town centre. Our website has lots of information, including suggestions for day trips and budget travel information.

www.bournemouthbackpackers.co.uk

Bournemouth Backpackers accommodates only those with a foreign passport and aged 18 or over.

CONTACT Receptionist, Tel: (01202) 299491, To email us use the booking form on website.
OPENING SEASON All Year
OPENING HOURS High Season (mid May - mid Sept) 08:30 - 10:30 & 16:00-19:00. Low Season: Limited hours-check website. No curfew.
NUMBER OF BEDS 26: 2 x 6, 2 x 4, 2 x 2/3.
BOOKING REQUIREMENTS Advised (essential in low season).
PRICE PER NIGHT From £11 (depending on season & room).

PUBLIC TRANSPORT
Three minutes' walk from main Bus/Train station.

DIRECTIONS
By Car Turn off A388 at the Travel Interchange. Turn left at next roundabout and make a U-turn at the following one. Take first left after B&Q superstore, then first right & left into Frances Rd. **Walk from main Bus/Train Station**. Walk down the side-street opposite Texaco and past the church. Turn right and then left into Frances Rd.

PORTSMOUTH AND SOUTHSEA BACKPACKERS LODGE

4 Florence Road, Southsea
Portsmouth
Hants, PO5 2NE

Britain's only island city, Portsmouth is a unique blend of seaside resort and naval heritage. Portsmouth and Southsea Backpackers is the city's only independent hostel for travellers. It offers a friendly cosmopolitan atmosphere within easy reach of the major tourist attractions including the ships (Victory, Mary Rose and Warrior), the D Day museum, and the new Gunwharf Quays. It is only 150m from the beach and in an area containing an excellent variety of pubs, restaurants and clubs. The accommodation is mostly in small dorms for 4 people, but there are also twins, doubles and family rooms, some with en-suite facilities. All hot showers are free. We have a large social area which has Sky TV, an internet facility, pool, darts and a dining area. There is a large fully equipped kitchen, and barbecue and seating in the garden area. Also secure cycle storage.

www.portsmouthbackpackers.co.uk

CONTACT Jane or Pete, Tel/Fax : (023) 92832495
Email: portsmouthbackpackers@hotmail.com
OPENING SEASON All year
OPENING HOURS (service) 8am to 11pm
NUMBER OF BEDS 68: 1x8, 1x6, 10x4, 7x2
BOOKING REQUIREMENTS Advisable, groups require deposit.
PRICE PER NIGHT Dorm £12, Double/Twin £26-£29

PUBLIC TRANSPORT
From any bus or train station catch a bus to Southsea and get off at the Strand. Walk back the way the bus has come and Florence Road is 2nd left. If there are 2+ people get a taxi. Ferries from Portsmouth go to France, Spain, the Channel Islands, and the Isle of Wight.

DIRECTIONS
From the M27 take the M275 to Portsmouth and follow signs to the seafront. Drive along the seafront until you see a blue glass building (The Pyramids) and here turn left. You will come to a mini roundabout. Turn right and Florence Road is then 1st on the left.

P 3m

GUMBER BOTHY

Gumber Farm
Slindon
Near Arundel
West Sussex
BN18 ORN

Gumber Bothy is a converted traditional Sussex barn on the National Trust's Slindon Estate in the heart of the South Downs. It provides simple overnight accommodation or camping for walkers, riders and cyclists, just off the South Downs Way. The bothy forms part of Gumber Farm and is 5 minutes' walk from Stane Street, the Roman Road that crosses the South Downs Way at Bignor Hill. Facilities include platforms in 3 dorms sleeping up to 30, good hot showers and basins, kitchen/diner with gas hob and washing up facilities, a few pots and pans provided, and breakfast foodstuffs available to order in advance. Paddock for friendly horses and racks for bikes. Wheelchair accessible (please phone for details). Sorry, but as we're a sheep farm we have to say no dogs and most definitely **NO CARS**. Under 16s accompanied by adults please. No under fives.

CONTACT Mark or Juliet, Tel/Fax: (01243) 814484.
Email: mark.wardle@nationaltrust.org.uk
OPENING SEASON Easter to the end of October.
OPENING HOURS Flexible.
NUMBER OF BEDS 30: 1 x 16 : 1 x 6 : 1 x 4 plus overflow area
BOOKING REQUIREMENTS Booking by telephone. Booking required for groups of six or more, with 50% deposit.
PRICE PER NIGHT £8 (adult), £4 (under 16's).

PUBLIC TRANSPORT
Train stations, Arundel (urban) 5 miles, Amberley (rural) 5 miles, Chichester (8 miles). National Express stop at Chichester. Bus service 700 from Chichester bus station (opposite train station) stops at Royal Oak pub on A27 every ½ hour Monday to Friday. The Royal Oak is a 3 mile walk from the hostel. Taxi fare from Arundel to Northwood Farm is £10, followed by a 2 mile walk across country.

DIRECTIONS
OS Sheet 197 GR 961 119 (Bothy), GR 973 129 (Nearest car park). No vehicular access. One mile off South Downs Way on Stane Street bridleway (a straight Roman Road).

BRIGHTON BACKPACKERS INDEPENDENT HOSTEL

75/76 Middle Street
Brighton
BN1 1AL

Brighton Backpackers is an independently owned and run hostel and offers the kind of open and stimulating atmosphere you find abroad. A laid back alternative for travellers from all over the world; there's no curfew here, no chores and the common room is open till late. There are two kitchens, a free pool table, showers, central heating, good hi-fi, satellite TV, cheap internet access, a restaurant and bar and friendly atmosphere. We are on the seafront, in the centre of town where all the good social/shopping areas are, including the historic lanes and the bohemian North Lanes. The hostel is in two buildings: the main part is on Middle Street, about 50 yards from the sea. This is where the reception is located.

On the seafront (around the corner) is the Brighton Beach Hotel Annexe, where we have rooms for 2-4 people (all en-suite), with spectacular views of the beach and piers.

www.brightonbackpackers.com

CONTACT Tel: (01273) 777717
OPENING SEASON All year
OPENING HOURS 9am till late.
NUMBER OF BEDS 80
BOOKING REQUIREMENTS Call for availability
PRICE PER NIGHT from £13pp to £15pp. Special weekly rate. Breakfast included in price.

PUBLIC TRANSPORT
Brighton has a train station and intercity coaches operate from Poole Valley coach station.

DIRECTIONS
From train station (10 mins), walk straight to the seafront, turn left and then first left. **From coach station** (3 mins), walk west along the sea front, Middle Street comes off the seafront between the two piers.

P H 1m

KiPPS INDEPENDENT HOSTEL

40 Nunnery Fields
Canterbury
Kent, CT1 3JT

Recommended by Lonely Planet and Let's Go travel guides, Kipps is an ideal 'home from home' for travellers, visitors or small groups looking for self-catering budget accommodation in Canterbury. Only a short walk from the city centre, Kipps is the ideal place to stay to experience the area's numerous pubs, restaurants, shops, café's and historical sites, including the renowned Canterbury Cathedral. Canterbury also makes an ideal base for day trips to Dover, Leeds Castle and the many local beaches. Everyone is welcome to enjoy the facilities on offer:- large backyard and garden (BBQ & hammocks), TV lounge and fully equipped kitchen, a small shop offering breakfast and other food items, bicycle hire (advice on the must-see pubs and local villages). Broadband internet access. Rooms vary from single/double/twin//family (with cots), to dormitories of up to 8 beds (most ensuite). Camping is available.

www.kipps-hostel.com

CONTACT Tony Oakey. Tel: (01227) 786121,
Email: info@kipps-hostel.com
OPENING SEASON All year
OPENING HOURS No curfew, reception 8am to 11pm
NUMBER OF BEDS 50:- 2 x 1 : 1 x 2 : 2 x 3 : 1 x 5 : 1 x 6 : 3 x 7 : 1 x 8
BOOKING REQUIREMENTS Advance booking recommended.
PRICE PER NIGHT £13 dorm to £18.50 single. Discounts available for longer stays and groups. All major credit cards accepted.

PUBLIC TRANSPORT
Canterbury East train station on London Victoria to Dover line, is ½mile by footpath (phone hostel for directions). The local C4 bus stops by the door of the hostel. Taxi from coach/rail stations is £3.

DIRECTIONS
By car :- Take B2068 to Hythe from City Ring Road (A28). Turn right at first traffic lights by church. KiPPS is 300 yds on left, with free parking meters.

P H 1m

OLD SCHOOL HOUSE

6, First Avenue, Cliftonville
Margate
Kent
CT9 2LG

Old School House is a friendly, family-run, seaside hostel with a '3 star' English Tourism Council rating. Accommodation varies from six-bedded dormitories to family and twin rooms, many with en-suite facilities. Guests are welcome to take advantage of our licensed club bar with TV, pool table and table tennis, or relax on the balcony whilst enjoying the sea views. Guest rooms and breakfast room are all non-smoking. Late night shopping is available close by.

The Isle of Thanet, which incorporates Margate, Broadstairs and Ramsgate, boasts 26 miles of safe sandy beaches and secluded bays. Nearby activities include water sports, indoor bowls, mini-golf, ten pin bowling, cliff top walks, museums, caves etc., many within walking distance. Thanet's Viking Coastal Cycle route connects with the National Cycle Network.

CONTACT Ray Ridley Tel: (01843) 223905,
Email: schoolhouseclift@aol.com
OPENING SEASON January to November
OPENING HOURS Reception 8am - 11pm No curfew
NUMBER OF BEDS **26**:- rooms x beds: 1 x 2 3 x 4 2 x 6
BOOKING REQUIREMENTS Booking advisable with 10% deposit.
PRICE PER NIGHT £9.00 - £15.00. Discounts available for groups. Credit cards accepted.

PUBLIC TRANSPORT
Margate train station from London Victoria. 15 mins' walk. £2 Taxi from Station. Bus numbers 8 or 88 to 'Oval' Cliftonville. National Express to Oval Green Cliftonville.

DIRECTIONS
Leave M2 at junction 7, take A299 to Margate, follow coast road approx 2 miles to Cliftonville. Old School House is on the first road after the 'Oval' Green.

P AM 1m

JOURNEYS KINGS CROSS

54-58 Caledonian Road
Kings Cross
London, N1 9DP

Welcome to Central London's premiere hostel, Journeys Hostel at Kings Cross. Newly refurbished with all new facilities this hostel accommodates the needs of any modern backpacker. Facilities include a chill out room, TV room, self-catering kitchen with dining area, and a range of room options. Located a short walk from the buzz of Camden Town and all other major attractions and transport links, our hostel is ideally situated to help you experience London life to the fullest. Whether you are looking for clubs, pubs, the sights or just good memories, Journeys Kings Cross places you on their doorstep at a price to suit any pocket. With friendly staff and a fun atmosphere this hostel has become THE place to rest a weary head after a day's exploration.

www.journeyshostels.com

CONTACT Tel: (0207) 833 3893 , Email:journeys_uk@hotmail.com
OPENING SEASON All Year
OPENING HOURS 24 Hours
NUMBER OF BEDS 96: 1x10, 5x8, 9x4, 3 doubles and 2 twins
BOOKING REQUIREMENTS Not essential
PRICE PER NIGHT Dorms: £15 (£90 per week); quads: £17.50 per person; doubles:£22.50 per person; twins: £20 per person.

PUBLIC TRANSPORT
Nearest Underground and train stations are Kings Cross St Pancras. **From Heathrow Airport, Waterloo and Victoria** use the Underground. **From Gatwick** use Gatwick Express Train to Victoria. **From Stansted** use London Eastern Train to Tottenham Hale, and continue on Underground. **From Luton Airport** use Thameslink Rail from Luton Airport Parkway to Luton Station, then take Midland Mainline to Kings Cross St Pancras.

DIRECTIONS
From Kings Cross St Pancras Station turn left onto Pentonville road. Continue, passing York Way on your left, coming to Caledonian Road shortly after.

AM 1m

JOURNEYS LONDON HOSTEL

73 Lambeth Walk
Lambeth
London
SE11 6DX

Fast becoming one of London's best loved hostels, Journeys London Hostel has just undergone a total revamp including a fantastic new sun terrace for chilling in the afternoon sun. It is situated just minutes away from Big Ben and Waterloo International Rail Station and within a short walk of everything that makes London such a vibrant city. With a self-catering kitchen, atmospheric bar with big screen entertainment, pool table, juke box and broadband internet access, we're your ideal choice for your 'home away from home'. We are experienced in hosting groups of up to 60 guests and FREE coach parking is available nearby

www.journeyshostels.com

CONTACT Tel: 0207 5823088, Email: Journeys_uk@hotmail.com
OPENING SEASON All year
OPENING HOURS 24 hours
NUMBER OF BEDS 60 : 4x8 2x10 2 x twin 2 x double
BOOKING REQUIREMENTS Not essential
PRICE PER NIGHT Dorms: £15 (£90 per week); Twin: £20 per person ; Double: £22.50 per person.

PUBLIC TRANSPORT
Nearest Underground station is Lambeth North on the Bakerloo Line. **From Heathrow airport** take Picadilly Line from terminals 1,2 or 3. **From Gatwick Airport** Take Thameslink Rail to London Bridge, then use Underground. **From Stansted airport** Take the London Eastern from Stansted Mountfitchet to Tottenham Hale, then use Underground. **From Luton Airport** take Thameslink Rail from Luton Airport Parkway to Farringdon, then use Underground.

DIRECTIONS
From Lambeth North Station follow signposts to Imperial War Museum. Turn right by the Day's Inn hotel. Turn left at the Lambeth Walk pub and follow the walk round to no. 73

AM 1m

 See page 34 for advert

DOVER CASTLE HOSTEL AND FLATSHARES

6 Great Dover Street
Borough
London, SE1 4XW

The Dover Castle Hostel is a friendly, privately run Hostel offering the best value accommodation for backpackers in central London. We have 68 beds in bright and clean dormitory style rooms which range in size from 4 to 12 persons. We offer daily and weekly rates and prices include breakfast, hot showers and free luggage lock-up. The hostel has great facilities, including it's own late licensed bar, internet café, lockers and laundry service. There is no curfew - you may party all night, sleep all day, and hostel guests get a discount card for food and drink. If you are an international traveller the Dover Castle is your home in London, whether you are here to sightsee, study, work or party. For longer term guests, we offer house/flatshares in central London. These apartments are all in zones 1 & 2. Single rooms are from £80 a week, twin rooms from £110. The apartments are clean and fully equipped and furnished. Just call us to arrange a free viewing. Member of the London Tourist Board.

www.dovercastlehostel.co.uk

CONTACT Martin Tel: (020) 74037773.Fax: (020) 77878654
Email: dovercastle@hotmail.com
OPENING SEASON All year
OPENING HOURS 24 hours.
NUMBER OF BEDS 68: 1x4 : 3x6 : 3x8 : 1x10 : 1x12
BOOKING REQUIREMENTS Booking advisable in summer. Credit card secures bed.
PRICE PER NIGHT £10-£15 per person including breakfast

PUBLIC TRANSPORT
Nearest main line station is London Bridge. Take underground Northern (black line) to Borough. By car the hostel is opposite Borough underground station between London Bridge and Elephant and Castle. We are located 10mins from Waterloo International Stn.

DIRECTIONS
From Borough Underground Station cross the road to Great Dover Street, we are 1 minute walk and located on the right hand side.

1m

ASHLEE HOUSE

261-265 Gray's Inn Road
King's Cross
London
WC1X 8QT

Ashlee House is ideal for those looking for a hostel in a convenient central London location, with great facilities and rock bottom prices. It has a mixture of rooms from shared dormitories down to twin rooms.

Ashlee House is in the centre of London, a short walk from the British Museum, Covent Garden, Soho, Oxford Street, Camden Market and many of London's major tourist attractions. Security is excellent with coded entrances to the building and rooms. There is a fully equipped self-catering kitchen. A big attraction is the cool design of the two guest lounge areas created by a leading design firm. Great for socialising with fellow travellers or unwinding after a busy day out in London. The reception has a blackboard of local tips and places of interest to visit on London.

www.ashleehouse.co.uk

CONTACT Tel: (020) 7833 9400, Fax: (020) 7833 9677,
Email: info@ashleehouse.co.uk,
OPENING SEASON All Year
OPENING HOURS 24 hours - no curfew or lockouts
NUMBER OF BEDS 172: 16x3 : 10x4 : 12x2 : 6x4 : 4x8 : 4x1
BOOKING REQUIREMENTS Booking in advance is recommended.
PRICE PER NIGHT From £13pp. inc. breakfast. Group discounts.

PUBLIC TRANSPORT

Kings Cross has excellent public transport: underground, local buses and direct links with all major airports - Heathrow, Gatwick, Luton and Stansted. Only 20 minutes from Waterloo International and Victoria.

DIRECTIONS

King's Cross station is 2 mins away by foot. From the station take the exit for Grays Inn Road, departing the exit McDonald's will be on right. Keep McDonald's right, walk straight ahead, passing an exchange bureau, the police station and KFC. The road curves to the right - this is Grays Inn Road - the hostel is 200 metres up the road on the right, opposite The Royal Throat Nose and Ear hospital.

P AM 1m

 See page 319 for advert

GENERATOR LONDON

Compton Place
(off 37 Tavistock Place)
Russell Square London
WC1H 9SE

Just minutes from Covent Garden and Leicester Square The Generator is located in the heart of Bloomsbury. It is the UK's largest tourist hostel, with over 800 beds offering an unbeatable combination of convenience and value.

We are open 24 hours a day, 365 days a year with friendly staff who are always on hand to help. There is a late bar (open 6.00 pm to 2.00 am) which provides the perfect environment to meet young travellers from all over the world. Other facilities include a laundry, games room with pool tables and satellite TV, internet café, safety deposit boxes and free luggage storage on departure. Breakfast is free for everyone, as are bed sheets, towels and 24 hour hot showers. Accommodation is available in singles, twins, triples, quads, multirooms and dorms. The hostel is generally suitable for 18-35s but there is no age limit.

www.generatorhostels.com

CONTACT Tel: (0207) 388 7666, Email: info@the-generator.co.uk
OPENING SEASON All year
OPENING HOURS 24
NUMBER OF BEDS 846: 39 x 2 : 38 x 3 : 104 x 4 : 2 x 5 : 17 x 6 : 11 x 8 2 x 12 1 x 14. = 214 rooms
BOOKING REQUIREMENTS You will need a credit card number to guarantee - 48 hr cancellation.
PRICE PER NIGHT From £10 per person in a dorm room.

PUBLIC TRANSPORT
Kings Cross/Euston Station are both approx 5 minutes' walk from the hostel. The nearest National Express station is Victoria and the closest tube station is Russell Square.

DIRECTIONS
From Russell Square Tube cross onto Marchmont Street, walk to traffic lights and turn right onto Tavistock Place - the hostel is at number 37.

ASTOR'S HYDE PARK HOSTEL

2-6 Inverness Terrace
London
W2 3HU

The Hyde Park Hostel is in a beautiful location, opposite Hyde Park and Kensington Palace and within only a few minutes' walk of bustling Queensway, Notting Hill (home to Europe's legendary Notting Hill carnival) and Portobello Market. The nearby Whiteley's Shopping centre offers cafés, shops and a large cinema complex.

This fun, exciting and friendly hostel offers all the facilities that the young, or young at heart, traveller requires. With great value for money accommodation ranging from £10 to £22 per person per night, including a full continental breakfast, unlimited hot water, clean bed linen, all tax, cooking facilities, satellite TV, communal lounge and valuables 'lock-up'. Other facilities include self-catering kitchen, bar, café, laundry, internet and games room.

www.astorhostels.com

CONTACT Reception. Tel: (020) 7 229 5101,
Fax: (020) 7 229 3170, Email: hydepark@astorhostels.com
OPENING SEASON All year
OPENING HOURS 24 hours
NUMBER OF BEDS 250: many rooms accommodating from 2 to 18
BOOKING REQUIREMENTS Summer popularity makes booking important. **16 to 45-year-old backpackers only. No DSS**

PRICE PER NIGHT £10.00 to £22.50 per person.

PUBLIC TRANSPORT
Tube Stations: Queensway and Bayswater.

DIRECTIONS
From Queensway tube station turn left onto Bayswater Road. Take the first left, Inverness Terrace, and the building is on your right hand side at the beginning of the street.

P 1m

 See page 202 for colour photo and page 33 for advert

PICCADILLY BACKPACKERS HOTEL

12 Sherwood Street
Piccadilly
London
W1F 7BR

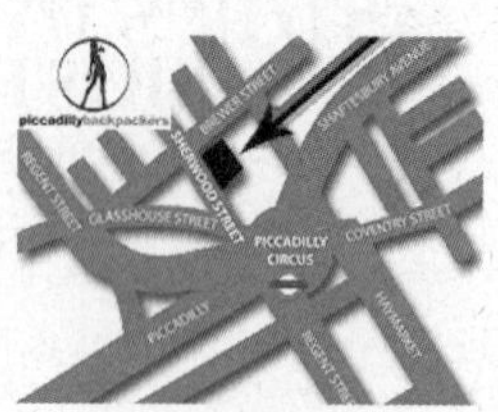

Piccadilly Backpackers Hotel is literally a hop, skip and a jump from Piccadilly Circus. London's most central hostel for travellers on a budget! Soak up the atmosphere from this vibrant area, as famous as the capital itself. Our award winning hostel, spread over 4 colourful floors, is surrounded with London's attractions; including the famous nightspot Leicester Square, the trendy area of Soho, shops of Oxford Street, and London's renowned Theatre Land.

Heaps of free facilities include wide screen TV, lockers, luggage storage and the all important breakfast, with access to high speed internet and a dedicated Travel shop and more! Come join us for a cheap drink in our funky bar - not a minute away - and nightly party events are organised daily. You're sure to have an awesome time! Overall, Piccadilly Backpackers offers an unbeatable blend of value, comfort and security, and is undeniably the greatest portal for visitors to London!

www.piccadillybackpackers.com

CONTACT Reception, Tel: (0207) 434 9009. Fax: (0207) 434 9010
Email: bookings@piccadillybackpackers.com
OPENING SEASON All Year
OPENING HOURS 24 Hours
NUMBER OF BEDS 550
BOOKING REQUIREMENTS Phone or book online.
PRICE PER NIGHT From only £12 per person.

PUBLIC TRANSPORT
From Heathrow via Underground take the Piccadilly Line to Piccadilly Circus. All buses to central London/Piccadilly Circus.

DIRECTIONS
Take exit 1 from Piccadilly underground to Glasshouse St, cross road onto Sherwood St, walk ½ minute to London's most central hostel.

P AM 1m

SMART HYDE PARK INN

48-50 Inverness Terrace
Bayswater
London
W2 3JA

Smart Hyde Park Inn is London's award winning Hostel which consistently is voted in the top ten hostels in the WORLD! It has also been voted best located hostel in LONDON, so stay with us and your journey to London will start with an experience that you won't forget.

The hostel is located in London's buzzing Bayswater and is set in a stunning grade I listed building. Hyde Park Inn is a clean, safe and secure place to stay with 24-hour access to the hostel facilities and your room. Each of our staff is highly trained, so they know what you are looking for and are there to assist you during your stay.

www.smartbackpackers.com

CONTACT Tel: 020 7229 0000. Fax 020 7229 8333.
Email bookings@hydeparkinn.com
OPENING SEASON All year
OPENING HOURS 24 hours (no curfew or lockouts)
NUMBER OF BEDS 223: 3x1 : 5x2 : 1x3 : 6x4 : 7x6 : 9x8 :3x10 : 2x12
BOOKING REQUIREMENTS Book by phone, fax, email or online www.smartbackpackers.com
PRICE PER NIGHT from £9 per person (inclusive of breakfast and linen)

PUBLIC TRANSPORT
Tube Stations: Bayswater (Circle and District line) and Queensway(Central line). Train Stations: Victoria, Paddington, Kings Cross, and Euston. Bus station: Victoria. Easy links from all major airports- Heathrow, Gatwick, Luton, City & Stansted.

DIRECTIONS
From Bayswater Station cross the road and walk down Inverness Place, at the end of the road is Hyde Park Inn. From Queensway Station turn left onto Bayswater Road, cross the road and take the first right into Inverness Place. At the end of the road is Hyde Park Inn.

P AM

SMART CAMDEN INN

55-57 Bayham Street
London
NW1 0AA

Smart Camden Inn is one of London's premier hostels and is located in London's legendary Camden Town area, set in a stunning building. Smart Camden Inn is a clean, safe and secure place to stay with 24-hour access to the hostel facilities and your room. All the rooms have washing facilities en-suite. There are many bath and shower rooms in our building with unlimited piping hot water.

We cater for all travellers, from groups to backpackers and provide the perfect place to meet and mix with like-minded people from all over the world. Camden Inn's staff are highly trained, so they know what you are looking for and are there to assist you during your stay.

www.smartbackpackers.com

CONTACT Tel: 020 7388 8900 Fax 020 7388 2008
email bookings@camdenhostel.com
OPENING SEASON All year
OPENING HOURS 24 hours (no curfew or lockouts)
NUMBER OF BEDS 90: 7x4 : 9x6 : 1x8
BOOKING REQUIREMENTS Book by phone, fax or email or online www.smartbackpackers.com
PRICE PER NIGHT from £9 per person including breakfast

PUBLIC TRANSPORT
Tube Stations: Camden Town (Northern Line). Train Stations: Euston, Kings Cross, Liverpool Street & Paddington. Bus station: Victoria. Easy links from all major airports- Heathrow, Gatwick, Luton, City & Stansted

DIRECTIONS
From Camden Town take the left exit. Walk down Bayham Street, which is opposite the station. We are on the right side of the street approx. 2 min from the station.

SMART HYDE PARK VIEW

11 Craven Hill Gardens
Bayswater
London W2 3EU

Hyde Park View is our newest hostel located in the buzzing area of Bayswater and a stone's throw away from Hyde Park and lots of other tourist attractions. It has also been voted in the top ten hostels in the WORLD! So stay with us and your journey to London will start with an experience that you won't forget.

Hyde Park View is a stunning listed building. It is a clean, safe and secure place to stay with 24-hour access to the hostel facilities and your room. Each of our staff is highly trained, so they know what you are looking for and are there to assist you during your stay.

www.smartbackpackers.com

CONTACT Reception, Tel: 44 (0)20 7262 3167, Fax: 44 (0)20 7262 2083 Email: hpvbookings@hydeparkinn.com
OPENING SEASON All Year
OPENING HOURS 24 Hours
NUMBER OF BEDS 104 = 2 x 4, 16 x 6
BOOKING REQUIREMENTS www.smartbackpackers.com online booking or book by phone. Deposit required for groups.
PRICE PER NIGHT From £9.00 per night per bed (inclusive of breakfast and linen).

PUBLIC TRANSPORT
Tube Stations: Bayswater (Circle and District line) and Queensway (Central line). Train Stations: Victoria, Paddington, Kings Cross, and Euston. Bus station: Victoria. Easy links from all major airports-Heathrow, Gatwick, Luton, City & Stansted.

DIRECTIONS
From Bayswater Tube Station cross the road (Queensway Road) and turn right. Walk for 2 minutes till you hit the Bayswater road. Turn left and walk for 5 min and turn left into Leinster Gardens Road. Keep walking and you will see Craven (Gardens) Hotel on your right. Take the turn just after the hotel and you will see Hyde Park View Hostel.

P H AM 1m

LEINSTER INN

7-12 Leinster Square
London
W2 4PR

The Leinster Inn is in a quiet square overlooking gardens yet close to Portobello Market, Hyde Park, Kensington Palace and Notting Hill (home to Europe's legendary Notting Hill carnival). Nearby Queensway offers bustling shops and restaurants as well as the combined shopping complex and cinemas at Whiteley's. The Leinster Inn is great for weeklies, with regular parties, great music and very lively atmosphere!

Prices range from £10.00 to £15 per night in multi-share rooms of four to eight people. Singles start from £25 and Twins and Doubles from £22 per person. Discounted weekly rates may be available in low season. The price includes continental breakfast, unlimited hot water, clean bed linen, all tax, cooking facilities, satellite TV, communal lounge and a valuables lock-up. Other facilities include a late night licensed bar, pool table, video games, internet lounge, fax service and a job board. There's no curfew and staff are available 24 hours.

www.astorhostels.com

TELEPHONE/FAX CONTACT Receptionist, Tel: (020) 7 229 9641, Fax: (020) 7 221 5255
OPENING SEASON All year
OPENING HOURS 24 hours, no curfew
NUMBER OF BEDS 380
BOOKING REQUIREMENTS Booking is essential in summer. Credit card or sterling cheque for first night secures reservation.
18-30 year old backpackers only. No DSS
PRICE PER NIGHT From £10 to £35 per person.

PUBLIC TRANSPORT
Take London underground to Bayswater or Queensway tube station.

DIRECTIONS From Bayswater or Queensway tube stations: turn left and walk down to Porchester Gardens and turn left, then walk to end and turn right, then second left, hostel is on the right.

1m

HARLOW INTERNATIONAL HOSTEL

13 School Lane Harlow
Essex CM20 2QD

Harlow International Hostel is situated in the centre of a landscaped park and is one of the oldest buildings in Harlow. The town of Harlow is the ideal base from which to explore London, Cambridge and the best of the South East of England. The journey time to central London is only 35 minutes from the hostel. Sustrans National Cycle Route One passes our front door. We are the closest hostel to Stansted Airport.
There is a range of room sizes from single to eight bedded, many with their own washing facilities. Self-catering facilities, refreshments and a small shop are all available. During your visit you can relax with a book from our large collection or enjoy a board game with other guests. There is also table tennis, bar billiards and even our own orienteering course. There are plenty of activities available within the park including an assault course, swimming pool, and outdoor pursuit centre. Meals can be provided for groups.

www.h-i-h.co.uk

CONTACT Richard or Iku, Tel: (01279) 421702
Email: mail@h-i-h.co.uk
OPENING SEASON All year
OPENING HOURS 08:00 - 24:00 (check in 16:00 - 22:30)
NUMBER OF BEDS 36: 2 x 1 : 2 x 2 : 3 x 4 : 3 x 6
BOOKING REQUIREMENTS Advance booking (can be taken 18 months in advance) is recommended. Deposit of £1 pppn of stay.
PRICE PER NIGHT £10.00 adults £7.50 under 16. Please contact hostel for information on group discounts and private rooms.

PUBLIC TRANSPORT
The rail station is only 600m from Hostel with links to London, Cambridge & Stansted Airport. Buses connect to London and airports.

DIRECTIONS
J7 of M11 take A414 into Harlow. At the 4th roundabout take 1st exit (First Ave). Drive to 4th set of traffic lights. Immediately after lights turn right (School Lane). Hostel is on left opp Greyhound Pub.

P AM 1m

OXFORD BACKPACKERS

9a Hythe Bridge Street
Oxford
OX1 2EW

Oxford Backpackers is a purpose built hostel, in the heart of Oxford the leading university town of England. The hostel is two minutes' walk from the train and bus stations and close to the Tourist Information Centre and all the City's attractions. It is safe, clean and friendly. Small dorms, fully equipped kitchen, well supplied bar, laundry, games room, internet access and organised activities add to the experience.

Oxford City is steeped in history and culture, you can explore Christ Church, Magdalen and New College of the University, Bodleian Library, the Oxford Story and Britain's oldest museum the Ashmolean Museum. Alternatively explore the canals and quiet villages of the Cotswolds.

www.hostels.co.uk

CONTACT Tel: (01865) 721761, Fax: (01865) 203293,
Email: oxford@hostels.co.uk
OPENING SEASON All year
OPENING HOURS 24 hour access, service 8am until 12 midnight
NUMBER OF BEDS 100
BOOKING REQUIREMENTS Booking is advised in summer (April to Sept), 7 days in advance with deposit by credit card.
PRICE PER NIGHT From £14 per person. Discounts for longer stays and groups. Discounts when you book ahead to Bath (01225) 446787 Backpacker hostel.

PUBLIC TRANSPORT
Oxford has train and National Express services. Hostel is 100m from train station and easy walking distance from the coach station.

DIRECTIONS
From train station turn left and walk 100 metres, hostel is on your right. From Oxford coach station turn right, hostel is over the bridge 100 metres on your left. By road follow signs to the train station.

NANFORD GUEST HOUSE

137 Iffley Road
Oxford
OX4 1EJ

Period guest house located 5 minutes on foot from the University of Oxford. Wide range and number of rooms at budget prices. All rooms have private shower, toilet, colour TV and tea and coffee making facilities. All prices include full English breakfast. Off road garage space available. Families and large groups welcome.

The University of Oxford rugby football and athletics track is adjacent. The River Cherwell is only 5 minutes' walk away and offers the usual riverside amenities including boating.

www.nanfordguesthouse.com

CONTACT Tel: (01865) 244743
Email: b.cronin@btinternet.com
OPENING SEASON Year round
OPENING HOURS 24 hours
NUMBER OF BEDS: **180** 10 Quad/10 triple/30 dbl/10 twin/30 single
BOOKING REQUIREMENTS Booking essential with credit card
PRICE PER NIGHT from £20pp per night - Groups welcome

PUBLIC TRANSPORT
National Express run a service to Oxford from Heathrow, every 30 minutes. By bus from Heathrow airport get off at St Clements and take 2nd exit on left at the plain roundabout.

DIRECTIONS
By car from London : M40, A40, A420 A4158 and from the south A34, A4144 and A4158 (this is Iffley Road). By train get No4 bus from the front of the station to James Street. Guest House is 20yds down Iffley Road on the left.

BERROW HOUSE BUNKHOUSE & CAMP SITE

Hollybush
Ledbury
Herefordshire HR8 1ET

Berrow House is situated in Hollybush between Rugged Stone Hill and Midsummer Hill of the Malvern Hills range. It is ideally suited for both families, groups and individuals (including those with special needs) to enjoy the countryside and the many attractions that the Malvern area has to offer. It is near the Forest of Dean and the Welsh border, at the start of the Worcestershire Way Walk, with towns of Malvern, Ledbury, Tewkesbury, Worcester, and Gloucester, all within a half hour drive. The Bunkhouse is a converted workshop, which made furniture for the Eastnor Estate. It includes sleeping accommodation for 5 in the main room, with sleeping accommodation for 3 on the upper floor. The main room has heating and easy chairs. The adjacent kitchen/dining room has hot water, cooker, cutlery, crockery and cooking utensils. Toilets, dryer and shower are adjacent. The Fold, which was formally used as lambing sheds, has sleeping accommodation for 4 in two rooms. There is a kitchen equipped as in main bunkhouse. Heating, toilet, shower and cloakroom provided. Camping also available. Picnic area and water garden, small chapel for private prayer. Car park.

www.berrowhouse.co.uk

CONTACT Bill or Mary Cole, Tel/Fax: (01531) 635845
OPENING SEASON All year
OPENING HOURS 24 hours
NUMBER OF BEDS 8 (bunkhouse), **4** (Fold) and 8 tents.
BOOKING REQUIREMENTS Not required for individuals.
PRICE PER NIGHT £7 per person.

PUBLIC TRANSPORT
Nearest train station and National Express service are in Ledbury, which is 3 miles from the hostel and would cost approx. £3 in a taxi.

DIRECTIONS
Take A449 from Ledbury towards Malvern. Turn right on to A438 through Eastnor up hill. Berrow House is behind the next phone box on right in Hollybush. Look for camp sign.

P 5m

STOKES BARN BUNKHOUSE

Newtown House Farm Office
Much Wenlock
Shropshire TF13 6DB

GROUPS ONLY

Stokes Barn is located on top of Wenlock Edge, an Area of Outstanding Natural Beauty and in the heart of Shropshire's countryside. The barn offers comfortable, centrally heated, dormitory accommodation for a wide range of groups. Self-catering or a catered service is available, with a large kitchen and dining area. Our cottage across the courtyard is often used as part of a booking for leaders, teachers or families.
Stokes Barn is an ideal base for field study groups, universities, schools, walkers or just a relaxing reunion with friends. The "Ironbridge World Heritage Site" is only 6 miles away and is a great attraction. Walk to our historic town of Much Wenlock to visit shops, pubs and sports facilities. Situated only a few miles from Church Stretton and the Long Mynd we find ourselves in a walking/ cycling haven. As always we aim to make your stay relaxing and enjoyable. **www.Stokesbarn.co.uk**

CONTACT Suzanne & Chris Hill, Tel: (01952) 727293, Mob: 07967 565266 Fax: (01952) 728130, Email: info@stokesbarn.co.uk
OPENING SEASON All year
OPENING HOURS 24 hours with prior notice
NUMBER OF BEDS 40: 1x10 : 1x12 : 1x5 : 1x8 : 4x2
BOOKING REQUIREMENTS Deposit required.
PRICE PER NIGHT from £9pp, special rate for groups of 20 plus.

PUBLIC TRANSPORT
Nearest train stations are in Telford (10 miles) and in Shrewsbury (10 miles). National Express coaches call at Shrewsbury from London, call (0839) 142 348 for information. Local Midland Red buses stop in Much Wenlock, call 01952 223766 for details.

DIRECTIONS
GR 609 999. When driving from the M6 take M54 Telford following Ironbridge Gorge signs. A4169 to Much Wenlock, joining A458 for Shrewsbury. Stokes Barn is then signposted 1 mile from Much Wenlock on the Shrewsbury Road.

5m

OLD RED LION

Bailey Street
Castle Acre
Norfolk
PE32 2AG

Visitors to Castle Acre are entranced by the special atmosphere of this medieval walled town which lies within the outer bailey of an 11th-century castle. Castle Acre is on the Peddars Way, an ancient track now a long distance path. The Old Red Lion, a former pub, is centrally situated and carries on the tradition of serving travellers who seek refreshment and repose. Guests can stay in private rooms or dormitories where bedding and linen are provided free of charge. There are quiet areas (with wood burning stoves) for reading, meeting other guests and playing. There are two large areas and studio space (one with kitchen and toilet) which are ideal for group use, courses and retreats. Communally served meals (wholefood) are available. The entire premises are available for hire. Secure bike store. Drying facilities. Good local shops, pubs etc. NO SMOKING. Tourism concern supporter.

www.oldredlion.here2stay.org.uk

CONTACT Alison Loughlin Tel: (01760)755557.
Email: old_red_lion@lineone.net
OPENING SEASON All year
OPENING HOURS Free time, by prior negotiation (day access).
NUMBER OF BEDS 23: 1x9 : 1x6 : 2xdouble (1en-suite) : 2 twin
Entire premises may be hired for SOLE OCCUPANCY.
BOOKING REQUIREMENTS Useful but not essential.
PRICE PER NIGHT £15 to £25 (inc full bedding and breakfast).

PUBLIC TRANSPORT
Train stations are at King's Lynn & Downham Market (14 miles). Buses from King's Lynn to Swaffham. Daily National Express coach between Victoria Coach Station & Swaffham. Approx taxi fare from Swaffham £3.50. Norfolk Bus info (0500) 626116.

DIRECTIONS
GR 818151. Castle Acre is 3½ miles north of Swaffham (A47) on the A1065. The hostel is on left, 75yds from Bailey Gate in village centre. Frontage on street line painted red.

DEEPDALE BACKPACKERS

Deepdale Farm
Burnham Deepdale
Norfolk
PE31 8DD

Get out of the smog to the stunning north Norfolk coast, 'An Area of Outstanding Natural Beauty'. What is your poison: adrenalin sports (kite surfing, windsurfing and paragliding); great pubs (two within a few hundred metres, plus many more locally); the great outdoors (walking, cycling, sailing, photography, sunsets and beaches) or the chance to chill!

A hostel where you will enjoy your stay, built by backpackers for backpackers. Facilities include en-suite shower rooms, fully equipped kitchen, sitting room with TV and hifi, laundry, BBQ area, drying room, café and tourist information centre. Dorms and twin/ double rooms available. Camping is also available. See also Deepdale Granary Group Hostel on page 64.

www.deepdalefarm.co.uk

CONTACT : Deepdale Information Tel: (01485) 210256
Email: info@deepdalefarm.co.uk
OPENING SEASON All year
OPENING HOURS All day (collect key from Deepdale Information)
NUMBER OF BEDS 37
BOOKING REQUIREMENTS Pre-booking is strongly recommended. Max group size 12
PRICE PER NIGHT from £10.50pp dorm room. £28 twin room. £63pp per week dorm room.

PUBLIC TRANSPORT
Train and national coach stations at King's Lynn (25 miles) excellent Coastal Hopper Bus to Burnham Deepdale. Coastal Hopper services the coast from King's Lynn to Cromer, including Sandringham and Titchwell Bird Reserve. Travel information: Travelline 0870 608 2 608

DIRECTIONS
GR 803443. On A149 coast road, halfway between Hunstanton and Wells-next-the Sea. Beside Deepdale Garage, opp Deepdale Church.

P 3m

DEEPDALE GRANARY GROUP HOSTEL

Deepdale Farm
Burnham Deepdale
Norfolk
PE31 8DD

GROUPS ONLY

Sleeping 18 Deepdale Granary is the ideal base for groups exploring the unique north Norfolk coast, 'An Area of Outstanding Natural Beauty'. The area offers fantastic beaches, birdwatching, cycling, walking, watersports and heritage.

The hostel has recently been upgraded and offers central heating, fully equipped kitchen, showers, toilets, drying room, laundry, café and tourist information centre. The rooms consist of two six bed dorms, a four bed dorm and a twin room. Camping is also available. See also Deepdale Stables Backpackers Hostel on page 63.

www.deepdalefarm.co.uk

CONTACT Deepdale Information Tel (01485) 210256
Email: info@deepdalefarm.co.uk
OPENING SEASON All year
OPENING HOURS All day (collect key from Deepdale Information)
NUMBER OF BEDS 18: 2 x 6 : 1 x 4 : 1 x 2.
BOOKING REQUIREMENTS Pre-booking essential, 20% deposit, with balance due one month in advance.
PRICE PER NIGHT £180 weekends & bank holidays. £130 weekdays. £1,010 for 7 nights (Friday and Saturday adjacent).

PUBLIC TRANSPORT
Nearest train and national coach stations at King's Lynn (25 miles) then excellent Coastal Hopper bus to Burnham Deepdale. Coastal Hopper services the coast from King's Lynn to Cromer, including Sandringham. For travel information contact: Travelline 0870 608 2 608

DIRECTIONS
GR 803443 On A149 coast road, halfway between Hunstanton and Wells-next-the-Sea. Beside Deepdale Garage & opposite Deepdale Church.

THE IGLOO BACKPACKERS HOSTEL

110 Mansfield Road
Nottingham
NG1 3HL

Located within walking distance of the city's historical sights and entertaining sounds, the Igloo is Nottingham's only backpackers' hostel. On offer to backpackers and youth groups is a clean, safe and warm overnight stay in a large, listed Victorian house. Just £13.50 per night per person buys a whole host of homely comforts; bunk bed dorms, hot power showers, lounge with games, TV & info and fully-equipped kitchen plus free tea, coffee and good company. Open in outlook and open all day all year, the Igloo is the ideal home-from-home for hostellers seeking rest and recuperation before pursuing the exploits of local hero, Robin Hood, or enjoying the energetic nightlife of this popular university city. Check out the web site for more details:

www.igloohostel.co.uk

CONTACT Steve, Tel: (0115) 9475250,
Email: reception@igloohostel.co.uk
OPENING SEASON All year
OPENING HOURS Open all day. 3am curfew.
NUMBER OF BEDS 36: 3 x 10 : 1 x 6.
BOOKING REQUIREMENTS Not essential, but advised for groups. Confirm large group booking in writing (deposit may be required).
PRICE PER NIGHT £13.50 per person. £54 per week.

PUBLIC TRANSPORT

Nottingham has a mainline train station with direct and regular services to London etc. National Express operates from Broadmarsh bus station. From bus/train stations the Igloo is 20 min' walk, a £3 taxi ride or catch Citybus 90 from opposite the train station to Mansfield Rd, ask for International Community Centre, walk uphill for 1 minute.

DIRECTIONS

From the Tourist Information Centre, Market Square, Nottingham, turn right out of TIC, take the next left onto Clumber Street, keep walking straight on for ten mins, past the Victoria Shopping Centre, until you reach the Golden Fleece Pub. The Igloo is diagonally opposite.

3m

MOORSIDE FARM BUNKHOUSE

Hollinsclough
Longnor, Buxton
Derbyshire SK17 0RF

Moorside Farm is a 300-year-old farmhouse set 1200 feet up in the beautiful Peak District National Park on the Derbyshire/Staffordshire border and approximately five miles from the historic town of Buxton. Sleeping accommodation is provided in two areas, one for 14 - this is alpine style with pine clad ceiling and a pine floor with bunk beds. The second area has 6 beds, also in bunks and is an ideal room for a small group or family. Downstairs there are showers, toilets and a large dining/general room. The farmhouse has full central heating and drying facilities are available.

We provide a three course breakfast, a packed lunch and a substantial dinner in the evening, vegetarians are catered for. A small kitchen is available for making tea and coffee. Ample parking space is provided. The farmhouse has a current fire certificate. All bookings have sole use of the accommodation.

www.moorsidefarm.com

CONTACT Charlie Tel: (01298) 83406
Email : Charliefutcher@aol.com
OPENING SEASON All year
OPENING HOURS 24 hours
NUMBER OF BEDS 20: 1 x 14 : 1 x 6
BOOKING REQUIREMENTS Booking with deposit required with two weeks' notice
PRICE PER NIGHT £22.00 per person, bed, breakfast and evening meal included. £14.00 per person bed and breakfast. (min 4 persons)

PUBLIC TRANSPORT
Nearest train station Buxton. Take bus to Longnor or Travellers Rest. Bus enquires (01332) 292200

DIRECTIONS
GR SK 055 670. Leave A53, Buxton to Leek road, at Travellers Rest, take 4th lane on left, down to T junction, take first left, Moorside Farm is first right entrance.

BARN FARM CAMPING BARNS AND CAMPSITE

Birchover
Matlock
Derbyshire
DE4 2BL

Barn Farm is a working livestock farm in the Peak District national park with fine views over the Derwent valley. It borders the mystical Stanton Moor with its Victorian stone carvings and ancient Nine Ladies stone circle. Robin Hood's Stride and other bouldering and climbing areas are nearby and the area is excellent for walking with the Limestone Way long distance path passing close by. Birchover has a village shop and two pubs which serve food, one of which is the famous 'Druid Inn'.

Barn Farm provides camping with good showers, toilet and laundry facilities and three camping barns, one of which is booked via the YHA. Sabine Hay Barn Bunkhouse and Hill Carr Barn provide well appointed accommodation which is available to all. Sabine Hay has 15 bunkbeds arranged around a communal space with fully fitted kitchen and table and chairs. Hill Carr barn has a similar arrangement with single beds. Both bunkhouses are heated and have their own private bathroom and shower facilities in adjacent barns.

CONTACT Tel: (01629) 650245, Email: gilberthh@msn.com
OPENING SEASON All Year
OPENING HOURS Accommodation available all day.
NUMBER OF BEDS 30: 2x15
BOOKING REQUIREMENTS Booking advisable 20% deposit.
PRICE PER NIGHT £100 per night per barn. Weekly rates available. Camping £5 per person, reduced to £4 for Dof E groups.

PUBLIC TRANSPORT
The 172 bus from Bakewell to Matlock runs approximately hourly.

DIRECTIONS
From the A6 between Matlock and Bakewell take the B5056 and follow signs for Birchover. In Birchover continue past the Druid Inn to the top of the village, where you will see the farm sign.

THE RECKONING HOUSE

Mandale Farm,Haddon Grove
Bakewell, Derbyshire
DE45 1JF

The Reckoning House camping barn has been recently renovated to a high standard including double glazing and insulation. It is situated on the edge of Lathkill Dale, 3 miles from Bakewell. Lathkill Dale is a nature reserve managed by English Nature to protect a variety of flora and fauna as well as some outstanding geological features. Horse riding, fishing, golf and cycle hire are all available locally. There are also many local walks including the Limestone Way.

The Reckoning House has a cooking area, 4 calor gas rings (gas supplied) a washing up sink with hot water, a toilet, washbasin and shower inside the barn. The sleeping area is upstairs and consists of two separate sleeping floors. There are electric heaters in all rooms.

CONTACT Tel: (01629) 812416, Email: juliafinney808@hotmail.com
OPENING SEASON All year
OPENING HOURS By arrangement
NUMBER OF BEDS 12
BOOKING REQUIREMENTS Sole use bookings have priority at weekends. 10% deposit, balance 2 weeks before arrival.
PRICE PER NIGHT £7.50 pp. Sole use Fri/Sat £75. Sun to Thurs £65

PUBLIC TRANSPORT
Train stations at Buxton (10 miles away) and Matlock (13 miles). National Express drop at Bakewell. Local buses (enquiries (01332) 292200) go to Bakewell from Monyash, Over Haddon and Buxton.

DIRECTIONS
GR 184 666. Take the B5055 out of Bakewell towards Monyash. Continue for approximately three miles. Look out for two sets of holiday cottages on your right. After passing Haddon Grove Farm holiday cottages (the second set), take the first turn left at the signpost to Haddon Grove. Bear left at the bottom of the lane beside Haddon Grove Farm Camp site. The camping barn is the first on the left about half a mile further on. Please contact us for directions if on foot.

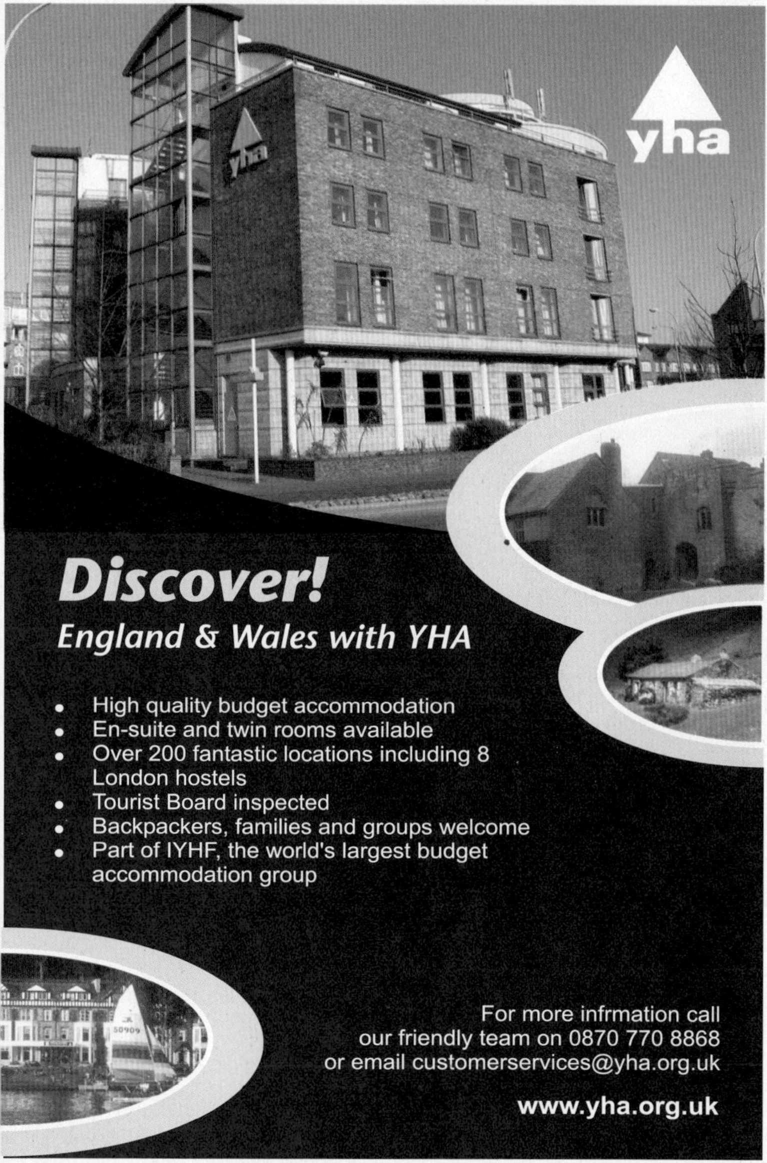
yha
Discover!
England & Wales with YHA
• High quality budget accommodation
• En-suite and twin rooms available
• Over 200 fantastic locations including 8 London hostels
• Tourist Board inspected
• Backpackers, families and groups welcome
• Part of IYHF, the world's largest budget accommodation group
For more infrmation call
our friendly team on 0870 770 8868
or email customerservices@yha.org.uk
www.yha.org.uk

take a breath of
fresh air and
explore Britain
by bike

International Inn page79

PINDALE FARM OUTDOOR CENTRE

Pindale Lane
Hope, Hope Valley
Derbyshire, S33 6RN

The Centre is situated one mile from Castleton in the heart of the Peak District. The centre comprises a farmhouse pre-dating 1340 and lead mine buildings from the 1850s. These have been completely rebuilt from a near derelict condition in 1988, and opened by HRH The Prince of Wales. The Centre now offers 5 different kinds of accommodation. The farmhouse offers traditional bed and (an AGA cooked) breakfast. The Barn has 6 independent self-catering units, the lower 3 of these can accommodate people with certain physical disabilities. The old Lead Mine Engine House, our logo, is a self-catering unit sleeping 8. The Powder House, originally the mine's explosive store, is a small camping barn with basic facilities for up to 4 people. A campsite, adjacent to the Centre, has showers, hot water, and toilet facilities. The Centre is the ideal base for walking, climbing, caving, horse riding etc. Instruction is available if required. Well behaved pets welcome.

www.pindale.fsbusiness.co.uk

CONTACT Tel: (01433) 620111, Fax: (01433) 620729,
Email: bookings@pindale.fsbusiness.co.uk
OPENING SEASON All year (Camping March-October)
OPENING HOURS 24 hours.
NUMBER OF BEDS 64 bunkbeds plus camping and B&B
BOOKING REQUIREMENTS Booking advisable for specific dates. Early booking is best. A deposit is required.
PRICE PER NIGHT All prices are per person, per night. Camping £4, Powder House £5, Engine House and Barn £8, B&B £20 with an AGA breakfast (some four poster beds).

PUBLIC TRANSPORT
Hope has a train station. The nearest National Express service is in Sheffield. Approximate taxi fare to Sheffield is £15-£20. On local buses ask for Hope. Hope is 15 minutes' walk from the hostel.

DIRECTIONS
GR 163 825 From Hope follow cement works signs, turn off main road between church and Woodroffe Arms.

 See page 201 for colour photo

THORPE FARM BUNKHOUSES

Thorpe Farm, Hathersage
Hope Valley Via Sheffield
S32 1BQ

Thorpe Farm Bunkhouses are situated a mile northeast of Hathersage, on a family run mixed/dairy farm. It is 2 miles from Stanage Edge and other popular climbing and walking areas are nearby. Castleton is 6 miles up the Hope Valley and Eyam is 6 miles southwest. The dormitories have individual bunks each with mattress and pillow. There is some sleeping space in the sitting rooms and room for camping outside. The bunkhouses have heating, drying facilities, hot showers, toilets, electric/gas cooking, fridges, freezers, electric kettles, toasters etc.

www.thorpe-bunk.co.uk

CONTACT Jane Marsden, Tel: (01433) 650659
OPENING SEASON All year
OPENING HOURS No restriction
NUMBER OF BEDS: The Old Shippon 31: 1x12 : 1x11: 2x4. **The Byre 14:** 1x5 : 1x4 : plus 4 in living room, one level throughout, disabled bathroom facilities. **The Old Stables 14:** 1x8 : 1x6. **Pondside 14:** 1x8 : 1x6
BOOKING REQUIREMENTS For weekends it is highly recommended to book or enquire.
PRICE PER NIGHT From £8 per person.Sole use from £94 per night.

PUBLIC TRANSPORT
Train station at Hathersage, 10 mins walk from bunkhouse. Bus service 272 operates from Sheffield to Hathersage. Weekends only bus service 257 operates from Sheffield via Stanage & Snake Pass to Hathersage. Details phone Busline (01298) 230980 or (01246) 250450.

DIRECTIONS
GR 223 824. **If walking** from A6187/A625 in Hathersage turn right (just past the George Hotel) up Jaggers Lane, turn second right up Coggers Lane and fifth turning on left (Signed Thorpe Farm). **If driving** follow the road from Hathersage towards Hope for ¾ mile, then turn right into private drive (signposted Thorpe Farm).

UPPER BOOTH CAMPING BARN

Upper Booth Farm
Edale, Hope Valley
Derbyshire. S33 7ZJ

"We found it - the most beautiful site we've ever encountered" Derby Express February 2003. The Camping barn is located adjacent to a small campsite alongside Crowden Clough on the National Trust's High Peak Estate. It is possible to hire the barn and additional pitches on the campsite.

There is space for cooking and tables for eating in the barn. Toilets, handbasins, washing up sinks and a shower are shared with the campsite. Upper Booth camping barn is located on a working hill-farm. Walking and biking are available from the farm, **the Pennine Way passes through the farmyard.** Climbing, riding, airsports and golf are all available locally.

www.upperboothcamping.co.uk

CONTACT Robert or Sarah Tel: (01433) 670250.
Email : mail@helliwell.info
OPENING SEASON All year. **No unaccompanied under 16s**
OPENING HOURS No restriction~not suitable for late night parties
NUMBER OF BEDS Sleeping space for 12
BOOKING REQUIREMENTS Pre-booking essential for weekends & bank holidays. 20% deposit. Balance 1 month in advance
PRICE PER NIGHT £4 per person. £55 per night sole use.

PUBLIC TRANSPORT
Nearest station, Edale (Sheffield/Manchester line) approx 40 mins walk on footpaths to Upper Booth. Nearest bus stop Barber Booth (15 mins walk from Upper Booth). Service 260 bank holidays and weekends. Service 200 weekdays. 3 buses a day go to Upper Booth.

DIRECTIONS
GR103 853. Follow signs for Edale village, then for Barber Booth, immediately after river bridge turn right for Upper Booth.

     🍴AM

HOMESTEAD AND CHEESEHOUSE

The Farm, Bamford
Hope Valley
Derbyshire S33 0BL

The Bunkhouses are situated in the middle of Bamford, on a small mixed farm, just a mile from Bamford Edge and 3 miles from Stanage Edge. Ladybower, Derwent and Howden reservoirs are between 1½ and 7 miles further up the valley. Castleton is 5 miles to the north, Chatsworth 10 miles and Haddon Hall 14 miles to the south west.

Both bunkhouses have individual bunks each with mattress, fitted sheets and pillow, gas central heating and drying facilities. **Homestead** has 22 beds in 3 rooms, there are 2 bathrooms with 2 toilets and showers in each, there is a large dayroom with oak seating. **Cheesehouse** is a self contained bunkhouse with four bunks, ideal for a small family or group, it has a shower and toilet and is equipped with a kitchen having cooking rings, a microwave oven, toaster and kettle.

The Bunkhouses are 2 minutes' walk from the Anglers Rest and Ye Derwent!!!

CONTACT Helena Platts Tel: (01433) 651298
OPENING SEASON All year
OPENING HOURS No restriction
NUMBER OF BEDS Homestead **22:** 1x10 : 2x6. Cheesehouse **4:** 1x4.
BOOKING REQUIREMENTS Recommended for weekends.
PRICE PER NIGHT £8 per person. Homestead sole use £150. Cheesehouse sole use £30

PUBLIC TRANSPORT
Nearest train station Bamford, 10 mins' walk. Bus 274 & 275 operates Sundays Bamford/Sheffield or to Castleton. Bus 272 Bamford to Sheffield and Castleton. Bus 175 Bamford/Bakewell.

DIRECTIONS
The farm is in the centre of Bamford on South View Lane (turn off A6013 at the 'Country Stores').

CHESTER BACKPACKERS

67 Boughton
Chester CH3 5AF

Chester Backpackers is located just a few minutes' walk from the ancient heart of the historic city of Chester in an original Tudor coaching inn (formally the Waterloo Inn). We offer clean, comfortable rooms all of which have en-suite facilities, with freshly laundered linen provided as standard. Free tea and coffee, free left luggage facilities and well-equipped rooms make Chester Backpackers an ideal base for walking the Roman walls of Chester, exploring the nearby Welsh mountains and dramatic coastline or day trips to Liverpool and Manchester. We can also assist with finding work for longer-term travellers and our attractive long-term rates make it an ideal location to spend time in this beautiful city. We are open 24 hours with no curfew, and our friendly well-trained staff (travellers themselves) are on hand to offer help and advice whenever needed.

www.chesterbackpackers.co.uk

CONTACT Tel: (01244) 400185,
Email: sales@chesterbackpackers.co.uk
OPENING SEASON All year
OPENING HOURS 24 hours, no curfew
NUMBER OF BEDS 32: 1 x 18 : 1 x 8 : 2 x 2 : 2 x 1
BOOKING REQUIREMENTS Book by phone or email. Strongly recommended at weekends, 2 to 4 day notice advisable at other times.
PRICE PER NIGHT Dorm £13pp Single £18.50pp Dbl/ twin £34 per room. (all rooms are en-suite). Long term rates available

PUBLIC TRANSPORT
Hostel is 10 mins' walk from train station and 10 mins' walk from National Express coach station. The Sustrans (cyclist and walkers) network is a few mins' walk away. International airports at Liverpool and Manchester are both 30 mins' drive from Chester.

DIRECTIONS
From railway station walk directly up City Road, at ring road (near Jones pub) bear left into Boughton (A41) we are 100 metres on left. From coach station walk into Northgate Street heading towards Tourist Info Centre(on right). Turn left into Foregate Street, go under clock situated on Roman wall and head straight on into Boughton (under the subway) we are 100 metres on left from the underpass.

P AM 1m

EMBASSIE HOSTEL

1 Falkner Square
Liverpool
L8 7NU

The Embassie is a terrace house in an unspoilt Georgian square used in the filming of '*In the Name of the Father*'. The house was built in 1820 and until 1986 it was the Consulate of Venezuela. It is only 15 minutes' walk from the city centre. Liverpool is known for its nightlife, a student population of 70,000 ensures a lively scene, bands start playing at 11pm and bars are regularly open till 2am. Hostellers have a key to come and go, the hostel is clean, safe and staffed 24 hours. Bedding is provided (including sheets) and free coffee, tea, toast and jam are available 24 hours, eat as much as you want. International, or UK regional travellers only, NO LOCALS.

www.embassie.com

CONTACT Kevin, Tel: (0151) 7071089
OPENING SEASON All year
OPENING HOURS Please book in between 9am and 12am (phone if arriving later). Key given for 24hr access.
NUMBER OF BEDS 40
BOOKING REQUIREMENTS Booking is not essential for individuals. Groups larger then 6 should book (20% deposit).
PRICE PER NIGHT (from 1.1.05) £14.50 (first night), £13.50 (consecutive nights).

PUBLIC TRANSPORT
Liverpool has a train station and is served by National Express Coaches. A £3.50 taxi fare will bring you from the train or bus station to the hostel door, (good idea if you have a heavy rucksack).

DIRECTIONS
From the Anglican Cathedral (the third largest in the world) continue uphill along Canning Street away from the city centre. This will bring you into Falkner Square (15-20 mins). The hostel has a red door and is by a phone box.

See page 72 colour photo montage

THE INTERNATIONAL INN

South Hunter Street
(off Hardman Street)
Liverpool 1

The International Inn is an award winning hostel, located in the heart of Liverpool City Centre's cultural quarter. Liverpool has a wealth of attractions for visitors and you will find theatres, the City's two Cathedrals, Philharmonic Hall, as well as the City's renowned nightlife venues just a stone's throw away. The Hostel is also ideally located for visiting students, being opposite the Students' Union Building and University. The Hostel provides fully heated accommodation in ensuite dormitories of 2, 4, 6, 8 and 10 beds. Facilities include a café, fully equipped kitchen/dining room, TV lounge/games room, laundry, baggage store, internet access and information desk. There are no curfews to curtail your evening's fun.

Winner! Mersey Tourism Award ~ Small Tourism Business of the Year 2002
NW Tourism Bronze for being Environmentally aware 2003
Nominated - Mersey Tourism Awards, Small Tourism Business 2004
Winner - Mersey Tourism Awards, Outstanding Customer Service 2004

www.internationalinn.co.uk

CONTACT Tel: (0151) 709 8135, Email: info@internationalinn.co.uk
OPENING SEASON All year
OPENING HOURS All day
NUMBER OF BEDS 100: 4 x 2 : 7 x 4 : 2 x 6 : 4 x 8 : 2 x 10.
BOOKING REQUIREMENTS Advisable but not essential, the hostel is very popular at the weekend.
PRICE PER NIGHT £15, (dorm) or £18 per person in twin room

PUBLIC TRANSPORT
Liverpool Lime Street Station 10 minutes' walk away. National Express Station 10-15 minutes' walk.

DIRECTIONS
From Lime St Station take the Skelhorn St exit. Turn left up hill & continue along Copperas Hill. At Main Road jnct. turn right along Russell St, continuing along Clarence St then Rodney St. At jnct. of Hardman St (HSBC bank on corner) turn left. The second road on left is South Hunter St & the hostel is 20 yards up on the right.

P AM 1m

THE HATTERS

50 Newton Street
Manchester
M1 2EA

Winners of the 2004 Manchester Tourism Outstanding Customer Care award, The Hatters has firmly established itself as the city's favourite hostel. Catering for independent travellers and groups it is the ideal spot to start exploring the north west.

Located in the Northern Quarter in the heart of the city centre, let our knowledgeable and friendly staff guide you to the best that this great city has to offer, from live music and football to restaurants, shopping, museums, pubs and clubs.

www.hattersgroup.com

CONTACT Tel: (01612) 369500.
Email: Manchester@hattersgroup.com
OPENING SEASON All year
OPENING HOURS 24 hours
NUMBER OF BEDS 168: 1x18 : 8x10 : 6x8 : 1x6 : 2x4 : 3x2 : 2x1.
BOOKING REQUIREMENTS Booking recommended, essential for groups with deposit. ID is required at check in. Booking not essential for individuals.
PRICE PER NIGHT From £14 in 18 bed dorm, £15 in 6 to 10 bed dorms, £17 in 4 bed dorms and £22.50 per person in private rooms. Check our website for special offers.

PUBLIC TRANSPORT
We are located only 5 minutes from Piccadilly railway station which is in the city centre. The main bus and tram station is on Piccadilly Gardens which is literally around the corner.

DIRECTIONS
Coming into Manchester follow signs for Piccadilly Station. Newton Street is at the top of Portland and London Piccadilly Road.

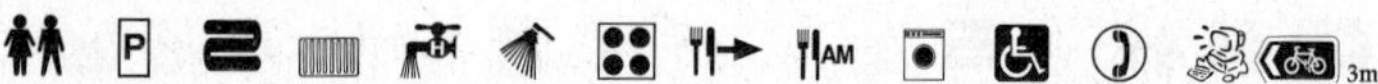

BRANSDALE MILL

Bransdale, Fadmoor,
York
YO62 7JL

GROUPS ONLY

The hostel occupies a converted Water Mill at the head of Bransdale, an unspoiled and hidden valley in the North York Moors. Accommodation is comfortable, but basic. It is an ideal base from which to get away from it all and to enjoy peace and tranquillity in beautiful countryside. There are many fine walks in the surrounding area, which is rich in wildlife. The nearest towns are Kirkbymoorside and Helmsley, both 10 miles away, and the North Yorkshire coast can be reached within an hour. The local pubs are 8 miles away, both of which serve food. Local attractions include the North Yorkshire Moors Railway; 'Heartbeat Country'; National Trust properties at Nunnington, Rievaulx, Bridestones, and the Yorkshire Coast; Pickering and Helmsley Castles and Duncombe Park. The surrounding farmland is owned by the National Trust and let to tenant farmers; please respect the working life of the Dale during your visit. *Under 16's to be accompanied by responsible adult.*

Mill unfortunately not equipped for wheelchair access.

CONTACT Anne Deebank Tel: (01751) 431693.
Email: anne.deebank@nationaltrust.org.uk
OPENING SEASON All year, but used for NT working holidays at peak spring/summer times.
OPENING HOURS All day
NUMBER OF BEDS 13: 1 x 7 : 1 x 6.
BOOKING REQUIREMENTS Essential at least 2 weeks in advance.
PRICE PER NIGHT £8.00 per person.

PUBLIC TRANSPORT
National Express to Pickering. Local buses Malton (18 miles) and Kirkbymoorside. Taxi Kirkbymoorside approx £10.

DIRECTIONS
From Kirkbymoorside Market Place left at the mini roundabout take left fork to Fadmoor continue 9 miles. Just before the head of Bransdale see a gate with sign 'Basecamp', follow track to Mill.

YORK YOUTH HOTEL

11/13 Bishophill Senior
York
North Yorkshire
YO1 6EF

York Youth Hotel provides Backpacker Hostel accommodation in city centre. We are 6 minutes' walk from the railway station and 3 minutes' walk from the bus terminus.

This is a beautiful Georgian house surrounded by York's historic treasures. No other transport needed, you can easily walk to all York's attractions, plus step straight into the York "Café Society" or very vibrant night life.

NO CURFEWS, NO MEMBERSHIP, Open 24 hours. More information available on our web site, or send us an email.

www.yorkyouthhotel.com

CONTACT Tel: (01904) 625904 Fax: (01904) 612494
Email: info@yorkyouthhotel.com
OPENING SEASON 12 months
OPENING HOURS 24 Hours
NUMBER OF BEDS 100
BOOKING REQUIREMENTS Advisable, particularly at weekends
PRICE PER NIGHT £14 per person

PUBLIC TRANSPORT
York Railway Station 400 metres. Bus Terminus either at the Railway Station or Rougier Street 200 metres away.

DIRECTIONS
From York Railway Station, turn right out of the station, turn 1st left into Micklegate, turn 2nd right into Trinity Lane, straight across the junction, we are 20 metres on the left.

YORK YOUTH HOTEL

www.yorkyouthhotel.com

info@yorkyouthhotel.com

NO MEMBERSHIP REQUIRED
NO CURFEW (OPEN 24 HOURS)

- DORMITORIES
- 4-6 BEDDED ROOMS
- TWIN ROOMS
- SINGLE ROOMS
- FAMILY ROOMS
- TV LOUNGE
- SHOP
- SNACKS
- REFRESHMENTS (24 hours)
- NIGHT PORTER
- INFORMATION SERVICE

PRICES FROM
£14
PER NIGHT

INDIVIDUALS & GROUPS WELCOME

♦ MEALS AVAILABLE ♦ BIKE HIRE ♦ TELEPHONE ♦ BEDS ♦ INTERNET ♦ GAMES ROOM ♦ KITCHEN ♦ LAUNDRY ♦ SHOWERS

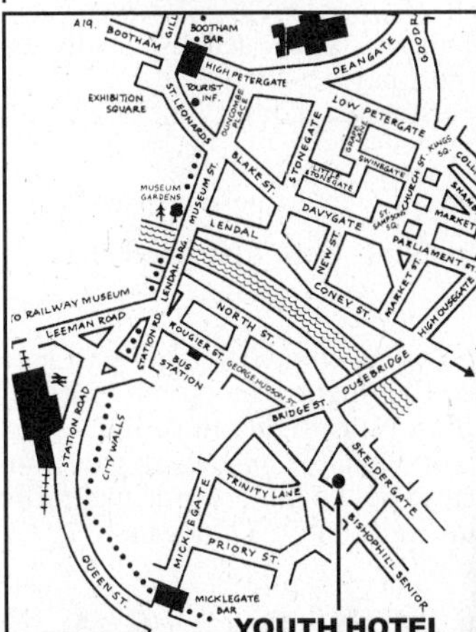

WE ARE HERE
ユース ホステル
YUNGDOMSHARBAGE
OSTELLO
AUBERGE DE JEUNESE
ALBERGUE JUVENIL
JUGENDHERBERGE

BISHOPHILL HOUSE
11/13 BISHOPHILL SENIOR,
YORK, YO1 1EF

Tel: (01904) 625904 or 630613

YORK BACKPACKERS

Micklegate House
88-90 Micklegate
York
YO1 6JX

York Backpackers is situated in a magnificent historic mansion, inside the medieval city walls and just 5 minutes from Rail and Coach stations. It is a short stroll from the gothic York Minster and the world-famous Jorvik Viking Centre. Open all year round with friendly staff who are always on hand to help.

Our Dungeons Bar is open till late providing the perfect environment to meet travellers from all over the world. Breakfast, bedding (including sheets) and hot showers are all free. There are 135 beds available in double rooms, family rooms and dorms. Other facilities include self-catering kitchen, laundry, TV and video room, internet & 24 hour security.

www.yorkbackpackers.co.uk

CONTACT Tel: (01904) 627720, Email:mail@yorkbackpackers.co.uk
OPENING SEASON All year
OPENING HOURS 24 Hours
NUMBER OF BEDS 135: 2x18, 1x17, 1x16, 2x12, 2x10, 1x8, 1x6, 2xfamily(5) & 1xTwin
BOOKING REQUIREMENTS Booking is advised especially on weekends and in summer. Deposit Full payment required.
PRICE PER NIGHT From £9 per person in a dorm room. (All prices include breakfast)

PUBLIC TRANSPORT
York has coach and rail stations 5 minutes' walk from the hostel.

DIRECTIONS
By Car: From A64 take A1036 into York. Continue straight past race course and into Micklegate. We're 100 metres along on the left opposite the church. **From Rail station**: Turn right out of the station for 300 metres. Take the first left through the medieval gate into Micklegate. **From Coach Station**: Head up the hill towards the traffic lights. At the end of Rougier St, turn right onto Micklegate.

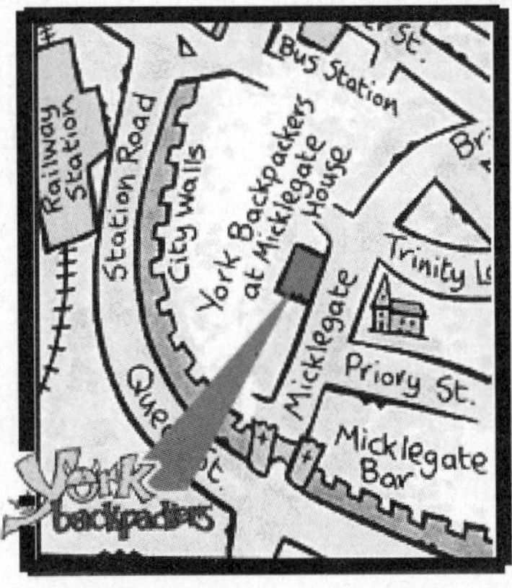

HISTORIC HOSTEL located on one of the **most popular streets** in York, **inside the medieval city walls** and close to pubs, clubs and shops.

From £9 pppn

incl. breakfast

- **5 mins walk from buses & trains •**
- TV room with videos •
- **Dungeon Bar with great atmosphere •**
- Georgian Café •
- **E-mail, Internet, fax and phone •**
- Self-catering kitchen •
- **Laundry •**

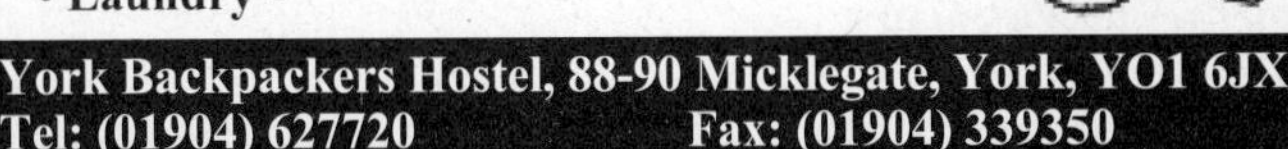

York Backpackers Hostel, 88-90 Micklegate, York, YO1 6JX
Tel: (01904) 627720 **Fax: (01904) 339350**
E-mail: mail@yorkbackpackers.co.uk

www.yorkbackpackers.co.uk

 See page 207 for colour photo

WHITBY BACKPACKERS AT HARBOUR GRANGE

Spital Bridge
Whitby
North Yorkshire YO22 4EF

Harbour Grange is Whitby's long established friendly, backpackers' hostel. It is beautifully situated on the River Esk, in Whitby itself, and only 5 minutes' walk from train and bus stations. The hostel is all on the ground floor and has good facilities for self-catering with a dining area and a separate lounge area, both big enough to seat 24 people. There are 5 dormitories and family rooms are available on request. The hostel is open all day but so that everyone can have a chance of a good night's sleep, there is a curfew at 11.30 (quiet at midnight). The premises are non-smoking.

Whitby is a beautiful little fishing town surrounded by beaches and moorland. Here you can find stunning views from cliff walks and visit lovely villages like Grosmont where steam trains run to Pickering & Goathland where Heartbeat is filmed. Take a look at where Captain Cook lived and the Abbey that has stood as a landmark for the last 800 years. **www.whitbybackpackers.co.uk**

CONTACT Birgitta Ward-Foxton, Tel: (01947) 600817
Email: backpackers@harbourgrange.co.uk
OPENING SEASON 1st March - 31st Oct (Open all year for groups booked in advance)
OPENING HOURS Hostel open all day. Check in 5pm-9pm.
NUMBER OF BEDS 24: 1 x 2 : 2 x 4 : 1 x 6 : 1 x 8.
BOOKING REQUIREMENTS Booking advised for weekends and for groups. A deposit of 10% is required.
PRICE PER NIGHT From £10 per person. The hostel can be hired for sole use by groups for £200 a night.

PUBLIC TRANSPORT
Whitby has a train station and a bus station.

DIRECTIONS
From Whitby train and bus stations: cross the bridge and turn right. Follow the river. First right after "The Bottom House" pub.

P H 1m

WHITEFIELDS COTTAGE

Fountains Abbey and
Studley Royal Park
Fountains, Ripon. HG4 3DY

Situated on a medieval deer-park, Whitefields Cottage offers self-catering accommodation within the Fountains Abbey and Studley Royal Estate. Cared for by the National Trust and awarded World Heritage Site status in 1986, the estate contains a beautiful water garden, Elizabethan mansion and a Cistercian abbey. Whitefields is a 19th-century cottage on the edge of Studley Royal Deer Park, home to around 500 Red, Fallow and Sika deer.

Whether you want to explore the water gardens and impressive abbey, or walk around the North York moors (1hr drive) or Yorkshire Dales, Whitefields is ideal. It is fully equipped to offer groups of up to 16 people, inexpensive but comfortable accommodation. Our facilities include showers, toilets, laundry, drying room and telephone.

GROUPS ONLY

CONTACT Kath Slinn. Tel (01765) 643172.
Email :- Kath.slinn@nationaltrust.org.uk
OPENING SEASON All year, except Christmas and New Year
OPENING HOURS No restrictions
NUMBER OF BEDS 16: 1 x 6 : 1 x 8 : 1 x 2.
BOOKING REQUIREMENTS Bookings required 2 weeks in advance, non refundable deposit £60
PRICE PER NIGHT £10 per person. Minimum charge equivalent to 6 people per night (£60 per night)

PUBLIC TRANSPORT
Train station and National Express coaches at Harrogate (15 miles). Regular bus service between Harrogate and Ripon. Taxis Ripon to Whitefields £5 - Harrogate to Whitefields £20.

DIRECTIONS
From B6265 turn to Studley Roger. Drive through village, bear sharp right, before the National Trust sign, into deer park, ½ mile up main avenue turn right sign-posted; "estate vehicles only". Turn right up the track at the end of this road, Whitefields is at top of track. Telephone estate office (during office hours) for gate code if arriving after 6pm Winter or 9pm Summer.

WEST END OUTDOOR CENTRE

West End
Summerbridge, Harrogate
HG3 4BA

Situated in the Yorkshire Dales amidst stunning landscape overlooking Thruscross Reservoir in a designated Area of Outstanding Natural Beauty on the edge of the Dales National Park, this self-catering accommodation centre offers excellent facilities for up to 30 people in 9 bedrooms with bunk beds. Leaders' en-suite accommodation has private catering, dining and lounge facilities. The centre is fully centrally heated. There are 4 showers, 4 hand basins and 4 toilets. There are no extra charges for heating, lighting and hot water. The well-equipped kitchen includes a 4-oven Aga cooker, two fridges and a freezer, together with all the cooking utensils and equipment. 3 star Hostel.

Ideal for Team Building Courses, Schools, Scouts, Guides and family parties etc. Located only 12 miles from Harrogate and Skipton, 30 miles from the City of York. Tourist Board inspected and managed by the owners. All teenagers must be accompanied by an adult (25+). Ask for one of our brochures or find us on the web.

www.westendoutdoorcentre.co.uk

CONTACT Tel: (01943) 880207. Email: m.verity@virgin.net
OPENING SEASON All year
OPENING HOURS Flexible
NUMBER OF BEDS 30 :- 4 x 2 : 3 x 4 : 1 x 6 : 1 x 4 en-suite
BOOKING REQUIREMENTS Advisable at weekends
PRICE PER NIGHT £10.00 pp. Sole use £220 (Sat/Sun/Bank Hol), £180 any other night, £550 for 4 nights midweek. Sunday night, if staying for more than 2 nights (not bank holidays) £100.

PUBLIC TRANSPORT
Nearest train stations are at Harrogate and Skipton, both 12 miles from the hostel. Taxi fare from either station would be approximately £15.

DIRECTIONS
GR 146 575. Leave A59 at Blubberhouses, signed West End 2½ miles. Do not turn off, centre is on left side.

AIRTON QUAKER HOSTEL

The Nook
Airton, Skipton
North Yorkshire
BD23 4AE

Airton Quaker Meeting house was built in 1690 by William Ellis and the adjoining hostel was originally a stable for the Quakers attending the meetings. The stable was converted into a wartime evacuee hostel in 1940 and used as a holiday hostel from 1943 with a modernisation in 1983. The meeting house is still used for worship. The hostel is situated in the centre of Airton, a typical Yorkshire Dales village on the banks of the River Aire. The Pennine Way passes the village and Malham Cove, Janet's Foss and Gordale Scar are within walking distance.

The hostel has a self-catering kitchen/common area, and three rooms of 6,4,2 bunks. Blankets and pillow are provided but you must bring your own sleeping bag. There is a farm shop and café at Airton (closed Mondays) but there are more facilities at Gargrave. Parties of children (except families) must be accompanied by two adults.

CONTACT Mr or Mrs Parker, (01729) 830263
OPENING SEASON All year
OPENING HOURS No Restrictions
NUMBER OF BEDS 12: 1 x 6 : 1 x 4 : 1 x 2
BOOKING REQUIREMENTS Advance booking is recommended with a deposit of 10%.
PRICE PER NIGHT £6 (adults) £3 (Children under 16). Exclusive use of the hostel is available for a supplement charge.

PUBLIC TRANSPORT
Nearest train stations Gargrave (4½miles), Skipton (8½miles). Buses from Skipton to Malham pass through Airton. Approx taxi fare from Skipton £12.

DIRECTIONS GR 904 592 Block of buildings at the end of Airton Village on the top of the hill leading down to the river bridge.

DALESBRIDGE

Austwick
Nr Settle
LA2 8AZ

Dalesbridge is located on the A65 at Austwick, on the edge of the Yorkshire Dales National Park, just five miles from both Ingleton and Settle. It is a comfortable venue for those visiting the Yorkshire Dales, whether you are a family, a group or an individual.

The six bed units have a kitchen area with a cooker, fridge, washing up sink, shower and toilet. Crockery, cutlery and cooking pots are provided and there is a seating area in the middle of the room. The four bed units have a shower and toilet, small seating area with kettle, toaster, microwave crockery and cutlery. These rooms are ideal for the smaller group not requiring full self-catering facilities. Utilising all the units provides group accommodation for up to 40. You will need to bring your own sleeping bag and pillow, alternatively bedding is available to hire. We have a great deal to offer: Bar, drying room, functions, B&B, and campsite.

www.dalesbridge.co.uk

CONTACT Jon Tel: (015242) 51021, Email: info@dalesbridge.co.uk
OPENING SEASON All year
OPENING HOURS Reception open 9:00-17:00 (out of hours messaging system)
NUMBER OF BEDS 40
BOOKING REQUIREMENTS Advance booking with deposit
PRICE PER NIGHT £12 per person. ~ £65 - 6 bed unit ~ £45 - 4 bed unit.

PUBLIC TRANSPORT
Settle railway station is 5 miles away and Clapham station 1½ miles. There are infrequent buses but if you would like collection from either railway station please give us a call.

DIRECTIONS
GR 762 676. The hostel is on the main A65. When travelling from Settle towards Ingleton we are situated on the left hand side just after the Shell Petrol Station.

P H 1m

See page 210 for colour photo

TIMBERLODGE

Pinecroft, Ingleton
Carnforth
Lancashire
LA6 3DP

Timberlodge is a Scandinavian pine lodge for self-catering groups or individuals, situated half a mile from Ingleton on the edge of the Yorkshire Dales. The surrounding limestone landscape is renowned for its excellent underground systems. The famous Gaping Ghyll system is popular with cavers and for those that like to keep dry there are show caves featuring stalagmites, stalactites and a massive 200,000-year-old ice age cavern. The Three Peaks Race route is accessible to the enthusiastic walker and from Ingleton there is a pleasant 4-mile walk on maintained footpaths through spectacular waterfall and woodland scenery.

The lodge is fully double glazed and centrally heated. It has spacious bunkrooms for 3 to 6 people, hot showers, sauna, and an excellent drying room. The kitchen is well equipped with gas and electric cookers, dishwasher, fridge freezer, microwave and a food warmer which will hold 48 meals. The large dining room has a soft drinks machine and satellite television and video. There is a payphone for incoming/ outgoing calls (015242) 42119.

www.pine-croft.co.uk

CONTACT Robin and Dorothy Hainsworth, Tel/Fax: (015242) 41462, Email: enquiries@pine-croft.co.uk
OPENING SEASON All year
OPENING HOURS 10am - 10pm
NUMBER OF BEDS 48:- 4 x 3 6 x 6
BOOKING REQUIREMENTS Booking (with deposit) is advised with as much notice as possible, particularly for groups.
PRICE PER NIGHT £10 per person. Exclusive use available.

PUBLIC TRANSPORT
Nearest train station is at Bentham (3 miles away). Local buses call at Ingleton (1 mile away).

DIRECTIONS
GR 699719, The hostel is ¾ of a mile south of Ingleton on the A65.

THE GOLDEN LION BUNKROOM

Horton-in-Ribblesdale
Nr. Settle
North Yorkshire
BD24 0MB

The Golden Lion Bunkroom is part of the Hotel and is situated in the Yorkshire Dales overlooking Pen-y-ghent. It makes an ideal base for the adventurous who are tackling the 'Three Peaks' or a welcome break for Pennine Way Walkers. It is believed that The Golden Lion was a coaching inn during the sixteenth century and the old coach highway can still be followed on foot.

Three public bars provide a good selection of real ales and The Flag Floored Tap Room makes an ideal place for people who enjoy outdoor activities - even in wet weather there is no need to remove boots to enjoy a refreshing drink. At weekends this bar is used extensively by the local pothole clubs and singing sessions are not uncommon. Visitors with musical instruments and plenty of enthusiasm are welcome! A variety of food can provide anything from a beefburger to an a la carte menu. Vegetarian meals are also available.

CONTACT Michael Johnson, Tel/Fax: (01729) 860206,
Email tricia@goldenlionhotel.co.uk
OPENING SEASON All year (except Christmas Day)
OPENING HOURS 11.00 am to 11.00 pm
NUMBER OF BEDS 15 (1 room)
BOOKING REQUIREMENTS Booking recommended with deposit of full amount £8 per person.
PRICE PER NIGHT £8.00pp

PUBLIC TRANSPORT
Nearest train stations are Settle (6 miles) and Horton (½ mile). Three buses a day stop near to the Golden Lion Hotel.Taxi to Settle £5 - £6.

DIRECTIONS
Follow signs from Settle to Horton-in-Ribblesdale. We are opposite the Church.

5m

SKIRFARE BRIDGE DALES BARN

Kilnsey
Skipton
North Yorkshire
BD23 5PT

Skirfare Bridge Dales Barn is a traditional stone barn and is a distinctive feature of the beautiful Dales landscape, standing at the confluence of Upper Wharfedale and Littondale with the Climbers' Challenge, Kilnsey Crag, providing a spectacular backdrop. The area has long been famous for walking, cycling and touring with several footpaths easily accessible from the barn including the Dales Way. Kilnsey is nearby where you can find The Kilnsey Park providing day fishing and food as well as The Tennant Arms Hotel for those who prefer a bar snack. Pony trekking is available at Conistone.

Although altered little on the outside, internally the Barn has been converted to provide centrally heated accommodation in six ground floor bedrooms with fully equipped kitchen, common room, drying room and showers on the upper floor. Ample car parking and a grass recreation area.

CONTACT Mrs J Foster, Tel: (01756) 761028
OPENING SEASON All year
OPENING HOURS 4.00 pm to 10.30 am
NUMBER OF BEDS 25 in 6 bedrooms
BOOKING REQUIREMENTS Booking essential, up to 6 months in advance for weekend block bookings (Friday, Saturday nights)
PRICE PER NIGHT £10 per person or £190 for full Barn booking.

PUBLIC TRANSPORT
Skipton Railway Station is 12 miles away. There are also buses from Bradford, Keighley and Harrogate. A Dales bus service runs directly past the Barn, phone (01756) 753123 or (01535) 603284.

DIRECTIONS
From Skipton take B6265 to Threshfield then the B6160 towards Kettlewell for 3 miles. Past the Crag the Barn is a further 400m North. One mile from the Dales Way at Conistone-with-Kilnsey, turn into the Barn just before Arncliffe T junction.

GRANGE FARM BARN

Grange Farm, Hubberholme
Buckden, Skipton
North Yorks
BD23 5JE

Grange Farm Barn was formerly the stables and coach-house for Grange Farm, Hubberholme, which used to be the vicarage for the 13th-century church nearby. The author and dramatist, J B Priestley wished to be buried at Hubberholme and a plaque in the church in his memory states "he found Hubberholme one of the smallest and most pleasant places in the world".

The barn is situated in the Yorkshire Dales National Park in ideal walking country. It sleeps 18 people in 4 separate rooms (2x6 1x4 1x2) on the ground floor, with drying room, showers and toilets. Upstairs is a fully equipped kitchen and a large dining and recreation room in traditional "Dales Style", giving magnificent views of Langstrothdale. The barn has central heating, is open all year and there is plenty of parking space. It is ideal for family and school parties and reunions, with group bookings only at weekends. Smaller groups or individuals are welcome mid-week.

All teenagers must be accompanied by an adult.

CONTACT Mrs A Falshaw Tel: (01756) 760259
OPENING SEASON All year
OPENING HOURS All day
NUMBER OF BEDS : 18 2x6 : 1x4 : 1x2
BOOKING REQUIREMENTS Booking not essential but advised, deposit required with confirmation.
PRICE PER NIGHT £8 pp £6 children. Sole use Weekends £288. (Group bookings only) Bank Holidays (3 nights) £432.

PUBLIC TRANSPORT
Train station; Skipton 20 miles. Buses from Skipton to Buckden.

DIRECTIONS
From Skipton B6265 to Threshfield. B6160 to Buckden. Turn left at signpost to Hubberholme (Hawes Rd). Grange Farm is ¾ mile on left.

THE BARNSTEAD

Stackstead Farm
Ingleton
Carnforth
Lancs
LA6 3HS

The Barnstead is situated in the beautiful Yorkshire Dales, one mile from Ingleton village centre. It has panoramic views of Ingleborough and Whernside, and is within easy access of the Lake District and Lancashire coast. Local attractions include rambling, fell walking, pot-holing, climbing and geological and historic sites.

The Barnstead provides bunk-style self-catering accommodation, in two separate units, for individuals, families or groups. Both units are centrally heated, sleeping bag liners, duvets and pillows are provided, inclusive of price. Unit One has:- 22 beds in 4 dorms, large lounge/dining area, drying room, large fitted kitchen (with cookers, fridges, freezer, crockery and utensils) and male & female washrooms with showers. Unit Two has:- One 6 bed dorm, kitchen/lounge and washroom with shower. No extras.

www.stacksteadfarm.co.uk

CONTACT Wendy/Steve Moorhouse, Tel: (015242) 41386,
Email: Enquiries@Stacksteadfarm.co.uk
OPENING SEASON All year
OPENING HOURS 9am to 9pm
NUMBER OF BEDS (Unit 1) **22:** beds 2x4 : 1x6 : 1x8 (Unit 2) 1x 6 beds.
BOOKING REQUIREMENTS Pre-booking advised with as much notice as possible. Deposit required.
PRICE PER NIGHT (Unit 1) £10 per person or £180 for full use. (Unit 2) £10 per person (minimum of 4 at weekends).

PUBLIC TRANSPORT
Nearest train station (Bentham) 3 miles, buses (Ingleton) 1 mile.

DIRECTIONS
GR 686 724. On main A65 Kirkby Lonsdale to Settle road. When travelling south turn right at Masons Arms pub in Ingleton. In 300 yards turn right into farm.

           1m

THE OLD SCHOOL BUNKHOUSE

Chapel-le-Dale
Ingleton Carnforth
Lancs LA6 3AR

Situated 4½ miles from Ingleton in Yorkshire Dales limestone country. Located between Ingleborough and Whernside with superb views of both, the bunkhouse makes an ideal base for sporting or nature holidays. The area is well known for its scenery including the Three Peaks walk, (Ingleborough, Pen-y-ghent and Whernside), the waterfalls walk and for having some of the best caves and potholes in the country including the famous Gaping Ghyll system and the White Scar show cave.

This is a stone property, which has been converted from an old school, with much of the character remaining and provides self-catering accommodation for up to 30 people. The property comprises lounge, dining room, drying room, 3 shower rooms with hand basins and toilets. Well equipped kitchen with industrial cooker, toaster, fridge, freezer, dishwasher, microwave, and payphone. Nearest Pub 100 yds

www.oldschoolbunkhouse.co.uk

CONTACT Tel/Fax: (01524) 242327. Neal and Tanya Wild.
Email:- info@oldschoolhouse.gbr.cc
OPENING SEASON All year
OPENING HOURS 24 hours
NUMBER OF BEDS 30: 5 x 6
BOOKING REQUIREMENTS Booking essential up to 5 months in advance for popular times, £100 deposit for 2 nights, 25% for 3 +.
PRICE PER NIGHT £8 per person, minimum £160 per night, minimum 2 nights at weekend.

PUBLIC TRANSPORT
Ribblehead station 1 mile. Local buses run from Ingleton 4½ miles.

DIRECTIONS
4½ miles on the B6255 Ingleton to Hawes Road, just after Chapel-Le-Dale village on left hand side. 11 miles from Hawes on B6255.

HARRIS HOUSE

The Old School
Hardraw, near Hawes
Wensleydale
North Yorkshire
DL8 3LZ

Harris House is the outdoor pursuits centre of the William Hulmes Grammar School (Manchester). The centre occupies an old village school, with attached headmaster's house, on the edge of the hamlet of Hardraw. It is a grade II listed building built in 1875 in attractive Dale stone. Ample parking is available in the old playground and the large schoolroom is used for communal activities. The well appointed and practical accommodation is centrally heated throughout and can accommodate groups of up to 34.

Hardraw has a camp site, a café and the Green Dragon Inn (adjacent to Hardraw Force waterfall). Many groups use these facilities to complement their visit. The café offers good value, substantial home cooking for groups. In the locality are opportunities for caving, rock climbing, fell walking and cycling (secure storage). The Pennine Way passes the centre. The local town of Hawes has a full range of shops. Harris House is a ideal base for Duke of Edinburgh's award expedition training or educational visits.

www.whgs.co.uk

CONTACT Warden, Tel: (0161)226 2054, Email: hardraw@whgs.co.uk
OPENING SEASON All Year
OPENING HOURS 24 Hours
NUMBER OF BEDS 32: 3x8, 2x3, 1x2
BOOKING REQUIREMENTS Essential (20% deposit) but short notice bookings are often available.
PRICE PER NIGHT £11 per person, Minimum £110, maximum £160

PUBLIC TRANSPORT
Garsdale Station is 8 miles away, connected by infrequent buses. Hawes, a pleasant 1½ mile walk away, has more frequent buses.

DIRECTIONS
Turn north off A684 1 mile to the west of Hawes and proceed for ½ mile. Harris House is at the west end of the hamlet of Hardraw.

FELL END BUNKHOUSE

Ravenstonedale
Sedbergh
Cumbria
CA17 4LN

Fell End provides bunk-house style accommodation for people wishing to explore this beautiful and wild area. Overlooking the Howgill Fells and 6 miles from any town, it provides an ideal remote base for those interested in walking, cycling, caving and canoeing. Perfect for small groups and families and only 20 miles from the Lake District. Fell End is owned by the Bendrigg Trust, a charity offering outdoor activities for disabled people.

Fell End accommodates 12 people in bunks in the central communal area, plus a single bed in an adjoining room. The beds have a covered mattress and pillow. The main feature in the living area is a beautiful multi-fuel-burning stove, which also heats the radiators. There is a fully equipped kitchen with fridge/freezer and electric cooker. The bathroom area consists of two toilets, one electric shower and four washbasins. Entry is by a touch lock system. Dogs are allowed but only under strict supervision. Fell End is not wheelchair friendly.

CONTACT Lynne Irish. Tel: (01539) 723766, Fax (01539) 722446
Email: office@bendrigg.org.uk
OPENING SEASON All year
OPENING HOURS 24 hours
NUMBER OF BEDS **13:** 1 x 12 : 1 x 1.
BOOKING REQUIREMENTS Advance booking required with 20% deposit
PRICE PER NIGHT £7 per person

PUBLIC TRANSPORT
Nearest train station is Kirkby Stephen (6 miles) Carlisle/Settle/Leeds line. Then take bus 564 Mon to Sat (4 per day) Tel (017683) 71199 for times.

DIRECTIONS
GR 723 983, detailed directions will be given on booking.

      3m

MARSETT BARN

c/o Low Mill Outdoor Centre
Askrigg, Leyburn
North Yorkshire DL8 3HZ

Marsett Barn is a "back to nature" experience, it is an old barn in an old landscape. The barn is basic but full of character and charm and has been sympathetically restored to retain its special place in this Dales' setting.

On the ground floor there is an entrance area with living and dining space, a wood burning stove, a fully fitted kitchen, a drying area, and a toilet for people with disabilities. Upstairs there are two sleeping areas, each with platform to sleep 10 people (20 in total). Also there are toilets with handbasins and showers.

Activities may be available at Low Mill Outdoor Centre from £70 per session. A list of activities is available on request.

www.lowmill.com

CONTACT Tel: (01969) 650432
Email: lowmill@gofree.co.uk
OPENING SEASON All year
OPENING HOURS All day
NUMBER OF BEDS: 20 2 platforms x 10
BOOKING REQUIREMENTS Booking is essential
PRICE PER NIGHT £6per person (min£20) includes gas

PUBLIC TRANSPORT
The nearest bus stop is Bainbridge (4 miles) and nearest train station Garsdale (11 miles)

DIRECTIONS
From Marsett Green, access is normally on foot or cycle. From the green, follow the track on left towards Stalling Busk. The Barn is in a field on the right, approximately ½ kilometre from the green.

THE WALKER'S HOSTEL

Oubas Hill
Ulverston
Cumbria, LA12 7LB

On the edge of the Lake District, the Walker's Hostel has 30 beds with between 2 and 7 beds to a room. One room is a family room with a cot. We do not normally expect strangers to share rooms. Breakfasts and evening meals are home cooked and meat free. We have a book exchange, local maps, games and toys. We have a no smoking policy in the house, a cycle lockup, a drying room and an open fire. We play good music and enjoy the company of our guests.

Ulverston is an old market town with plenty of good pubs. The Cumbria Way starts at Ulverston and there are street markets on Thursdays and Saturdays as well as other attractions. The lighthouse on Hoad Hill is a famous land mark. The Walker's Hostel is ideally suited for long and short walks. We are happy to give advice on how to get the most from your visit.

www.walkershostel.co.uk

CONTACT Jean Povey, Tel/Fax: (01229) 585588,
Email: povey@walkershostel.freeserve.co.uk
OPENING SEASON January to October
OPENING HOURS Flexible
NUMBER OF BEDS 30: 1 x 2 : 1 x 3 : 3 x 4 : 1 x 6 : 1 x 7.
BOOKING REQUIREMENTS Booking is advisable, not essential.
PRICE PER NIGHT £14 Bed and Breakfast; £8 for evening meal. Reductions for children.

PUBLIC TRANSPORT
Ulverston has a good train service. National Express Coaches and local Stage Coach buses also come to Ulverston phone 0870 608 2608.

DIRECTIONS
From M6 Jn 36 take the A590. On the edge of Ulverston there is a roundabout. Turn left, and left again. From the bus or train station, walk towards town. Turn right down A590. We are just beyond the second roundabout.

GRIZEDALE HOSTEL

Hawkshead
Ambleside
Cumbria
LA22 0QJ

The Grizedale Hostel is situated in the heart of the Grizedale Forest Park, between Lake Windermere and Coniston Water, just three miles south of Hawkshead. The Grizedale Park offers lots of facilities for visitors which include, self-guided walking and cycling trails, (bikes can be hired), "go ape" high wire course, orienteering routes, education service, 80 forest sculptures, and some of the most beautiful scenery. Visitor centre staff will be happy to help you plan to get the most out of your time.

The hostel provides affordable self-catering group accommodation. It is divided into three main rooms, two dorms each sleeping 8 visitors with their own shower, wash basin and toilet facilities and a common room/kitchen with tables and chairs. The hostel is equipped with crockery, cutlery, fridge/freezer, cooker and wood burning stove.

www.forestry.gov.uk/northwestengland

CONTACT Tel: (01229) 860010. Email: grizedale@forestry.gsi.gov.uk
OPENING SEASON All year
OPENING HOURS Arrive by 5pm if possible and vacate by 10am.
NUMBER OF BEDS 16: 2 x 8
BOOKING REQUIREMENTS Booking essential, deposit of £30.00.
PRICE PER NIGHT Peak (Easter-Oct, Xmas, New Year & Feb half term) £200 3nights, £225 4nights, £400 7nights. Off Peak: £170 3nights, £200 4nights, £350 7nights.

PUBLIC TRANSPORT
Train stations at Windermere 10 miles & Ulverston 12 miles. National Express travels to Ambleside 8 miles. Some local buses available.

DIRECTIONS
2½ miles south west of Hawkshead. From the south follow the signs from A590 at Haverthwaite - Grizedale is 1½m north of Satterthwaite village. From north A593 & B5286 from Ambleside to Hawkshead.

ROOKHOW CENTRE

Rusland
Grizedale
South Lakeland
Cumbria
LA12 8LA

Perhaps the best situated small hostel in the Lake District. Peaceful, in 12 acres of its own woodland, but close to the heart of the Lakes, ten minutes from Coniston Water and Windermere, and on the edge of the famous Grizedale Forest Park with its trails and sculptures. Superb area for walking, cycling and all outdoor activities. Also for quiet retreat, relaxation, study and artistic pursuits.

The Rookhow Centre is within the former stables of the nearby historic Quaker meeting house which is also available for conferences and group sessions. Guests find the centre warm, comfortable and well equipped. There are sleeping areas, a self-catering kitchen/dining area and picnic tables and barbecue for warm days. There is a camping area and a spectacular canvas and oak framed 'Yurt', in the woods.

CONTACT Warden, Tel: (01229) 860231,
Email: rookhow@britishlibrary.net
OPENING SEASON All year
OPENING HOURS All day
NUMBER OF BEDS 20: 1x8 : 1x 9. plus several extra on bed-settees
BOOKING REQUIREMENTS Booking is essential (deposit).
PRICE PER NIGHT from Adult £11. Under 16's £6.

PUBLIC TRANSPORT
Nearest train station (Ulverston) is 8 miles from the hostel. Approximately £12 taxi fare from station.

DIRECTIONS
GR 332 896. **From A590** leave at Greenodd (A5092) junction and follow sign for Workington for ¼ mile. Take minor road to right signed Oxen Park. Continue through Oxen Park for a further 2 miles more, Rookhow is on left. **From Ambleside** : to Hawkshead, then to Grizedale. Continue beyond Grizedale for 3½ miles (Satterthwaite to Ulverston Road). Rookhow is on the right.

STICKLEBARN BUNKHOUSE

Sticklebarn Tavern
Great Langdale
Cumbria
LA22 9JU

The Sticklebarn is beautifully situated amidst some of the finest mountain scenery in England. It is at the very foot of the famous Langdale Pikes and Dungeon Ghyll waterfalls and seven miles north west of Ambleside. The Sticklebarn is privately owned and is available to the general outdoor public and traveller on foot. The bunkhouse has no common room or self-catering facilities but there is a TV room and meals service provided in the pub. Sorry no pets. A brochure is available on request.

CONTACT The Manager Tel: (015394) 37356
Email: Sticklebarn@aol.com
OPENING SEASON All year
OPENING HOURS Open all day. Food served. Summer; 12noon to 9.30pm; Winter 12noon to 2.30 and 6pm to 9.30pm. Breakfasts available between 8am and 10.30am weekends, 8.30am and 10.30am during week.
NUMBER OF BEDS Winter *20*, Summer **16**
BOOKING REQUIREMENTS Pre-booking is advised for weekends and groups (at least 7 days in advance) and requires a deposit.
PRICE PER NIGHT £10 per person.

PUBLIC TRANSPORT
Bus service 516 to Great Langdale from Ambleside, ask for New Dungeon Ghyll Hotel, walk 5 mins (phone (01946) 632222 for timetable).

DIRECTIONS
From the A591 Windermere to Keswick road at Ambleside take the A593 turn to Coniston / Torver. After two miles take the B5343 to Great Langdale via Chapel Stile. The Bunkhouse is adjacent to the Sticklebarn Tavern.

AMBLESIDE BACKPACKERS

Iveing Cottage
Old Lake Road
Ambleside Cumbria LA22 0DJ

Ambleside Backpackers is the ultimate clean, comfortable, secure, budget, centrally heated accommodation for single backpackers & groups. No lock out, no curfew; a manager on site. Included in the price are free tea/coffee and light breakfast plus lockers for hire. We are 5 minutes' walk from the centre of the local market town of Ambleside, situated at the northern end of Lake Windermere.

The 1871 building has been totally refurbished retaining all the traditional features. There are 12 dorms ranging from 4 to 11 bunks. All dorms have new matresses, duvets, bunk sheets, carpets, curtains, washbasins and views of the local fells. We offer a fully equipped commercial kitchen plus dining room together with a large common room with fire, satellite TV, video, & hi fi. In our own grounds there is a barbeque and sitting area overlooking the local fell. Only 7 minutes' walk to the Lake with steamers, ferries, rowing boats and sailing. Local pubs and restaurants are within 5 minutes' walk. Many of the local walks can be started from the Hostel, the local tour bus has a stop a few yards away.

www.englishlakesbackpackers.co.uk

CONTACT Martin, Michael or Carol (01539) 432340:
Email : enquiries@englishlakesbackpackers.co.uk
OPENING SEASON All year
OPENING HOURS 24 hours
NUMBER OF BEDS 74: 2 x 10 : 1 x 7 : 4 x 6 : 4 x 4 : 1 x 5 : 1 x 2
BOOKING REQUIREMENTS Essential for groups - 25% deposit.
PRICE PER NIGHT £14.00. Discount on 3 or more nights.

PUBLIC TRANSPORT
Windermere train station 4 miles (555 bus to Ambleside).

DIRECTIONS
A591 Windermere to Ambleside. Opp Hayes Garden Ctr turn right, Old Lake Road half way up on right.

P 1m

GRASMERE INDEPENDENT HOSTEL

Broadrayne Farm, Keswick Road
Grasmere, Cumbria, LA22 9RU

This small deluxe hostel is situated on a farm right at the heart of the Lakes. See the best of Lakeland right from our doorstep. Give the car a holiday. Take the Wordsworth walk around Grasmere and Rydal Lake, or do a mountain classic, climb Helvellyn or Fairfield from our door. The Coast to Coast footpath goes right through the farm. Over 101 other local attractions and activities, including a good pub with fine bar meals just 300 yds down the road.

Our English Tourism Council 4 star graded hostel has ensuite bedrooms with made up beds (sheets & duvets) lockers, bedside lights, a coin operated sauna, commercial laundry, drying room, dining room, 2 self-catering kitchens with microwaves, fridges, toasters etc. A stunning common room with large TV, a lockable bike/luggage store and private parking. We are resident proprietors. Cleanliness and friendliness assured. Totally non-smoking. Individuals, families and groups all welcome. *If you want the best, be our guest* visit our informative website:-

www.grasmerehostel.co.uk

CONTACT Mr Bev Dennison, Tel: (015394) 35055,
Email: Bev@grasmerehostel.co.uk
OPENING SEASON All year (notable superb winter walking base)
OPENING HOURS 8am to 10pm, (keys for resident guests)
NUMBER OF BEDS 24: 1 x 3 : 1 x 4 : 1 x 5 : 2 x 6.
BOOKING REQUIREMENTS Advisable, credit card confirms bed.
PRICE PER NIGHT £14.50 per person (bedding inc). Groups please apply for rates.

PUBLIC TRANSPORT
Train to Windermere Station (11 miles from hostel), catch 555 bus from Windermere or Keswick, ask for Travellers Rest Pub. There is also a National Express coach that runs between London/Grasmere daily.

DIRECTIONS
GR 336 094.1¼ miles north of village. Stay on main A591 right to our drive, 400m north of Travellers Rest Pub,on the right hand side.

P AM 3m

LAKE DISTRICT BACKPACKERS

High Street
Windermere
Cumbria. LA23 1AF

Situated in the heart of Windermere and central Lakeland, you will find our cosy, friendly hostel ideally situated for exploring the surrounding area. We can advise you on routes for walks and cycle rides and provide you with maps or you can join one of our guided days out. We are often asked to help organise abseiling, canoeing, sailing, windsurfing even caving! There is easy access to the lake and fells from our door and we are adjacent to the main 555 bus route through Lakeland.

The hostel itself with its small dormitories provides you with every comfort but at a budget price. We are right next to a number of pubs, restaurants and take-aways and only minutes away from the rail and bus stations. Internet access and Sky keep you in touch with the world! A well equipped kitchen and comfortable common room help to make your stay one to remember. Check us out on:-

www.lakedistrictbackpackers.co.uk

CONTACT Paul. Tel: (015394) 46374.
Email: enquiries@lakedistrictbackpackers.co.uk
OPENING SEASON All year
OPENING HOURS 24 hours
NUMBER OF BEDS 22:- 1 x 7 : 1 x 5 : 1 x 4 : 2 x 3.
BOOKING REQUIREMENTS Booking is essential, 24 hours in advance - deposit required.
PRICE PER NIGHT From £11.00pp.

PUBLIC TRANSPORT
Windermere train station is 2 minutes' walk. National Express Coach stop 2 minutes' walk.

DIRECTIONS
Turn left out of station, walk to information centre, Hostel is opposite, next to Simpson and Parsons Insurance Company.

P H 1m

MAGGS HOWE CAMPING BARN

Maggs Howe
Kentmere
Kendal, Cumbria. LA8 9JP

Kentmere is a quiet, unspoilt valley within the Lake District National Park. It's a ramblers' paradise with woods, fields, lanes, a scattering of traditional lakeland farms and dwellings, and of course the fells with their walks so favoured by Wainwright. The Lakeland to Lindisfarne Long Distance path passes this way as well as the mountain bikers' and horse riders' Coast to Coast. Kentmere offers plenty of activities which include biking, riding and fishing, but most of all quiet enjoyment. A pleasant day's visit can be found at the market town of Kendal and Lake Windermere which are only 20 minutes away.

The recently converted Barn has two sleeping areas, fully fitted kitchen, two showers and toilets. All you need is your sleeping bag, mattresses provided. Breakfasts and suppers are available next door at the bed and breakfast.

www.smoothhound.co.uk/hotels/maggs.html

CONTACT Christine Hevey, (01539) 821689
OPENING SEASON All year
OPENING HOURS 24
NUMBER OF BED SPACES: 14: 1 x 4 1 x 10
BOOKING REQUIREMENTS Recommended with 50% deposit for groups. Individuals can book but not essential.
PRICE PER NIGHT £7.00 per person or £80 sole use.

PUBLIC TRANSPORT
Staveley 4 miles with train and bus service. Oxenholme train station is 10 miles (taxi £18). Kendal/Windermere National Express 8 miles.

DIRECTIONS
GR 462 041, MAP OS English Lakes South East. Green Quarter. Leave the A591 and come into Staveley, proceed to Kentmere for 4 miles, then take right fork to Green Quarter keeping right until you reach Maggs Howe.

LOW GILLERTHWAITE FIELD CENTRE

Ennerdale, Cleator
Cumbria CA23 3AX

Towards the head of Ennerdale valley, one of the most beautiful, least spoilt and quietest valleys in the Lake District, sitting at the foot of Pillar and Red Pike you will find Low Gillerthwaite. An ideal base for fellwalking, classic rock climbs, bird and wildlife watching, mountain biking, orienteering (we have our own permanent course), canoeing (instruction available for groups) and environmental studies.

Originally a 15th-century farmhouse, the Centre has group self-catering facilities, drying room, library of environmental books and a group lecture room. Due to its remoteness the Centre generates its own electricity and in the evening when the generator ceases lighting is supplied by gas lamps. Vehicle access is by forest track and a BT payphone is on site (most mobiles do not work here). With 40 beds Low Gillerthwaite is an ideal base for clubs, extended family groups, school and youth groups. Video available for group leaders; more information can be found on our website.

www.lgfc.org.uk

CONTACT Tel: (01946) 861229
Email: Warden@lgfc.org.uk
OPENING SEASON All year, except Christmas and Boxing Day
OPENING HOURS 24 hours
NUMBER OF BEDS **40:** 2x4 : 1x8 : 1x10 : 1x14
BOOKING REQUIREMENTS Always phone to check availability
PRICE PER NIGHT from £7. per person.

PUBLIC TRANSPORT
Whitehaven Station 12 miles. Buses to Ennerdale Bridge from Cleator Moor or Cockermouth (5miles).

DIRECTIONS
GR NY 139 141. From Ennerdale Bridge take road east, via Croasdale, 3.5 miles to Ennerdale Forest. Continue on forest track 3 miles. Hostel is the first building below the road on the right, 200m before the YHA.

DENTON HOUSE

Penrith Road
Keswick
Cumbria CA12 4JW

Denton House is a purpose built hostel and outdoor centre in the heart of the Lake District. The hostel is designed for group use so has plenty of hot water for showers, central heating throughout and a commercial kitchen, a large dining room and solid bunkbeds! Now that we welcome individuals too, we're constantly upgrading the facilities to be homely as well as functional. We hope to have an outdoor garden/seating area ready for summer 2005.

We are also an outdoor centre and can provide traditional activities for groups of all ages (must be pre-booked) as well as paintball and motorised sports. The centre is particularly suitable for those wanting to explore the great outdoors; we have storage for kayaks and bikes and there's access/egress to the River Greta just across the road. We have well qualified instructors available to provide advice as well as to run trips and help organise expeditions. We are primarily an adult hostel; under 16s are welcome in supervised groups or in exclusive use dorms with parents. We welcome dogs in some rooms if pre-booked. We take a large number of school, youth and military groups, corporate teambuilds and celebration weekends, so booking early is preferable.

www.vividevents.co.uk

CONTACT Tel: (017687) 75351. Email: sales@vividevents.co.uk
OPENING SEASON All year
OPENING HOURS 24 hours
NUMBER OF BEDS 56: 1x4 : 2x6 : 1x8 : 2x10 : 1x12.
BOOKING REQUIREMENTS Preferred (25% deposit for Groups)
PRICE PER NIGHT £12per bed. Group discounts available Oct - March

PUBLIC TRANSPORT
Nearest train station Penrith, buses hourly to Keswick.

DIRECTIONS
From bus centre out of town towards Windermere, keep the park on your left (approx 10mins). We are on the right after post sorting office.

P 1m

ST JOHN'S-IN-THE-VALE CAMPING BARN

Low Bridge End Farm
St John's-in-the-Vale
Keswick, CA12 4TS

St John's-in-the-Vale Camping Barn makes an ideal retreat throughout the year, with double glazing and a wood burning stove. It is on a traditional Lakeland farm, overlooking St John's Beck, surrounded by 50 acres of meadow and woodland. The location is ideal for walking, touring or simply enjoying the peace and abundant wildlife of the area. The star filled skies are spectacular because there is no light pollution. There is a woodland trail, which helps you appreciate the views and variety of wildlife that live on the farm. You can spot red squirrels, deer, badgers, dippers, kingfishers, herons, owls and bats to name but a few. Keswick is 6 miles away, offering a full range of shops, pubs, restaurants, leisure pool, climbing wall, museums, theatre and cinema. Sailing, canoeing, pony trekking and golf are also nearby.

www.campingbarn.com

CONTACT For details contact Graham or Sarah, Tel :(017687) 79242, Email: 1be@sjitv.freeserve.co.uk. To book Tel: (017687) 72645
OPENING SEASON All year
OPENING HOURS 24 hours
NUMBER OF BEDS 8: 1x8
BOOKING REQUIREMENTS Booking in advance is advised. Credit card booking available on (017687) 72645. Online booking www.lakelandcampingbarns.co.uk
PRICE PER NIGHT £5.50 per person.

PUBLIC TRANSPORT
Trains terminate at Windermere. From there take a 555 bus towards Keswick. Get off at Thirlmere Dam Road End (Smaithwaite). Climb over ladder stile and we are 1/2 mile north along a footpath.

DIRECTIONS
Leave M6 at junction 40. Take A66 towards Keswick for 14 miles. Turn left onto B5322 St John's in the Vale Road. We are 3 miles along the road on the right

Camping Barns offer a special opportunity to stay in ancient farm buildings at an affordable price (£5.50 per person per night). You can experience Cumbria's stunning lakes and lofty peaks literally from your doorstep.

The living and sleeping areas are usually communal, so unless you book the sole use of the barn, you may have to share with others.

Facilities are usually basic but they do vary between barns. As a general rule imagine you are camping but you don't need a tent!! As a minimum, they have a sleeping area, tables and benches for eating and preparing food, a water supply and a flush toilet. Many have basic heating; some have hot water and showers– see the individual barn entries for details.

For the more active... walking and cycling routes between the barns have been developed.

Contact: Lakeland Camping Barns Booking Office, Tel: 017687 72645Fax: 017687 75043, Moot Hall, Market Square, Keswick, CA12 4JR On-line booking is now available.

www.lakelandcampingbarns.co.uk

JOIN US NOW FOR AN UNFORGETTABLE EXPERIENCE

MILL COTTAGE BUNKHOUSE

Nenthead Mines Heritage Centre
Nenthead
Alston
Cumbria
CA9 3PD

Mill Cottage Bunkhouse is set amidst the sweeping Cumbrian fells and was once part of the home of the Smelt Mill manager. This is an 18th-century lead mining site which is now a Heritage and Visitor Centre. Guests at Mill Cottage have the opportunity to walk in the countryside which is an Area of Outstanding Natural Beauty and there is also the C-2-C cycle route which passes through the site.

The bunkhouse is fully heated, with hot water and showers, fully fitted self-catering kitchen with washing and drying facilities. There is a café on site as well as two pubs in the village.

www.npht.com

CONTACT Paul Mercer, Tel: (01434) 382037 or (01434) 382726, Email: info@npht.com
OPENING SEASON Bunkhouse open all year. Heritage Centre from Easter to October.
OPENING HOURS 24 hours, Heritage Centre open 10.30am to 5pm.
NUMBER OF BEDS 9: 1 x 9
BOOKING REQUIREMENTS Booking is preferred but not essential, depending on availability. Deposit is required.
PRICE PER NIGHT £10 per person.

PUBLIC TRANSPORT
Train stations at Hexham (24 miles away) and Penrith (25 miles away). Limited bus service (Wright Bros Buses (01434) 381200) from Hexham and Penrith to Alston.

DIRECTIONS
In Nenthead village, off the A689 Alston to Stanhope road. The bunkhouse is on the Nenthead Mines site.

ALSTON TRAINING & ADVENTURE CENTRE

High Plains Lodge
Alston
Cumbria
CA9 3DD

Alston Training and Adventure Centre is a purpose built Hostel and Outdoor Activity Centre situated in the Heart of Alston Moor in the North Pennines, an Area of Outstanding Natural Beauty, it has been established for 20 years. Within close proximity to the C2C cycle route and the Pennine Way it makes an ideal overnight stopping place.

The Centre, which is under the personal ownership of Dave and Gill Simpson, has been designed for group use with separate male and female floors and en-suite staff rooms, making it an ideal base for a multi-activity week or weekend. The Centre can provide Instructors for all activities and is licensed with the AALA to provide a range of activites (RO 304). Most activity sites are within a 15 minute drive with Hadrian's Wall just 30 minutes away for field trips and Ullswater just a 50 minute drive for a day's climbing and canoeing.

www.alstontraining.co.uk

CONTACT David Simpson, Tel: (01434) 381886, Fax: (01434) 382725, Email: alstontraining@btconnect.com
OPENING SEASON All year
OPENING HOURS All day
NUMBER OF BEDS 56: 4x8 4x6 1x4 (2x3 staff rooms)
BOOKING REQUIREMENTS Booking is essential for groups
PRICE PER NIGHT From £10 pp

PUBLIC TRANSPORT
Wrights Coaches - Newcastle to Alston and Carlisle to Alston stop at Alston (2 miles) Pickups can be arranged from Alston.

DIRECTIONS
Two miles from Alston B6277 (Alston to Middleton in Teesdale Rd) 300 metres from golf course. Close to C2C and Pennine Way.

H AM 1m

THE MINERS ARMS BUNKHOUSE

Nenthead
Alston
Cumbria CA9 3PF

At 1500ft above sea level, the Miners Arms can probably lay claim to be the highest village pub in England. If you like excellent food (National Prize Winning Cuisine), great beer (guest ales changed weekly), and friendly family hospitality or you just like drinking at altitude - you must try The Miners Arms in Nenthead, it's well worth a visit.

Accommodation is in a bunkhouse which sleeps 12 in four 3 tier bunks plus 3 pull-out beds, with washing and changing facilities which include 2 sinks and shower/toilet rooms. All bedding is provided, but there are no cooking facilities. Family, double, twin and single accommodation is available for bed and breakfast in the main house. The Hostel has a secure lockup for bikes and underground equipment. We are the official Stamping Post in Nenthead for the C2C Cycle route, and the Alternative Pennine Way passes through the village.

www.nenthead.com

TELEPHONE CONTACT Alison Clark (01434) 381427
Email: minersarms@cybermoor.org.uk
OPENING SEASON All year
OPENING HOURS All day
NUMBER OF BEDS 15
BOOKING REQUIREMENTS Booking recommended, group bookings must have 50% deposit.
PRICE PER NIGHT £11.00 bed, £15 B+B, accommodation in the main house £20.

PUBLIC TRANSPORT
There are train stations at Penrith and Hexham. There are National Express services at Carlisle and Newcastle. For details of local buses phone Wrights Bus Co (01434) 381200.

DIRECTIONS
On the main road A689 between Durham and Brampton.

1m

COMPASST

Townhead
Alston
Cumbria
CA9 3SL

Compasst Bunkhouse is situated at the top of the old cobbled street in Alston, the highest market town in England. The town is in the heart of Alston Moor and the North Pennines Area of Outstanding Natural Beauty, and the bunkhouse has uninterrupted views over the moor to Crossfell, 2930ft (893m).

Compasst is a unique facility within the walls of a former Methodist chapel and school. The C2C cycle route and Pennine Way cross paths outside the door. The complex offers total independence and facilities include a 24 bed cubicle bunk room, a 14 bed dormitory, a large combined kitchen/dining room with lounge, games room, sauna and large individualised shower block and launderette, all centrally heated. There is a large garden with stunning views of Crossfell.

Compasst is a versatile facility, suitable for individuals, small groups and parties up to 40. As qualified teachers we welcome school parties. We will also arrange custom-made holidays for groups, including all activities and visits.

www.compasst.co.uk

CONTACT Simon Tel: (01434) 382505. Mob: 07866 395731
Email: info@compasst.co.uk
OPENING SEASON All Year
OPENING HOURS All Day
NUMBER OF BEDS 38: 1 x 24, 1 x 14
BOOKING REQUIREMENTS Preferred but not essential
PRICE PER NIGHT From £12 per person

PUBLIC TRANSPORT
Train stations at Penrith and Hexham. National express services at Carlisle and Newcastle. Local bus information from Wrights Bus Company (01434) 381200

DIRECTIONS
GR 719 463. At the top of Alston Town (Townhead).

DEMESNE FARM BUNKHOUSE

Demesne Farm,
Bellingham, Hexham
Northumberland, NE48 2BS

Demesne Farm Bunkhouse is a self-catering unit which was converted in 2004, from a barn on a working hill farm. The farm is situated on the Pennine Way, Route 68 cycle route, Reivers cycle route and is within 100 metres of the centre of the North Tyne village of Bellingham on the edge of the Northumberland National Park. The bunkhouse provides an ideal base for exploring Northumberland, Hadrian's Wall, Kielder Water and many climbing crags. It accommodates 15 and is perfect for smaller groups, individuals and families. The bedrooms, which are heated, are fitted with hand-crafted oak man-sized bunk beds, high quality mattresses, pillows and curtains with cushion flooring. The communal living area with potbelly stove and fitted kitchen includes microwave, hob, fridge, kettle, toaster, crockery, cutlery, cooking utensils, farmhouse tables, chairs and easy chairs. It has 2 bathrooms, which are fully tiled including hot showers, hand basins and toilets. Outside in the courtyard there is ample parking, bike lock up and a gravelled area with picnic tables. No dogs or smoking in the bunkhouse.

www.demesnefarmcampsite.co.uk

CONTACT Robert Telfer, Tel: (01434) 220258,
Email:telfer@demesne.plus.com
OPENING SEASON All Year
OPENING HOURS Flexible, but no check in after 9pm
NUMBER OF BEDS 15: 1 x 8, 1 x 4, 1 x 3
BOOKING REQUIREMENTS Please book in advance.
PRICE PER NIGHT £10 per person

PUBLIC TRANSPORT
Nearest train station - Hexham 17 miles, regular bus service from Hexham to Bellingham. Bellingham bus stop 100 metres from Bunkhouse. Newcastle nearest city 45 minutes by car, Scottish Border 20 minutes by car, Kielder Water 10 minutes by car.

DIRECTIONS
100 metres from centre of village, located next to Northern Garage.

BONNY BARN

Harbottle, Nr Rothbury
Northumberland
NE65 7DG

Bonny Barn, (self catering/non-smoking) was built in 2002 to accommodate cyclists using Route 68 Penine Cycleway North which runs through Harbottle village. A mezzanine floor, laminated and with access to the upper garden, has 6 mattresses, sleeping bags, liners and pillows. There is a shower room with toilet and wash basin. Towels are provided.

The building is centrally heated, has a kitchen area, dining table & chairs, settee & TV. The kitchen is equipped with crockery, cutlery, fridge, toaster, kettle and a two hob gas burner. Basic provisions are available, other groceries can be ordered at the time of booking.

Its location in the Northumberland National Park, the Coquet Valley and the foothills of the Cheviots makes Harbottle an ideal base for walkers, cyclists, bird watchers and nature lovers. Vegetarian B&B with evening meals, is also available in the main house.

www.bonnybarn.co.uk

CONTACT Rosemary. Tel: (01669) 650476
Email : Rosemary@bonnybarn.co.uk
OPENING SEASON All year
OPENING HOURS No restrictions
NUMBER OF BEDS **6** sleeping places.
BOOKING REQUIREMENTS Advance booking with 50% deposit.
PRICE PER NIGHT 1-2 persons £40, 3 persons £45, 4 persons £50, 5 persons £55, 6 persons £60.

PUBLIC TRANSPORT
Nearest train station - Morpeth 25 miles. Post bus once a day from Rothbury. Approx taxi fare from Rothbury £5.

DIRECTIONS
NCN Route 68 Map ref 80/936047. We are situated in the main street in Harbottle. Entry is next to Village Hall and by the bus stop.

1m

JOINERS SHOP BUNKHOUSE

Preston
Chathill
Northumberland
NE67 5ES

The Joiners Shop Bunkhouse is an attractive 17th-century building retaining much of its historical charm and character. It is situated in a quiet hamlet only 7 miles from Alnwick, the seat of the Duke of Northumberland, 5 miles from the beautiful Northumberland Coast and 10 miles from Wooler and the Cheviot Hills. The area offers opportunities for walking, climbing, mountain biking, all water sports or simply sightseeing.

The Joiners Shop Bunkhouse has full cooking facilities and a dining area along with a log fire and cosy sitting area. The 18 large pine beds are in heated dormitories of twos and threes. Indoor space is available for bikes and other equipment and there is ample parking. Dogs welcome. NB There are dogs on site!

CONTACT Wal Wallace. Tel: (01665) 589245. Mob 07745 373729. Email: bunkhouse.wal@btinternet.com
OPENING SEASON All year
OPENING HOURS No Restrictions
NUMBER OF BEDS 18
BOOKING REQUIREMENTS Advised for weekends and holidays.
PRICE PER NIGHT £9.00 per person.

PUBLIC TRANSPORT
There are train stations at Chathill (1½ miles) limited service and Alnmouth (10 miles). There are National Express services at Alnwick (10 miles) and Berwick (24 miles). The local bus company is called ARRIVA and the nearest stop is Brownieside on the A1 (1½ miles).

DIRECTIONS
GR 183 254 Seven miles north of Alnwick on the A1 to Brownieside. Turn off A1 at sign for Preston Tower, hostel is 1½ miles on the left.

TACKROOM BUNKHOUSE

Annstead Farm
Beadnell
Northumberland
NE67 5BT

The Tackroom Bunkhouse is situated on a mixed working farm between the seaside villages of Beadnell and Seahouses, yards from a beautiful sandy beach on the spectacular Northumberland Coast. The area is ideal for walking, watersports, climbing, cycling, diving or sightseeing.

Accommodating 12, the bunkhouse is ideal for smaller groups, individuals and couples. The two bedrooms are each fitted with 6 man sized bunk-beds and a locker for each visitor. Sleeping bags are preferred but linen and towel hire are available. The communal area has a mini kitchen with hob, microwave, fridge, toaster etc, a dining table to seat 12 and colour TV. All crockery, cutlery and cooking utensils are supplied. Adjoining the bunkhouse is a shared shower/toilet block complete with washing machine and tumble drier. Also available is a lock-up, and off road parking. The Tackroom Bunkhouse is heated.

www.annstead.co.uk

CONTACT Sue Mellor, Tel: (01665) 720387 Fax: (01665) 721494
Email: susan@annstead.co.uk
OPENING SEASON Easter-October (by arrangement out of season).
OPENING HOURS Flexible, but no check-in after 10pm.
NUMBER OF BEDS 12: 2 x 6.
BOOKING REQUIREMENTS Recommended but not essential
PRICE PER NIGHT £8.50pp weeknights, £10.00pp Friday and Saturday.

PUBLIC TRANSPORT
Nearest train station is Berwick Upon Tweed. There are intermittent local buses to Seahouses and Beadnell, passing ½ mile away from the hostel.

DIRECTIONS
From A1 take the B1340, follow road to Beadnell (signed Seahouses/ Beadnell). Annstead farm is approx ½ mile past Beadnell on the left.

1m

THE OUTDOOR TRUST

Windy Gyle Bunkhouse
& Beal Expedition Centre
Belford
Northumberland NE70 7QE

Windy Gyle Bunkhouse and Beal Expedition Centre are both ideally situated in North Northumberland, the Cheviot Hills, Northumbrian Heritage Coast, Farne Islands; Rivers Till and Tweed and many fine crags and forests are nearby. Windy Gyle Bunkhouse is in the village of Belford (includes two-bed en-suite); Beal Expedition Centre is approx 7 miles north of Belford (no laundry or internet facilities). Windy Gyle and Beal Expedition Centre have easy access to the A1.

Both properties comprise a kitchen and dining room, shower and toilet facilities, the dormitories range from 3 to 12 beds. Exclusive use and catering services can be arranged. A full range of outdoor activities and instruction is available including; canoeing, kayaking, climbing & abseiling, windsurfing and sailing.

www.outdoortrust.co.uk

CONTACT Helen Tel: (01668) 213289
Email : info@outdoortrust.co.uk
OPENING SEASON All Year
OPENING HOURS 24 hours
NUMBER OF BEDS 41/30:- 1x2 : 1x5 : 1x6 : 2x8 : 1x12 and 5 x 6

BOOKING REQUIREMENTS Booking in advance is advised.
PRICE PER NIGHT £10.00. per person, self catering

PUBLIC TRANSPORT
Both Windy Gyle and Beal Expedition Centre are accessible on main 502/505 bus service that runs between Newcastle upon Tyne and Berwick-upon-Tweed.

DIRECTIONS
Windy Gyle; take the Belford turning off A1, we are near the centre of Belford. Take the 'Wooler' road opposite Spar Supermarket, we are 300 metres on right. **Beal Expedition Centre** is on A1, 8 miles south of Berwick-U-Tweed, heading north on the right side of the A1 at Beal/ Holy Island turn off between Plough Inn and Gulf Service Station.

BERWICK-ON-TWEED BACKPACKERS

56 Bridge Street
Berwick-on-Tweed
Northumberland
TD15 1AQ

Berwick-on-Tweed Backpackers has the perfect location inside the Elizabethan walls of this ancient market town and only a short walk from the bus and train stations. Berwick is an ideal stop-off on the train and road route from London to Edinburgh. Stop for a last taste of England just 50 miles from Scotland's capital or stay longer and explore the bracing Northumberland Coast.

Berwick-on-Tweed Backpackers is in a quiet courtyard and has an informal *come and go as you please* atmosphere. The hostel has self-catering facilities and there is a covered area for dry secure storage of bicycles. The hostel is next to Berwick Quayside, the Maltings Art Centre, Barrels Ale House, Brilliant Bikes and the Green Shop.

www.berwickbackpackers.co.uk

CONTACT Ian or Angela, Tel: (01289) 331481
Email: bkbackpacker@aol.com
OPENING SEASON All year
OPENING HOURS 11am until 7pm-summer. 4pm until 7pm winter
NUMBER OF BEDS 20: Lots of twins and doubles
BOOKING REQUIREMENTS Advisable in summer but not essential.
PRICE PER NIGHT From £10 to £16 per person.

PUBLIC TRANSPORT
Berwick-on-Tweed railway station is 10 minutes' walk away and the bus station is 5 minutes' walk away.

DIRECTIONS
In Berwick town centre, follow the main street towards the town hall. Take first right turn after the town hall, down Hide Hill, turn first right at the bottom of the hill into Bridge Street. The hostel is half way along Bridge Street on the right opposite the bookshop.

MAUGHOLD VENTURE CENTRE BUNKHOUSE

The Venture Centre
Maughold
Isle of Man
IM7 1AW

Maughold Venture Centre Bunkhouse is built of Manx stone, overlooking farmland with views in the distance to the sea. It offers self-catering facilities with the option of purchasing meals from the neighbouring adventure centre if required (subject to availability). All bedrooms are en-suite with full central heating, facilities include a basic but functional games room and kitchen. The number of beds in each room can be altered to suit your requirements.

The local beach of Port e Vullen, 10 mins' walk away, is popular with our visitors and we can arrange sessions of kayaking, abseiling, air rifle shooting, archery, gorge walking, dingy sailing, power boating and team challenge events. We have our own stop "Lewaigue Halt" on the unique Manx Electric Railway giving access to Douglas, Ramsay and to mountain walks and tranquil glens. The bunkhouse is suitable for Scouts, Guides, groups, families and individuals.

www.adventure-centre.co.uk

CONTACT Simon Read, Tel: (01624) 814240,
Email : Contact@adventure-centre.co.uk
OPENING SEASON February to November
OPENING HOURS 24 hours
NUMBER OF BEDS : 52 2x2 : 1x6 : 4x8 : 1x10
BOOKING REQUIREMENTS Telephone reservation essential
PRICE PER NIGHT £10-£15 per person

PUBLIC TRANSPORT
No 3 Bus or Manx Electric Railway from Douglas or Ramsey, get off at Dreemskerry (bus - 5 mins' walk away) or Lewaigue Halt (railway). Taxi from Ramsey £5. Taxi from Douglas £25.

DIRECTIONS
GR 469922. From Douglas take the A2 coast road, when the road begins to descend into Ramsey the Venture Centre is signposted on the right hand side, follow the signs it is the first building on the left.

JUNIOR HOUSE

King William's College
Castletown
Isle of Man
IM9 1TP

King William's College is the only independent school in the Isle of Man and is located on Castletown Bay in the south of the island. The Isle of Man has lots to offer, including an interesting transport system, great beaches, mountainous heathland, historic sites, charming villages and loads of fresh fish!!!!

Junior House - formally used for junior boarding, is set in the expansive College grounds and provides a mix of accommodation options ranging from single rooms to dormitory style accommodation.

The building has recently been refurbished and all the bathroom facilities upgraded. There is a lounge, laundry room, drying room and a new kitchen area. Junior House is an ideal location for all the attractions in the south of the island and the Junior House facilities are well matched to those looking for outdoor activity holidays. Catering can be provided at most times although guests should check at the time of booking. Junior House is a relaxed, clean and well maintained property.

www.kwc.sch.im

CONTACT Ruth Watterson Tel:(01624) 820470 /400. Fax: 820402
Email: rooms@kwc.sch.im
OPENING SEASON All year (except Christmas and New Year)
OPENING HOURS All day
NUMBER OF BEDS 54: 2x12 : 1x11 : 1x10 : 4x2 : 1x1
BOOKING REQUIREMENTS book with deposit for large parties and TT races.
PRICE PER NIGHT £12.50 per person. Breakfast extra.

PUBLIC TRANSPORT
The airport is located next to the College. Ferries dock at Douglas from Liverpool, Heysham, Dublin and Belfast (approx return fare £40)

DIRECTIONS
From Douglas follow signs to Castletown and the Airport. Bus stop is located opposite the entrance to King William's College.

P AM

KEY

45 – Hostel page number

45 – Page number of group only accomodation

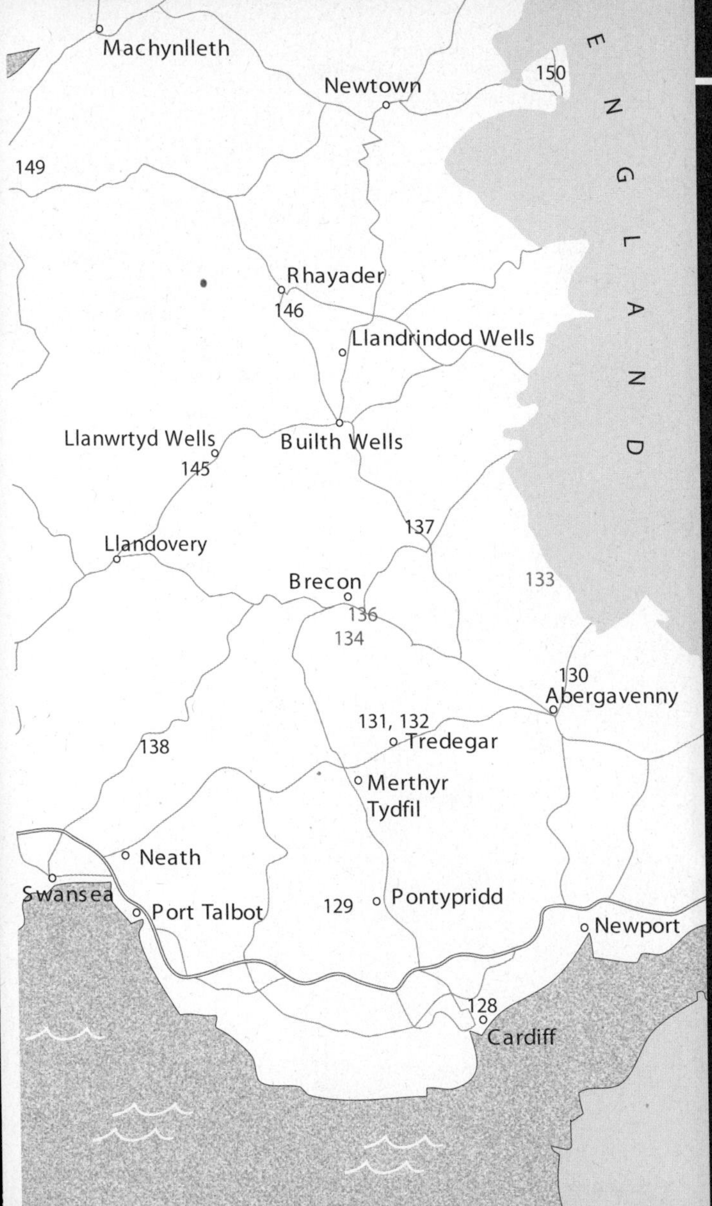
152
Machynlleth
Newtown
150
ENGLAND
149
Rhayader
146
Llandrindod Wells
Llanwrtyd Wells
145
Builth Wells
137
Llandovery
Brecon
133
136
134
130
Abergavenny
131, 132
Tredegar
138
Merthyr
Tydfil
Neath
Swansea
Port Talbot
129
Pontypridd
Newport
128
Cardiff

0
miles
25
0
kilometres
40
Holyhead
164
Colwyn Bay
Llandudno
160
Conwy
161
159
Bangor
163
Caernarfon
165
162
158
Betws-y-coed
157
166
167
Ffestiniog
169
170
168
Porthmadog
171
Criccieth
Pwllheli
172
Donlgellau
151
152
Machynlleth
Aberdyfi

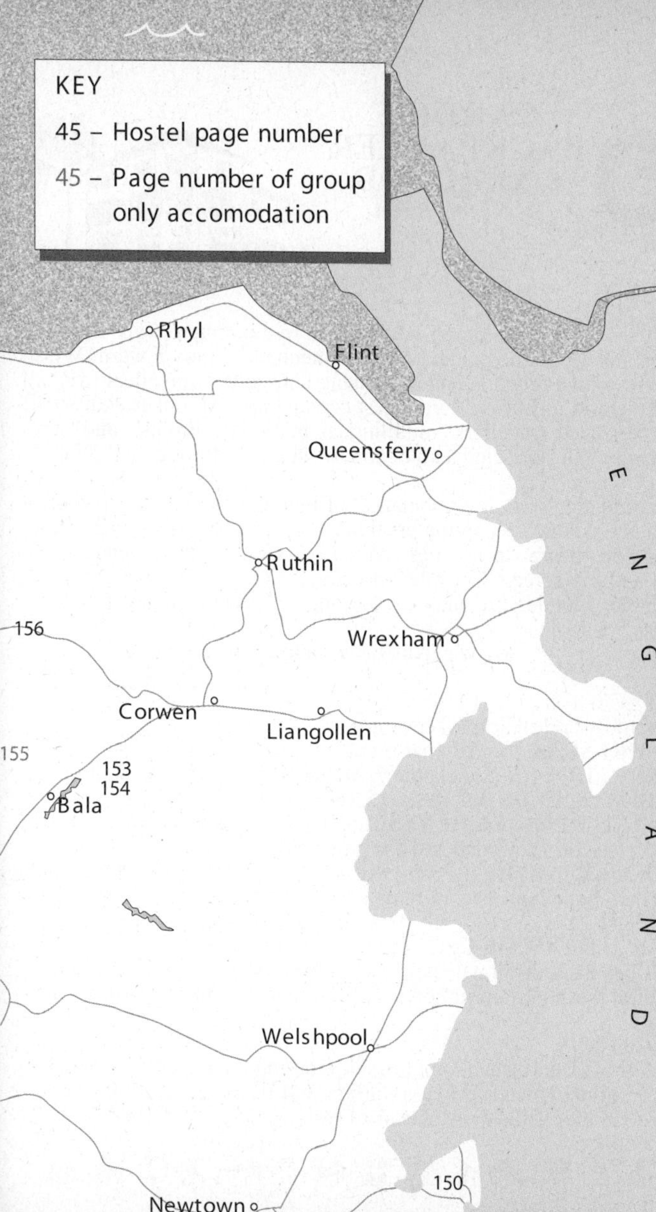
KEY
45 – Hostel page number
45 – Page number of group only accomodation
Rhyl
Flint
Queensferry
Ruthin
Wrexham
156
Corwen
Liangollen
155
153
154
Bala
Welshpool
150
Newtown
ENGLAND

 See page 216 for colour photo

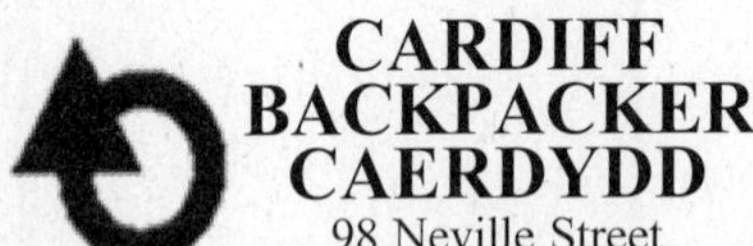

CARDIFF BACKPACKER CAERDYDD

98 Neville Street
Riverside
Cardiff
CF11 6LS

Cardiff's only central tourist hostel, only five minutes' walk from the stations and all municipal and central amenities. Enjoy a warm Welsh welcome, whilst relaxing and socialising with fellow travellers from all over the world in Europe's youngest capital city. All our friendly staff are experienced travellers; multilingual in Welsh, English and other languages; and knowledgeable about activities throughout Wales.

Accommodation is in a combination of twin/double and group rooms. Facilities include reception/breakfast area with *essentials* shop; information desk; telephones and fax; comfortable lounge with digital and big screen TV; internet centre; roof garden; guest bar with pool table, launderette and car parking. Foreign passport holders only.

www.cardiffbackpacker.com

CONTACT Tel: (029) 20 345577
Email: info@cardiffbackpacker.com
OPENING SEASON All year round
OPENING HOURS Sun-Thurs 7.30 to 2.30 Fri+Sat 24 hours
NUMBER OF BEDS 70: 4x2 1x5 1x4 3x6 3x8 1x10
BOOKING REQUIREMENTS Booking recommended for individuals and essential (with deposit) for groups.
PRICE PER NIGHT From £16.00p per person, including light breakfast. Excellent weekly rates available.

PUBLIC TRANSPORT
Cardiff has train, National Express and local bus services all calling at the central bus and train station (5 to 10 minutes' walk from the hostel).

DIRECTIONS
From Cardiff Central Station, turn left crossing the River Taff. Follow the river embankment upstream, turning left past the Riverbank Hotel. We are on the roundabout ahead of you.

P AM 1m

GLYNCORNEL ENVIRONMENTAL CENTRE

Nant-y-Gwyddon Road
Llwynypia
Rhondda CF40 2JF

Glyncornel is a unique and friendly place to stay for groups visiting the valleys of South Wales for study or recreation. The Centre is set on a hillside in its own nature reserve of ancient woodland and meadows. It is ideal for geographical and biological field study groups. Our experienced teaching staff can offer advice and assistance in running your own fieldwork. Alternatively, we can teach your group for an additional cost. Teaching rooms and a wide range of equipment are available. Cyclists and walkers will find plenty to occupy them with miles of footpaths and forest trails in stunning scenery both around the Centre and in the nearby Brecon Beacons National Park.

www.rhondda-cynon-taff.gov.uk/glyncornel

CONTACT Tim Orrell, Tel: (01443) 431727, Fax: (01443) 431734
Email: glyncornel@rhondda-cynon-taff.gov.uk
OPENING SEASON All year (except Christmas)
OPENING HOURS 5pm arrival time
NUMBER OF BEDS 59: 3 x 8 : 1 x 4 : 1 x 3 : 1 x 16 : 1 x 12
BOOKING REQUIREMENTS Booking is essential. 25% deposit required for group bookings.
PRICE PER NIGHT From £10 to £25 depending on age and type of board (self-catering, B&B or full board).

PUBLIC TRANSPORT
Trains run from Cardiff to Llwynypia station, 500m from the hostel. X9 and X10 buses run from Cardiff to Llwynypia Magistrates Court. From there, walk to the traffic lights and turn left. After 100m, turn left again into the hostel.

DIRECTIONS
Take J34 off M4 and follow A4119 for 11 miles to Llwynypia. From the North, take the A4061 off the A465 to Treorchy, then the A4058 to Llwynypia. The Centre is signposted from the crossroad with lights.

SMITHY'S BUNKHOUSE

Lower House Farm
Pantygelli,Abergavenny
Monmouthshire
NP7 7HR

Located on a working hill farm, Smithy's Bunkhouse lies in the Black Mountains within the Brecon Beacons National Park, some two miles from the historic market town of Abergavenny. Designed to accommodate 24 persons in two dormitories of 12 bunks, additional space is available above the common room if required. The bunkhouse is equipped with showers, toilets, fully equipped kitchen, drying area, coin operated washer and dryer and a common room with a wood burning stove. It is heated during the winter by night storage heaters, hot water and electricity are supplied at no extra cost, some firewood is provided and extra may be purchased. A 16th-century coaching inn is located at the top of the farm drive which serves bar snacks, restaurant meals and traditional ales. The area is ideal for walking, climbing, caving, mountain biking, canoeing, water sports, pony trekking.

www.smithysbunkhouse.com

CONTACT, Neil or Katy Smith, Tel: (01873) 853432
Email: info@smithysbunkhouse.com
OPENING SEASON All year
OPENING HOURS 24 hours by arrangement
NUMBER OF BEDS 24: 2 x 12.
BOOKING REQUIREMENTS Booking is advised with £100 deposit for groups. Cheques payable to Smithy's Bunkhouse.
PRICE PER NIGHT £9.50 per person, Group bookings £8.50.pp.

PUBLIC TRANSPORT
Nearest train station Abergavenny (2 miles). Taxi fare from station approximately £5. No local buses.

DIRECTIONS
GR 304 178. Pantygelli village is located two miles north of Abergavenny on the old Hereford Road. Access to the bunkhouse is down the farm drive opposite the Crown Inn.

BRYN BACH PARK

The Visitor Centre
Merthyr Road
Tredegar
Gwent
NP22 3AY

Nestling in 400 acres of beautiful country park, Bryn Bach offers self-catering accommodation within our Countryside Centre. All rooms have heating and washing facilities, and a fully fitted kitchen diner with satellite TV & video overlooks the lake. Early breakfasts or packed lunches can be ordered from our restaurant which serves delicious hot meals throughout the day. The centre also provides tourist information, gift shop, shower block, laundry etc.

The location is ideally situated for exploring the Brecon Beacons and South Wales Valleys. The park hosts several groups including Angling, Windsurfing, Model Boat and Flying Clubs. Also available are a range of instructor led activities such as caving, climbing, hill walking, kayaking and mountain biking are available on site. The park contains a 36-acre lake, adventure playground, picnic area, orienteering courses and BBQ hire. Caravan and camping is also available on site. A warm Welsh welcome is guaranteed here.

CONTACT Jon Kivell Tel: (01495) 711816, Fax: (01495) 725093, Email : parcbrynbach@blaenau-gwent.gov.uk
OPENING SEASON All year
OPENING HOURS 8.30am, flexible close but approx. dusk.
NUMBER OF BEDS 18 : 1 x 2 : 4 x 4
BOOKING REQUIREMENTS preferred, phone for availability.
PRICE PER NIGHT £10.25 per adult, £5.15 junior, OAP, student, UB40. Bedding £1 per night. 10% reductions for groups of 14 or more.

PUBLIC TRANSPORT
Nearest train stations are at Rhymney (3 miles from hostel) Merthyr (8 miles)both Cardiff line. Abergavenny(12miles) Newport-Hereford line. Buses from Abergavenny, Newport, Cardiff, and Merthyr call at at Tredegar (2 miles). Buslink, Park to Tredegar & Rhymney station.

DIRECTIONS
GR 126 100. From M4 ~ Tredegar. Well signposted from A465 'Heads of the Valley' road and Rhymney or Tredegar roundabouts.

5m

HOBO BACKPACKERS

& Holiday Cottages
Tredegar,
NP22 3NB

Association of Bunkhouse Operators

Located on the southern edge of the Brecon Beacons National Park, within the picturesque Sirhowy Valley, with good road and bus links; an ideal base for hill walks, waterfall walks, mountain biking, with long distance cycle routes nearby. Local activities we can book for you include horse riding, quad biking and paint balling. Visit a castle or two, ride on a steam train, or go down a mine (it's free). At weekends enjoy a wide variety of live music, from rock groups to Welsh choirs. Hobo is owned & run by experienced backpackers, who can provide you with lots of info on mountain biking, walking and kayaking.

Double bed/family rooms/all bedding provided
Fully equipped self-catering kitchen/free tea & coffee
Secure storage/drying room for all outdoor gear
www.hobo-backpackers.com

CONTACT Gill or Horace Tel: (01495) 718422,
Email: info@hobo-backpackers.co.uk
OPENING SEASON All year
OPENING HOURS Flexible
NUMBER OF BEDS 26: 2 x 6 : 2 x 7, plus 2 cottages sleep 6 each.
BOOKING REQUIREMENTS Phone/email to check availability.
PRICE PER NIGHT £12 per person. Sole use £275.

PUBLIC TRANSPORT
Bus; Nat Exp **509** from London Vic/Earls Court to Merthyr then **X4** every 30 mins to Tredegar. Stage Coach **X4** from Cardiff or Hereford. Nat Exp. **X321** from B'ham. **56** from Newport. Train to Cardiff then Valleys train to Rhymney, bus to Tredegar meets train and will carry bikes.

DIRECTIONS: M4 turn off Junction 28, sign Risca, then Tredegar (A4048). At **A465** follow Tredegar sign. At Bedwellty roundabout take town centre sign. Find the town clock, we're downhill from it.

THE WAIN HOUSE

Court Farm
Llanthony
Abergavenny
Monmouthshire
NP7 7NN

This old stone barn continues the tradition of 900 years when Llanthony Priory provided shelter and accommodation. Surrounded by the Black Mountains in the Brecon Beacons National Park, this spectacular setting is a superb base for walking, riding, pony trekking and other mountain activities.

Sixteen bunks are split into three separate areas for sleeping; there is a fully equipped kitchen, hot water for showers, heating throughout and a wood burning stove in the eating area. Small or large groups are welcome, but there is a minimum charge at weekends. Two pubs offer real beer and bar food.

Just 50 minutes from the M4 Severn Bridge and 1 hour from the M5/ M50 Junction, this must be one of the easiest bunkbarns to reach from the motorways - and yet you feel you are miles from anywhere.

The Wain House is only 100 yds from Cycle Route 42

www.llanthony.co.uk

CONTACT: Tel: (01873) 890359, Email: courtfarm@llanthony.co.uk
OPENING SEASON All year
OPENING HOURS 24 hours no restrictions
NUMBER OF BEDS **16:** 1 x 8 : 1 x 4 : 1 x 6
BOOKING REQUIREMENTS Booking and deposit required.
PRICE PER NIGHT £8.00 per person. Minimum charge of £180 at weekends (2 nights).

PUBLIC TRANSPORT
Abergavenny railway station 12 miles.

DIRECTIONS
GR 288 278. Map on website. Turn west off A465 Abergavenny to Hereford road at Llanvihangel Crucorney 5 miles north of Abergavenny. Llanthony is 6 miles along country lane - follow signs to Priory. On cycle route 42.

See page 215 for colour photo

FOREST LODGE

Libanus
Brecon
LD3 8NY

Forest Lodge farmhouse is in a wonderful position with spectacular views of the Brecon Beacons. Built in the 1820s and renovated it has the character of an olde worlde farmhouse but with modern amenities. It has 6 bedrooms, a large well equipped kitchen, drying / laundry room, dining room and 2 sitting rooms. A large grassed area to the front is an ideal play area. Sleeps 24.
Four cottages on the estate provide the following accommodation:

Charlotte's Cottage: Sleeps 6 in 3 bedrooms, with well equipped kitchen, utility room, sitting room and bathroom. Pets welcome.

Ivy Cottage: Sleeps 5 in 2 bedrooms, with kitchen, sitting/dining room, bathroom. Pets welcome.

Fern Cottage: Sleeps 4/5 in 2 bedrooms, with dining kitchen, sitting room and bathroom.

Shepherds Cottage: Sleeps 4/7 in 2 bedrooms, with sitting room, kitchen, bathroom and walled garden, so pets welcome.

www.breconcottages.com

CONTACT Elizabeth Daniel, Tel :(01874) 676446, Fax :(01874) 676416, Email: enquiries@breconcottages.com
OPENING SEASON All year
OPENING HOURS 24 hours
NUMBER OF BEDS 24 in main farmhouse and 24 in 4 cottages
BOOKING REQUIREMENTS Booking essential with 20% deposit
PRICE PER NIGHT Forrest Lodge = £770 for 3 nights, Charlotte = £220 for 3 nights, Ivy = £210 for 3 nights, Fern = £190 for 3 nights and Shepherds = £210 for 3 nights.

PUBLIC TRANSPORT
National Express buses run to nearby Brecon.

DIRECTIONS
Supplied with booking confirmation.

CANAL BARN BUNKHOUSE

Ty Camlas
Canal Bank
Brecon
Powys LD3 7HH

GROUPS ONLY

Nestling between the river Usk and the Canal, Canal Barn Bunkhouse has a superb setting and yet is near Brecon town centre. The Bunkhouse is at the hub of activity in the Brecon Beacons National Park with easy access to the numerous exciting outdoor activities available in this beautiful part of Wales. While Brecon town has a range of pubs, restaurants, takeaways and entertainments to satisfy most tastes and pockets, and all nearby in a safe walking distance.

Sleeping up to 24 people, the Bunkhouse offers award winning environmentally friendly, competitively priced, group accommodation of exceptional quality that is accessible by disabled people. Specifically designed as a base for your outdoor activities club, the Bunkhouse is equipped to a very high standard indeed and is an excellent venue for team building and residential training courses, or the place for an action packed get together with friends and family.

www.canal-barn.co.uk

CONTACT Ralph or Liz, Tel: (01874) 625361,
Email: ihg@canal-barn.co.uk
OPENING SEASON All year
OPENING HOURS No restrictions
NUMBER OF BEDS 24 (in 6 rooms)
BOOKING REQUIREMENTS Booking essential. (Minimum of 4)
PRICE PER NIGHT From £10.40

PUBLIC TRANSPORT
Train/bus to Merthyr Tydfil or Abergavenny, then bus to Brecon.

DIRECTIONS
GR 052 279. On the canal towpath close to Brecon town centre. Vehicular access is via the canal bridge next to the Safeway Petrol Station on the nearby Abergavenny to Brecon road (B4601).

TRERICKET MILL BUNKHOUSE

Erwood, Builth Wells
Powys
LD2 3TQ

Across the stream from Trericket Corn Mill this stone bunkhouse in an old cider orchard overlooks the River Wye. It is particularly suitable for small groups and individuals with two rooms sleeping four people each and an additional ensuite bunkroom for two in the mill. The bunkhouse is clean and cosy; heating, hot water and showers are all inclusive. Limited self-catering facilities are provided in a covered outdoor kitchen. Alternatively breakfasts and packed lunches can be provided and good pub meals are available locally. There are heated drying and common rooms in the mill and camping is also available.

Trericket Mill is situated on the Wye Valley Walk and National Cycle Route Eight. An ideal stop-over for walkers, cyclists and for others wishing to spend time in the beautiful countryside of Mid Wales. Canoeing, pony trekking, gliding, mountain bikes, rope centre and white water rafting all available locally.

www.trericket.co.uk

CONTACT Alistair/Nicky Legge, Tel: (01982) 560312
Email: mail@trericket.co.uk
OPENING SEASON All year
OPENING HOURS 24 hour access
NUMBER OF BEDS 10 bunks: 2 x 4 : 1 x 2. plus 6 veggie B&B beds
BOOKING REQUIREMENTS Advanced booking advised.
PRICE PER NIGHT £10.pp ~ £11.pp en-suite.

PUBLIC TRANSPORT
Train stations at Builth Wells (10 miles) Hereford (30 miles) Merthyr Tydfil (30 miles) daily bus service - ask to be dropped at Trericket Mill. National Express coaches drop off at Hereford and Brecon (13 miles). For transport enquiries(01597)826678(office hours).

DIRECTIONS
GR SO 112 414. We are set back from the A470 Brecon to Builth Wells road between the villages of Llyswen and Erwood.

1m

MERLINS BACKPACKERS

44-46 Commercial Street
Ystradgynlais, Swansea
SA9 1JH

Exciting, untamed, & beautiful - do you see yourself in Wales? Ko Samui, Goa, London, Dublin, Merlins Ystradgynlais - what never heard of us? You will be describing us to your friends as a "must go" place. Merlins offers basic but comfortable rooms the majority of which have en-suite facilities. Merlins has a warm and welcoming atmosphere and we pride ourselves on our Welsh hospitality. We have a bar and café. We are Wales Tourist Board accredited, they say ***"very comfortable hostel accommodation presented to a very good overall standard and very worthy of the 3 star quality rating awarded".*** Being on the very edge of the Brecon Beacons National Park the area has lots of castles and historic sites to visit, is steeped in folklore and is famous for its natural beauty. Merlins is well placed to offer a range of 'in your face' high adrenalin adventure activities such as canyoning, caving, climbing, abseiling, coasteering, hill walking, kayaking, canoeing, quad biking, paintballing, adventure days, and nearby Swansea has excellent nightlife.

www.backpackerwales.com

CONTACT Connie Tel: (01639) 845670.
Email: info@callofthewild.co.uk
OPENING SEASON All year
OPENING HOURS 24 hours
NUMBER OF BEDS 40:- 1 x 13 : 1 x double : 2 x 2 : 1 x 5 : 4 x 4
BOOKING REQUIREMENTS Booking essential
PRICE PER NIGHT £11 includes bedding (weekend supplement during June, July and August).

PUBLIC TRANSPORT
Hourly train services from London Paddington to Neath & Swansea, buses connect. Regular ferry between Swansea and Cork.

DIRECTIONS
M4 Junc.45. North on A4067 for 10 miles, right for Ystradgynlais, left at mini roundabout, over bridge, left after pedestrian crossing, we are 50m down on right.

PANTYRATHRO INTERNATIONAL HOSTEL

Pantyrathro Country Inn
Llansteffan, Carmarthen
SA33 5AJ

Llansteffan is a beautiful quaint village set at the tip of the Towi River and Carmarthen Bay. The sandy beaches nestled below the castle offer swimming and relaxation. The virtually traffic free country lanes make this area ideal for cycling. For the walker Carmarthenshire offers coastal walks and country walks. Carmarthen (Wales' oldest city) and ancestral home to Merlin of King Arthur's Legends, offers most social and cultural activities.
The Pantyrathro International Hostel provides both dorm and double room accommodation. Facilities include self-catering kitchen, dining area, TV lounge, showers and internet. Our two Mexican bars offer pool, darts, TV and weekly drink specials, food (eat-in or take-out). Horse riding, cycle hire and excursions for trekking, canoeing and surfing offered. Take a day trip or relax on the beaches or have a drink in our bars - something for everyone.

www.pantyrathrocountryinn.co.uk

CONTACT Ken Knuckles, Tel/Fax: (01267) 241014,
E-mail: kenknuckles@hotmail.com
OPENING SEASON Open all year
OPENING HOURS 24 hours
NUMBER OF BEDS 34 : 3 x 4 : 1 x 5 : 1 x 3 : 1 x 6 : 1 x 8
BOOKING REQUIREMENTS Booking recommended. 50% depost required in advance for groups.
PRICE PER NIGHT £12pp bunk, £26 dbl. £36 trple. Group discounts.

PUBLIC TRANSPORT
Carmarthen has both coach and train stations servicing South Wales, SW England and London. Local bus runs 6 times a day to Llansteffan. Ask driver to let you off at Pantyrathro.

DIRECTIONS
Pantyrathro is 6 miles from Carmarthen on the B4312, midway between Llangain and Llansteffan. Two miles from Llangain you will see the hostel signposted, turn right and follow signs to top of lane.

P 3m

TWR Y FELIN

St Davids
Pembrokeshire
SA62 6QS

GROUPS ONLY

Twr y Felin is a converted windmill within walking distance of the Pembrokeshire Coast Path, sandy beaches and the centre of St Davids. It is open as a hotel throughout the main tourism season Easter - October but offers self-catering accommodation for groups from October - March. As a bunkhouse this is top-end quality! Large kitchen, lounge and garden. All meals and a bar are available by arrangement.

Ty Hir is an adjoining self-catering cottage suitable for small groups or as an overflow to the main building.

Sea kayaking, climbing, surfing and Coasteering® are also available through TYF Adventure: the world's first Carbon Neutral® adventure company.

www.tyf.com

CONTACT Tel: (01437) 721678, Email: stay@tyf.com
OPENING SEASON All year
OPENING HOURS Flexible
NUMBER OF BEDS Twr y Felin 26 Beds: (3x1; 6x2; 1x3; 2x4). Ty Hir 8 beds (4x2)
BOOKING REQUIREMENTS Booking is essential. First night's payment required as deposit.
PRICE PER NIGHT October - March. Twr y Felin £150 per ten people, Ty Hir £120 per night. Twr y Felin operates as a hotel throughout the spring/summer high season. Please enquire for prices.

PUBLIC TRANSPORT
Train or coach to Haverfordwest. Bus/taxi services to St Davids.

DIRECTIONS
Situated behind St Davids visitor centre. GR SM758250. Signposted "Twr y Felin Outdoor Centre".

1m

CAERHAFOD LODGE

Llanrhian, St. Davids
Haverfordwest, Pembrokeshire
SA62 5BD

Ideally situated between the famous cathedral city of St Davids and the Irish ferry port of Fishguard, the Lodge overlooks the spectacular Pembrokeshire coastline. It is within easy walking distance of the well known Sloop Inn at Porthgain and the internationally renowned Coastal Path. The Celtic Trail cycle route passes the bottom of our drive making it an ideal stopover for cyclists. The Lodge is a good base for all outdoor activities. Boat trips around Ramsey Island or to Grassholm to see the Gannets can be arranged, as well as surfboard, wetsuit and cycle hire. The lodge is centrally heated and sleeps 23 in 5 separate rooms (4,4,4,5,6) all en-suite "great showers"! There is a modern fully equipped kitchen/diner with patio and picnic tables, "glorious sunsets".On site washing/drying room and secure storage area. Dogs welcome by prior arrangement. Smoking allowed outdoors. *Wales Tourist Board 3 star.*

www.caerhafod.co.uk

CONTACT Siôn or Carolyn Rees. Tel: (01348) 837859,
Email: Caerhafod@aol.com
OPENING SEASON All year
OPENING HOURS 24 hours
NUMBER OF BEDS 23: 3x4 : 1x5 : 1x6.
BOOKING REQUIREMENTS Advised in high season 25% deposit.
PRICE PER NIGHT Adult £12.00 Under 18 £9.50. Group rates.

PUBLIC TRANSPORT
Fishguard station 9 miles. Haverfordwest station 15 miles. Stena Sealink ferry Fishguard/Rosslare 9 miles. National Express coaches Haverfordwest 15 miles. 411 Bus Haverfordwest-St.Davids-Fishguard 50yds from Lodge. Seasonal coastal shuttle service for walkers. Bike hire available.

DIRECTIONS
GR Landranger 157, SM 827 317. A40 from Haverfordwest, left at Letterston (B4331) to Mathry. Left onto A487 to St Davids, right in Croesgoch for Llanrhian, at crossroads right for Trefin. After ½ mile turn into our drive.

1m

HAMILTON BACKPACKERS

21/23 Hamilton Street
Fishguard
Pembrokeshire
SA65 9HL

Hamilton Backpackers Lodge is an excellent overnight stop on the stunning Pembrokeshire Coast Path. It is also an ideal overnight stay five minutes from the ferries to Rosslare in Ireland. Pembrokeshire has a wealth of natural beauty and local history and many beautiful secluded beaches. The Backpackers Lodge is a very comfortable and friendly hostel with small dormitories and double rooms, all centrally heated. There is a dining room and TV lounge with Sky. The garden at the back of the hostel has a hammock, barbecue and picnic tables. We provide free tea, coffee and light breakfast. There is parking close by and the hostel is in the centre of town near to a number of pubs serving good meals. There is no curfew. Smoking is permitted only in the Garden Patio. To view web page see:

www.hamiltonbackpackers.co.uk

CONTACT Steve Roberts, Tel: (01348) 874797,
Email: hamiltonbackpackers@yahoo.co.uk
OPENING SEASON All year
OPENING HOURS 24 hours
NUMBER OF BEDS 27: 2 x 6 : 2 x 4 : 1 x 3 : 2 x 2.
BOOKING REQUIREMENTS Booking advised to confirm beds. 50% deposit required from groups.
PRICE PER NIGHT £13 (bunk), £16 (double) per person.

PUBLIC TRANSPORT
Fishguard ferry port has a train station and ferries to Rosslare in Ireland. The port is 1 mile from the hostel (approx taxi fare £3). National Express coaches call at Haverfordwest (15 miles). For details of local buses in Pembrokeshire phone Richard Bros (01239) 613756.

DIRECTIONS
From Haverfordwest (A40) to Fishguard Square, across first right by tourist office, 50 yds on left. From Cardigan A487 (North Wales Road) up hill and first left. From Harbour 1 mile to Fishguard Square, left, first right, 50 yards on left.

See page 211 for colour photo

TYCANOL FARM CAMPING BARN

Tycanol Farm
Newport
Pembrokeshire
SA42 0ST

Tycanol Farm offers accommodation for four in a camping barn close to the beautiful Pembrokeshire coast. For larger groups there is a camp site for tents and caravans which overlooks the whole of Newport Bay. Showers are available for the barn and camping and the hot water is free. There are no meals provided on the site but the camping barn has self-catering facilities and there are pubs and restaurants within a 10-minute walk. Laundry facilities are available on the site and there is also access to a drying room.

There are many activities to enjoy in the surrounding area. Pony trekking and a golf club are within a mile of the site. The area is also ideal for canoeing and sailing. The site is a five-minute walk to the coastal path and ten minutes to Newport itself. There is also a nature trail which contains badger setts. Free Barbecue cvery night at 6.30pm. Evcrybody greeted with a warm welcome.

www.caravancampingsites.co.uk/pembrokeshire/tycanolfarm.htm

CONTACT Hugh Harries, Tel: (01239) 820264
OPENING SEASON All year
OPENING HOURS 24 hours
NUMBER OF BEDS **4** in the barn plus camping.
BOOKING REQUIREMENTS Booking not always necessary.
PRICE PER NIGHT £10pp (camping barn), £5pp (camping).

PUBLIC TRANSPORT
Nearest train station is at Fishguard (7 miles away). Nearest National Express coaches are at Haverfordwest (18 miles away). Local buses pass the farm drive every hour; call (01239) 613756.

DIRECTIONS
Tycanol Farm is near beach a mile outside of Newport, Pembrokeshire on the A487 towards Fishguard, turn right at milk-stand signpost.

THE LONG BARN

Penrhiw, Capel Dewi
Llandysul
Ceredigion
SA44 4PG

The Long Barn is a traditional stone barn providing comfortable and warm bunkhouse accommodation. It is situated on a working organic farm in beautiful countryside, with views over the Teifi Valley. The stunning Ceredigion Coast and the Cambrian Mountains are both an easy drive away and the busy small town of Llandysul (1½ miles away) has all essential supplies. The barn's location is ideal for exploring, studying or simply admiring the Welsh countryside. Activities enjoyed by guests in the surrounding area include: horse riding, fishing, swimming, climbing, abseiling, canoeing, farm walks and cycling. The barn is open all year, having adequate heating with a lovely warm Rayburn, log fire, roof insulation and double glazing throughout.

www.thelongbarn.co.uk

CONTACT Tom or Eva, Tel/Fax: (01559) 363200,
Email: cowcher@thelongbarn.co.uk
OPENING SEASON All year
OPENING HOURS All day
NUMBER OF BEDS 34
BOOKING REQUIREMENTS Essential, deposit required.
PRICE PER NIGHT £7.50 pp (adult), £5.50pp (under 18s). Discount of 10% for groups of 20 or more.

PUBLIC TRANSPORT
Carmarthen (16 miles) has a train station and National Express service. Taxi fare from Carmarthen is approximately £16. Llandysul (1½ miles away) has a local bus service, phone 0870 6082608 for details.

DIRECTIONS
GR 437 417. In Llandysul, at the top of the main street, take right hand lane. Turn sharp right down hill. After 100 yds turn sharp left. Another ½ mile turn first right. Continue for 1 mile, Long Barn is on your right.

STONECROFT LODGE

Dolecoed Road
Llanwrtyd Wells
Powys
LD5 4RA

Stonecroft Lodge, our self-catering guest house, is situated in Llanwrtyd Wells, "The Smallest Town in Britain". Surrounded by the green fields, mountains and glorious countryside of Mid-Wales, Llanwrtyd is renowned Red Kite country and is the centre for mountain biking, walking, pony trekking etc. The town hosts many annual events such as the Man v Horse Marathon, World Bog Snorkelling Championships and the Mid-Wales Beer Festival. The Hostel offers a warm welcome and a comfortable stay. We are Wales Tourist Board Star Graded and have private or shared rooms with fully made up beds. There is a fully equipped kitchen, TV, video, free laundry and drying facilities, central heating, large riverside garden and ample parking. The Hostel adjoins our Good Beer Guide pub, Stonecroft Inn (where great food is available), and is truly your "home away from home", offering the best of everything for your stay.

www.stonecroft.co.uk

CONTACT Jane Brown. Tel: (01591) 610327, Fax: (01591) 610304, Email: party@stonecroft.co.uk
OPENING SEASON All year
OPENING HOURS All day - phone on arrival
NUMBER OF BEDS 27: 1 x 1 : 3 x 4 : 1 x 6 : 4 x family (dbl + 1 sgl)
BOOKING REQUIREMENTS Welcome, 50% deposit.
PRICE PER NIGHT £14.00. Whole house exclusive use rates are available.

PUBLIC TRANSPORT
Llanwrtyd Wells Station on the Heart of Wales line is a few minutes' walk from the hostel.

DIRECTIONS
GR 878 468. From Llanwrtyd town centre (A483) take Dolecoed Road towards Abergwesyn. Hostel is 100 yds on left. Check in at Stonecroft Inn.

BEILI BARN

Beili Neuadd
Rhayader
Powys
LD6 5NS

Beili Barn is a recently converted 16th-century stone barn beautifully positioned in quiet, secluded countryside with delightful views, its own stream, trout pools and woodland. The barn is situated just 2 miles from the small market town of Rhayader - the gateway to the Elan Valley reservoirs, known as "The Lakeland of Wales".

The centrally heated barn sleeps 16 in 3 en-suite rooms and includes a fully equipped kitchen/dining room, drying room and facilities for wheelchair users. A separate 3-bedroomed chalet is also available for families and small groups. Situated in Kite country, half way between the coast and Offas's Dyke (English border), we offer a comfortable base to explore the magnificent Elan Valley, Upper Wye and Cambrian Mountains. The nearby area offers a wide range of countryside activities including cycling, mountain biking, fishing, pony trekking, canoeing and of course bird watching and walking.

www.midwalesfarmstay.co.uk

CONTACT Ann or Carl Edwards, Tel: (01597) 810211,
Email: ann-carl@thebeili.freeserve.co.uk.
OPENING SEASON All year
OPENING HOURS All day access
NUMBER OF BEDS 16:- 2 x 6 1 x 4 (2x2 & 1x1) Chalet
BOOKING REQUIREMENTS Booking preferred (with deposit).
PRICE PER NIGHT £10.50 per person.

PUBLIC TRANSPORT
The nearest train station is Llandrindod Wells -12 miles. There are intermittent local buses to Rhayader.Taxi from Rhayader is approx £2.

DIRECTIONS
OS Explorer 200/OS147 GR 994698 Take the A44 east bound from Rhayader town centre (clock). Within ½ mile turn left on unclassified road signposted "Abbey Cwm-hir". Beili Neuadd is on the right.

P H AM 3m

PLAS DOLAU

Lovesgrove
Aberystwyth
Ceredigion
SY23 3HP

Plas Dolau is set in quiet countryside just 3 miles from the popular coastal town of Aberystwyth. Ideal for exploring West Wales, walking, cycling, riding, fishing and golf etc. The holiday centre includes a warm country mansion (WTB 4 star hostel) with mainly dormitory style accommodation and an adjoining scandinavian style farmhouse (WTB 2 star guesthouse) set on a 22 acre smallholding.

Plas Dolau includes meeting rooms, dining rooms, games room, small tuckshop and walks and sports areas. The centre can accommodate groups of up to 45 people. Various options for accommodation, provision of food, cooking facilities, etc are available. We are ideally suited for youth groups, field courses, retreats, house parties and many other groups or individuals. Please phone to discuss your requirements.

www.dolau-holidays.co.uk

CONTACT Tel: (01970) 617834 Email: pat.twigg@virgin.net
OPENING SEASON All year round
OPENING HOURS 24 hours
NUMBER OF BEDS 45: + cots etc. Plus 16 in farmhouse.
BOOKING REQUIREMENTS Booking is recommended, especially for large groups.
PRICE PER NIGHT Ranges from £14.00 (including basic breakfast) to £26.00 (private room, en-suite with full breakfast). From £400 per night for the whole mansion.

PUBLIC TRANSPORT
Nearest train station is in Aberystwyth. Taxi from the station will cost around £5. National Express coaches and local buses (525 and 526) will set down at the end of the hostel drive.

DIRECTIONS
GR 623 813, OS map 135. On the A44, 3 miles from Aberystwyth, 1 mile from Llanbadarn railway bridge, 0.6 miles from turning to Bow Street. Sign on roadside says "Y Gelli", B+B. We are about 250 yards along the drive. Reception in "Y Gelli".

P 1m

 See page 213 for colour photo

MAES-Y-MOR

25 Bath Street
Aberystwyth
Ceredigion Wales
SY23 2NN

Maes-y-Mor is located in the Cardiganshire coastal town of Aberystwyth. It is a new luxury hostel in a detached house with 8 bedrooms, 2 bathrooms, a kitchen/diner and launderette. All bedrooms have colour TV and tea/coffee making facilities and are furnished to a high standard. Beds are of a superior quality to ensure a good night's sleep, linen, towel and soap are provided. Halls and landings are themed in Welsh history pictures. There is a car parking area at rear and a secure shed for bikes.

Aberystwyth is an ideal base for both North and South Wales. Visit Devil's Bridge with its dramatic waterfalls or the Vale of Rheidol narrow gauge railway. There is the National Library of Wales, the Castle and the Harbour. Aberystwyth is a University town so there is plenty of night life. We offer a personal and helpful service.

*Croeso Cymraeg Cynnes i bawb/*Warm Welsh Welcome to all
www.maesymor.co.uk

CONTACT Gordon or Mererid, Tel: (01970) 639270 or 0770 2184463
Email mererid@maesymor.fsnet.co.uk
OPENING SEASON All year
OPENING HOURS 8am to 10pm
NUMBER OF BEDS 16: 8 x 2.
BOOKING REQUIREMENTS Booking advisable.
PRICE PER NIGHT £15pp.

PUBLIC TRANSPORT
Bus and Train Stations are within approximately 400m.

DIRECTIONS
From Bus and Train Stations follow Terrace Road in a straight line towards beach. Turn right at Tourist Board Shop, you will find us approx 30m along next to the cinema.

See page 211 for colour photo

MAESNANT CENTRE

Maesnant, Ponterwyd
Aberystwyth
Ceredigion SY23 3AG

Maesnant is set in the remote hillsides of the Plynlimon mountain. The Centre is an ideal location for hillwalking and mountain biking. The Centre is designed for use by youth groups, but family and other groups are welcome. Inside the centre there are 3 bunk rooms, two wash rooms (each with shower, wc's etc), kitchen and a large common room with dining facilities.

Accommodation in the Centre is limited to 16 persons, though camping is possible in the 12 acres of grounds. Maesnant is hired out on a self-catering basis.

There are many attractions in the area; Devils Bridge waterfalls and steam powered railway, Llywernog Mine Museum, Bwlch Nant Yr Arian Forest Centre and Powergen Rheidol Hydro Electric Power Scheme centre. *Groups under 16 years of age must include 2 adults.*

www.maesnant.org.uk

CONTACT Julie Bellchambers Tel: 07747 017371
Email info@maesnant.org.uk
OPENING SEASON March to November
OPENING HOURS No restrictions
NUMBER OF BEDS 16: 2 x 6 : 1 x 4
BOOKING REQUIREMENTS Telephone Booking essential. Deposit (£30) required 4 weeks in advance.
PRICE PER NIGHT £5 per person.

PUBLIC TRANSPORT
Nearest mainline railway station Aberyswyth, bus services to Ponterwyd.

DIRECTIONS
A44 from Aberystwyth to Ponterwyd, take scenic route to Nan y Moch via mountain road, (east end of village by 30mph sign) after 6 cattle grids and before 7th take a right turn, Maesnant is 1½ miles at the end of the road.

BROUGHTON BUNKHOUSE

Lower Broughton Farm
Nr Bishops Castle, Montgomery
Powys SY15 6SZ

Broughton Bunkhouse offers comfortable accommodation in 17th-century barn with a wealth of exposed beams and full of character. The bunkhouse is clean and cosy, central heating, hot water and showers are all inclusive. There is a fully-equipped kitchen with cookers, fridge-freezer, dishwasher and all the utensils you will need. Clothes washing and drying facilities are also provided.

We are just outside Bishops Castle in South Shropshire, an excellent area for walking on the nearby Stiperstones and Longmynd, cycling around Clun or just enjoying the real ale brewed in two of Bishop Castle's own pubs.

www.virtual-shropshire.co.uk/lower-broughton-farm

CONTACT Tom or Kate Tel/Fax: (01588) 638393.
Email: broughtonfarm@micro-plus-web.net
OPENING SEASON All year
OPENING HOURS 24 hours
NUMBER OF BEDS: 12 2 x 6
BOOKING REQUIREMENTS Helpful to book ahead for availability and to arrange check-in. Deposit required for advance bookings.
PRICE PER NIGHT From £10.00pp. Can be hired for sole use by groups per night or per week. Please telephone for prices.

PUBLIC TRANSPORT
Train Station at Craven Arms (12 miles). Taxi or bus service to Bishops Castle or pick up from hostel for £10 fee. National Coach stop in Shrewsbury. Local bus service to Bishops Castle, free pick-up to hostel from Bishops Castle.

DIRECTIONS
GR 313 906. From Bishops Castle take B4385 (signposted Montgomery). Lower Broughton Farm is 2 miles out of town on the right (on the B4385).

CANOLFAN CORRIS

Old School
Corris, Machynlleth
Powys, SY20 9QT

In the land of Druids and Myths, the Dyfi ECO Valley offers a unique experience. It is centred in the market town of Machynlleth the 'alternative' capital of Wales, once home of the last Welsh Parliament (1404) and the legendary Owain Glyndwr; it is now a national centre for ECO tourism. The mystery and magic of the Celtic race can be discovered at Celtica. Up the valley is the world renowned Centre for Alternative Technology with practical solutions for a world of green living. At Corris there is King Arthur's Labyrinth with its spectacular underground settings, the craft centre and narrow gauge railway. A biosphere of nature reserves, ancient sites, sandy beaches plus the lofty mountain of Cader Idris.

Canolfan Corris is an award-winning (Green Dragon environmental standards) hostel that is community run on Celtic and environmental themes and focuses on conservation and inner harmony. Come and share a community life style in a caring holistic atmosphere. Green Tourism Award Winner (WTB 3 star); a former village school in a friendly village community with a quaint pub. Vegetarian focused.

www.canolfancorris.com

CONTACT Michael Parish Tel/Fax : (01654) 761686.
Email: corrishostel@canolfancorris.com
OPENING SEASON March to December, or by arrangement.
OPENING HOURS All day access. Arrival by appointment
NUMBER OF BEDS 38: 1 x 6, 1 x 22 & 1 x 10 (in 4 bedded cubicles).
BOOKING REQUIREMENTS Phone, fax or email to check.
PRICE PER NIGHT From £11.50 - 12.50.

PUBLIC TRANSPORT
Buses 30/32/34 pass Machynlleth train station-Cambrian Coast line and Birmingham. Trawscambria 701.

DIRECTIONS
We are in the mountain village of Corris 6 miles north of Machynlleth just off the A 487 (GR 753 080). Turn off A487 into Corris. At Slaters Arms pub turn left uphill, hostel is 150 yds on right.

 See page 209 for colour photo

BRAICH GOCH BUNKHOUSE & INN

Corris, Machynlleth
Powys SY20 9RD

The Braich Goch is a 16th-century coaching inn situated 3 miles from Cadair Idris. There are stunning views of the Dulas valley and Dyfi Forest. We have converted from an hotel to bunkhouse accommodation specifically with outdoor enthusiasts in mind. Our facilities include drying room, secure bike storage and workshop, large well equipped self-catering kitchen. There are 6 bedrooms, 4 en-suite and a further two bathrooms. The location is ideal for walking, cycling, climbing and canoeing at all levels as well as bird watching or simply chilling out. New Oct 2004 Dyfi Forest mountain bike trails.
The Braich is also a pub - with pool table, darts, table football and other games to keep you entertained in the evening! We provide activity packages with qualified instructors, all equipment for kayaking, canoeing, climbing at various levels (see website for details). Indoor climbing and rope training area. In the area are King Arthur's Labyrinth and Corris Craft Centre, Centre for Alternative Technology, Machynlleth, Coed-y-Brenin Forest Park and the coast. WTB 3 star. GDL2 award. Walkers and cyclists welcome awards.

www.braichgoch.co.uk

CONTACT: Ann or Andy Tel: (01654) 761229 mobile 07881 626734
Email: AnnBottrill@aol.com
OPENING SEASON All year
OPENING HOURS All hours by arrangement
NUMBER OF BEDS 26 5 x 4 : 1 x 6
BOOKING REQUIREMENTS Essential for groups. 20% deposit, balance 2 weeks before arrival.
PRICE PER NIGHT From £12.50 per person

PUBLIC TRANSPORT
Nearest train station Machynlleth. Bus stops outside the Inn.

DIRECTIONS
GR 754 075 On A487 between Machynlleth and Dolgellau at Corris turning. 2½ miles north of Centre for Alternative Technology ½ mile south of King Arthur's Labyrinth.

BALA BACKPACKERS HOSTEL

32 Tegid Street
Bala, LL23 7EL

For adventure and experience within the Snowdonia National Park, Bala Backpackers offers opportunity within everyone's budget. Bala Backpackers has a homely atmosphere and is friendly hostel-style accommodation with 27 comfortable single beds in an early 1800s character building, located in a quiet, sunny chapel square, in the bustling market town of Bala, Mid North Wales.

Bala boasts a five mile long **Lake**, a white-water **River**, which is very popular for raft rides, and nestles beneath three 900 metre **Peaks**. The hostel has an equipped dining room and fully catered services are available from the warden. A Leisure Centre, complete with fun pool, is located at the lakeside just ten minutes' walk away. Or just soak up the atmosphere of this sunny bustling market town by day or evening, where there is a choice of 22 eating places and town shops 100 metres away. Curfew 11.30pm.

www. Bala-Backpackers.co.uk

CONTACT Stella, Tel: (01678) 521700
Email: info@bala-backpackers.co.uk
OPENING SEASON All year, midweek winter by prior arrangement.
OPENING HOURS Reception 5pm-10pm & 8am-10am.Secure access
NUMBER OF BEDS 27: 3x4 : 3x5
BOOKING REQUIREMENTS On-line , by phone or email.
PRICE PER NIGHT £10 per person (includes sheetbag and bedding)

PUBLIC TRANSPORT
Nearest Train Station Wrexham 30 miles. Buses daily from Wrexham and Barmouth (Bus 94). Connections in all directions from London to the North West Coast. Ferry Terminal: Holyhead (60 miles) on Anglesey to/from Dublin, Ireland.

DIRECTIONS
GR 926 358. Bala is on A494, off the A5 between Llangollen and Betws-y-Coed. From South, take M6, M54, A5 and A494 just after Corwen. A494 in Bala town, towards Dolgellau, turn left at the end of Bala High St. for Plassey St. Car Park. Tegid Street one minute.

1m

BALA BUNK HOUSE

Tomen Y Castell
Llanfor
Bala
Gwynedd
LL23 7HD

The coach house is a converted 200-year-old Welsh stone building. It carries WTB two star approval and is set back from the road in over an acre of picturesque grounds with a river and stream. Modernised to provide accommodation for outdoor activity groups, it is light, airy and comfortable with night storage heating and drying facilities. There is a large lounge/dining area and bunk rooms for 2, 4 and 8 plus annexe for 6. Separate ladies' and gentlemen's toilets have washing areas and hot showers. Fully equipped self-catering kitchen. The Little Cottage, a newly converted self-contained bunkroom sleeping 6, with kitchenette, shower and toilet/washing area. Ideal for smaller groups & families. Sheets & pillowcases are provided - bring a sleeping bag. From the Tomen there is a splendid view of the Berwyn Hills; together with the Aran and Arenig hills they provide superb walking. Bala Lake and the National White Water Centre are brilliant for water sports. Good pubs, restaurants and shops in Bala.

www.balabunkhouse.co.uk

CONTACT Guy and Jane Williams, Tel/Fax: (01678) 520738,
Email: thehappyunion@btinternet.com
OPENING SEASON All year
OPENING HOURS No restrictions
NUMBER OF BEDS 26 : 1x2 : 1x4 : 1x6 : 1x8. 1x6 self contained
BOOKING REQUIREMENTS Book if possible, ring or write with 20% deposit. Weekends are usually busy.
PRICE PER NIGHT Single night £12pp, two or more nights £10pp.

PUBLIC TRANSPORT
Nearest train station is at Wrexham (30 miles away). Nearest National Express at Corwen (10 miles away). Local buses call at Bala (1.6 miles from hostel). Call hostel for a taxi.

DIRECTIONS
GR 950 372. From England take M6, M54, A5 through Llangollen then A494 for Bala. We are on the A494 1½ miles before Bala (on the right).

H AM 1m

CORNERSTONE QUEST ADVENTURE CENTRE

Gwern-y-Genau
Arenig
Bala
Gwynedd LL23 7BP

The Cornerstone Quest achievement centre is at the foot of Arenig, the second highest mountain in Wales. Being seven miles from Bala and 25 miles from Porthmadog, the centre is ideally located for a variety of local pursuits to suit everyone's tastes. The Centre is developing a conversation area on the shores of Llyn Celyn. All this is set within the natural beauty of the Snowdonia National Park.

We have two houses on site which can be booked separately or jointly. There is a real homely atmosphere at Cornerstone Quest with great facilities for self-catering. Each house is self-contained with lounge/ dining area, kitchen, shower, toilets. Bed linen is provided. There is a shared meeting room, games room and 29 acres of land to explore. Restricted facilities for people with disabilities

www.cornerstonequest.co.uk

CONTACT Tel: 0121 643 1984 leaflet & bookings (check availability)
Email:- info@cornerstonequest.co.uk
OPENING SEASON All year
OPENING HOURS All day
NUMBER OF BEDS 30: 2x6 : 3x4 : 3x2
BOOKING REQUIREMENTS Booking essential, 25% deposit. Final payment 4 weeks prior to holiday.
PRICE PER NIGHT Farmhouse £216 (sleeps 18) , Celyn House £144 (sleeps 12). Guide prices (lower prices at different seasons)

PUBLIC TRANSPORT
Nearest Train Station; Wrexham (30miles) . Own transport essential.

DIRECTIONS
From Bala take the A4212 Trawsfynydd road, after ½ mile fork left signposted Rhyduchaf and Llidiardau. Five miles, two cattle grids later pass Bryn Ifan Cottage, turn first right. Gwern-y-Genau is ¼ mile on the left, about half way along the railway cutting.

TYDDYN BYCHAN

Cefn Brith
Cerrig y drudion
LL21 9TS

Tyddyn Bychan is an 18th-century traditional Welsh farmhouse, set in two and a half acres of private grounds surrounded on all sides by farmland with a large parking area well away from the road. Situated in an excellent location for fieldwork in Hiraethog and Snowdonia, climbing, fishing and numerous watersports including whitewater rafting, and many local walks. The Bunkhouse is luxurious with two sleeping areas containing 8 and 10 bunks which are of a very high standard. There are showers, washbasins and toilets for each room and a well equipped kitchen/dining room. Additional room is available in a small cottage. All bedding, heating and electricity are included, but bring your own towels. We can provide delicious homemade food in our licensed dining room and make up packed lunches. The bunkhouse and cottage are also equipped for self-catering. *Wales Tourist Board Three Star Bunkhouse*

www.tyddynbychan.co.uk

CONTACT Lynda, Tel: (01490) 420680.
Email :- tyddyn@tesco.net
OPENING SEASON All year
OPENING HOURS All day
NUMBER OF BEDS 24:- 1x10 1x8 1x6
BOOKING REQUIREMENTS Booking is advisable
PRICE PER NIGHT £10pp including bedding, discounts for groups and longer stays.

PUBLIC TRANSPORT
Nearest train station is at Llanrwst. Nearest National Express service at Colwyn Bay and Llandudno. Phone (01492) 575412 for details.

DIRECTIONS
GR 931 504. Turn off A5 at Cerrig y drudion. Take B4501 out of village for Llyn Brenig, take the turning on left for Cefn Brith. After about 2 miles you will see a phone box on left, chapel on right and the road widens for a layby. The gate for Tyddyn is on the left directly opposite junction on the right.

THE EAGLES

Penmachno
Betws-y-Coed
Conwy
LL24 0UG

The Eagles is a traditional inn offering real ales, and a very friendly atmosphere, a perfect setting for relaxing after a hard day in the hills! The very comfortable accommodation within The Eagles consists of 6 rooms sleeping 4 and 2 rooms sleeping 2. All rooms are centrally heated and with tea and coffee making facilities; duvets, pillows and sheets are supplied. There are two separate showers, a bathroom and two washrooms/toilets. A guest kitchen and secure bike storage are available. Breakfast is available on request.

The Eagles is situated on the edge of the peaceful village of Penmachno, in a secluded valley 4 miles south of Betws-y-Coed, within the heart of the Snowdonia National Park. Snowdon itself is about 15 miles away. Surrounded by mountain scenery, this is ideal accommodation for groups or individuals walking, climbing, cycling or canoeing - also perfect for families - self-catering cottages are also available.

www.eaglespenmachno.co.uk

CONTACT Gerry or Linda McMorrow, Tel: (01690) 760177,
Email inn@eaglespenmachno.co.uk
OPENING SEASON All year
OPENING HOURS Totally flexible
NUMBER OF BEDS 28: 6 x 4 : 2 x 2.
BOOKING REQUIREMENTS Recommended, essential for groups
PRICE PER NIGHT £12.50pp. Discount for groups of 10 or more.

PUBLIC TRANSPORT
Betws-y-Coed Station 3½miles. Bus 64 from Betws-y-Coed to Penmachno. From Ireland or London and points between London to Holyhead main line change at Llandudno Junction for Betws-y-coed.

DIRECTIONS
From A5, 2 miles east of Betws-y-Coed, at Conwy Falls Café, turn onto B4406 to Penmachno, cross bridge, The Eagles is in front of you.

BETWS-Y-COED YOUTH HOSTEL

yha AFFILIATED

Betws-y-Coed
Conwy
LL24 0DW

Situated just outside Betws-y-Coed, opposite Wales's most beautiful waterfall, nestling between majestic mountains, streams and rivers. Suberb for walkers, climbers or an ideal stop-over.

The Swallow Falls complex is a combinaton of hotel, hostel and camping site with full facilities. The hostel has been recently converted to include 44 beds, some en-suite with television We have a self-catering kitchen, drying room and launderette. The hostel has been refurnished and decorated to the highest standards.

Guests may use all the facilities of the hotel which include a quiet reading room, 2 bars with traditional food, a shop and Fudge Making Pantry. There is also a large car park, bike shed and landscaped gardens with a childrens' play area.

www.swallowfallshotel.co.uk

CONTACT Tel: (01690) 710796. Email: swallow.falls@virgin.net
OPENING SEASON All year
OPENING HOURS 8.00am - 11.00pm
NUMBER OF BEDS 52: 6x6 : 2x4 : 2x4 en-suite.TV
BOOKING REQUIREMENTS Book with first night as deposit
PRICE PER NIGHT From £9pp to £15pp

PUBLIC TRANSPORT
Nearest train station Betws-y-Coed. Buses from Betws-y-Coed to Swallow Falls.

DIRECTIONS
Situated 2 miles from Betws-y-Coed on the A5 to Bangor. Opposite Swallow Falls waterfall.

CONWY VALLEY BACKPACKERS BARN

Pyllau Gloewon Farm
Tal-y-bont, Conwy
Gwynedd
LL32 8YX

Conwy Valley Backpackers is situated on a peaceful working farm that is working towards organic status, in the heart of the beautiful Conwy Valley with excellent access to Snowdonia. Centrally heated, small dorms, fully equipped self-catering kitchen, log fires, hot showers and a fire alarm system. We have three separate dorms sleeping 6, 4 and 10, two of which have their own toilet facility. We can also provide secure bike/canoe storage, grazing for horses & tourist information. Beside the barn is a small stream and guests may picnic and BBQ on the river bank or swing lazily in the hammock, ideal space for restoration, relaxation and retreat. Breakfast/packed lunch/ light meals by arrangement. There are some great pubs and eating places within walking distance. Ample activities available from fishing, hiking to white water rafting and mountain biking. Groups are welcome. No dogs unless by prior arrangement.

www.conwyvalleybarn.com

CONTACT David, Claudia, Glyn or Helen, Tel: (01492) 660504
OPENING SEASON All year
OPENING HOURS All day
NUMBER OF BEDS 20: 1 x 4 : 1 x 6 : 1 x 10.
BOOKING REQUIREMENTS Not essential but recommended.
PRICE PER NIGHT From £10pp. Group bookings/sole use, from £10pp

PUBLIC TRANSPORT
Nearest train stations and National Express coach services are at Llandudno Junction and Conwy. Local bus 19 or 19a runs every 20 minutes from Conwy and Llandudno Junction, ask driver to drop you at Pyllau Gloewon farm gate.

DIRECTIONS
GR 769 697. Six miles south of Conwy on the B5106, look for Backpackers sign just before entering Talybont.

LLANDUDNO HOSTEL

14 Charlton Street
Llandudno
LL30 2AA

James and Melissa, with their five children, would like to invite you to their charming Victorian home. We are a friendly family-run hostel where individuals, families and groups (including school groups) are welcome all year. Some of the guests comments "friendliest hostel we've ever stayed in", "Wow isn't it clean", "these bathrooms are fabulous as good as any hotel". Come and try us, we love to meet new people and look forward to getting to know you.

Our elegant home is set in the heart of the Victorian seaside resort town of Llandudno, an ideal place to shop or explore the many varied local attractions. Excellent blue flag beaches, dry slope skiing, toboggan run, ten pin bowling, Bronze Age copper mine, traditional pier and many museums, fishing trips etc. Llandudno is within easy travelling distance to Snowdon, Bodnant Gardens and many local castles. We are able to book local attractions for groups and secure some discounts.

CONTACT Melissa or James Tel: (01492) 877430
Email:- postmaster@llandudnohostel.plus.com
OPENING SEASON All year. Telephone in winter prior to arrival
OPENING HOURS All day
NUMBER OF BEDS 40: 2x8 : 2x6 : 4x2 : 1x4 : 2 x family
BOOKING REQUIREMENTS Recommended, essential April to July
PRICE PER NIGHT From £13 adult. £9 child. £45 family (2+3). Group special prices on request.

PUBLIC TRANSPORT
Nearest train station Llandudno. Turn right as you exit train station, cross the road, turn left down Vaughan Street (towards the beach), left into Charlton Street, Llandudno Hostel is number 14 on the left.

DIRECTIONS
By car follow signs for Llandudno town centre, at one way system (Asda on right) turn left into Vaughan Street, then right into Charlton Street.

HOLISTIC HEALTH HOSTELS

'Bodlondeb' Village Road & Ty Refail, Mill Road
Llanfairfechan
County of Conway
LL33 0AA

Situated at the base of the Snowdonia National Park, within minutes' walk of the North Wales coastal route. This lovely town with the heart of a village offers easy access to all that Snowdonia has to offer whilst providing a superb stop-off location if you are travelling between Manchester/Liverpool and Dublin (via Holyhead). Llanfairfechan has 6 public houses and 6 churches, two languages, Welsh and English. A most balanced community - very yin/yang!

Holistic Health Hostels offer reflexology, aromatherapy and massage therapies on-site to visitors and guests. We also hope to offer coffee shop facilities in the future.

www.holistichealthhostels.com

CONTACT Joan Haggas. Tel: (01248) 680692, or 07711 556 157, Email: manchester.backpacker@good.co.uk
OPENING SEASON All year
OPENING HOURS By arrangement - no curfew
NUMBER OF BEDS 20 in hostel plus holiday cottage (sleeps 4 to 12)
BOOKING REQUIREMENTS Always telephone ahead for availability and to arrange check-in.
PRICE PER NIGHT £9 to £11 per person (dormitory) double/twin-share £16 per person.

PUBLIC TRANSPORT
Rail to Llanfairfechan or Llandudno Junction, local buses run from Bangor to Conway via Llanfairfechan.

DIRECTIONS
By car national route A55 (Conway to Bangor), follow signs for village. Conway to Bangor approx 15 miles. Llanfairfechan is midway. 'Bodlondeb' is next to the Post Office, facing the Village Hall.

P H 3m

 See page 215 for colour photo

WILLIAMS CAMPING BARN, BUNKHOUSE AND CAMPSITE

Gwern Gof Isaf Farm
Capel Curig
Betws-y-coed
Conwy LL24 0EU

Williams Camping Barn, Bunkhouse and Campsite is set on a 750 acre National Trust Farm. The accommodation is used by scouts, Duke of Edinburgh Award expeditions, climbers, ramblers, mountain bikers, canoeists, horse riders, schools and colleges.

The two bunkhouses sleep 16 and 6 and include hot and cold showers. The campsite can hold 100 tents. Larger groups can mix indoor accommodation with camping. The water is filtered and UV treated. A secure locked building is available for storing canoes or mountain bikes and there is a barbecue area. Climbing and abseiling are available on site. Short courses in canoeing, climbing etc, an artificial ski slope and a climbing wall are available at Plas y Brenin National Mountaineering Centre 3 miles away. There are four pubs/ restaurants and 3 climbing shops in nearby village of Capel Curig.

www.gwerngofisaf.co.uk

CONTACT David or Elizabeth, Tel: (01690) 720276
OPENING SEASON All year
OPENING HOURS 7.30am to 11pm
NUMBER OF BEDS 16 and 6 in 2 barns, plus 100 tent pitches.
BOOKING REQUIREMENTS Essential with 50% deposit
PRICE PER NIGHT £5 per person in barns, £3 per person camping

PUBLIC TRANSPORT
Sherpa buses run from Bangor (12 miles) and Betws-y-coed (8 miles) and stop at farm entrance. Nearest train stations are Betws-y-coed and Bangor.

DIRECTIONS
GR 686 602 (OS sheet 115). On A5 Bangor Road, 3 miles west of Capel Curig, opposite Carneod Llewelyn and Glyder mountain range.

      1m

JESSE JAMES' BUNKHOUSE

Penisarwaen
Nr Llanberis
Gwynedd, LL55 3DA

Established by Jesse in 1966, Snowdonia's Original Bunkhouse, a comfortable base for **non-smokers**. Perfectly situated between the mountains and the sea, there is a whole world to explore and enjoy - mountains and moorlands, rock climbing and scrambling, woodlands and beaches, with easy walks starting from the bunkhouse. Cyclists can experience everything from lovely quiet lanes to mountain bridleways and passes, where the views can be breathtaking and the silence deafening. There are two bunkhouses (like simple hostels), an apartment and a flat, all appropriately heated. All self-catering, with fully equipped kitchens and dining areas. There's a drying room, some camping space and off road parking. All you need is your sleeping bag, which can be hired, and your food. Ideal base for mountain courses. Jesse is a retired instructor/guide and a mountain rescue leader, who'll readily chat over a brew and maybe his famous flapjack! This is a Centre of Lo-Tech Pragmatism - keep it simple so long as it works. Here it really does. Ring or write for a leaflet. **Sorry no pets.**

CONTACT Jesse James, Tel: (01286) 870521 (24hrs)
OPENING SEASON All year, but enquire first.
OPENING HOURS All day
NUMBER OF BEDS 36, plus more in other grades
BOOKING REQUIREMENTS Ring or write, casuals take their chance. 50% deposit for two night weekends, less for longer.
PRICE PER NIGHT Hostel £9pp other from £11pp. Negotiable discounts for large or long stay groups.

PUBLIC TRANSPORT
Train/coach services to Bangor. Take bus 85,86 or 87 to Beran Esso Garage. Walk downhill 800 yds find Bunkhouse on right of main road.

DIRECTIONS
GR566 638. A5-A4085 to Llanberis then A4244(B4547)towards Bangor or A55 coast road to the Bangor turn-off then A4244(B4547) to Llanberis. See instructions from Beran Garage above.

OUTDOOR ALTERNATIVE

Cerrig-yr-Adar
Rhoscolyn, Holyhead
Anglesey. LL65 2NQ

Wonderfully situated in 7 acres of an 'Area of Outstanding Natural Beauty' 300m from a beach at south end of Holy Island, Anglesey. Nearby Holyhead has rail links and ferries to Ireland. The centre is an excellent base for so much in the outdoors and is immediately adjacent to the Anglesey Coastal Path. There is spectacular geology, a range of habitats and species of marine life, birds and plants. There are prehistoric remains and good walking on a varied and accessible coast. Kayakers have classic sea tours, overfalls, playwaves, surf and rockhopping. Climbers have Gogarth nearby and Rhoscolyn offers all grades in an attractive setting. Divers can beach launch for wrecks and scenic marine life. Birdwatching is excellent. Camping with toilets and showers is available and a pub within walking distance. We respect the environment and encourage careful energy use, composting & recycling. The Centre is a no-smoking area.

www.outdooralternative.org

CONTACT Jacqui or Andy Tel: 0845 1260609 (01407) 860469.
Email: centre@outdooralternative.org
OPENING SEASON All year
OPENING HOURS 24 hr access
NUMBER OF BEDS 36: 2 buildings 2x2 : 1x4 : 2x6 : and 1x3 : 2x4 : 1x5.
BOOKING REQUIREMENTS Essential
PRICE PER NIGHT £12.75 (inc VAT). (€ 18)

PUBLIC TRANSPORT
Nearest train station, Holyhead (10km) (London direct 4½ hrs) or (some) Valley (5km). National Exp Valley (6km). Bus 23/25 Holyhead Rhoscolyn (1km) or 4 & 44 Holyhead-Four Mile Bridge (3km). Ferry: Holyhead - Dublin or Dun Laoghaire. Taxi: Holyhead approx £12.

DIRECTIONS
GR SH 278 752. From A5 traffic lights at Y Fali/Valley take B4545 Trearddur. In 2km at Four Mile Bridge fork left at sign Rhoscolyn 2miles. After 2km sharp left at camping symbols. In 800m fork right at large white gatepost. The centre is 250m on the left.

1m

"TOTTERS"

Plas Porth Yr Aur
2 High Street, Caernarfon
Gwynedd LL55 1RN

'Totters' is situated in the heart of the historic castle town of Caernarfon. Sheltered by the castle's town wall, we are only 30 metres from the shores of the Menai Straits and get to see some fantastic sunsets. The town not only offers the visitor a huge selection of pubs and restaurants to choose from, but also acts as the perfect base for trips into the Snowdonia National Park. There is very good public transport in and out of the National Park.
The hostel is a 200-year-old, five floored town house, which is fully heated with all the comforts of home. Continental breakfast and all bedding is provided in the overnight charge. We have a common room with TV and games, drying room, book exchange, dining room, bicycle hire and a secure left luggage facility. The bedrooms sleep either 4 or 6 and can be arranged as mixed or single sex dorms. There is also a separate family room. We're easy going, flexible and WTB approved. Check us out in Lonely Planet, Let's Go & Rough Guides.

www.applemaps.co.uk/totters

CONTACT Bob or Henryette, Tel: (01286) 672963.
Email: bob@totters.free-online.co.uk
OPENING SEASON All year
OPENING HOURS All day access. Book in by 10pm.
NUMBER OF BEDS 30 : 5 x 6 (private rooms available on request)
BOOKING REQUIREMENTS Booking is essential for groups in June, July, August and September, 25% deposit required.
PRICE PER NIGHT £12 per person (includes breakfast and all bedding). Discounts for groups and long stays.

PUBLIC TRANSPORT
Bangor train station is 7 miles from the hostel. Catch a bus from outside the station to Caernarfon (fare £1.50). National Express coaches drop off in Caernarfon 200m from the hostel.

DIRECTIONS
Coming by road:- follow signs for town centre, turn right 200m after the big Celtic Royal hotel, keep going and Totters is the last house on the left (if you fall in the sea you've gone just too far!) The hostel is beside the castle wall next to the Royal Welsh Yacht Club.

1m

PLAS-Y-NANT

Betws Garmon
Caernarfon
Gwynedd LL54 7YR

Plas-y-Nant is 7 miles from Caernarfon in the foothills of Snowdon. Set amidst the rugged mountain scenery of the National Park, it is an ideal base from which to explore the mountains and coast. It could also provide a spectacular venue for your wedding or other special event for which we can offer exclusive use. There is a licensed bar, dining room and spacious lounges which are ideal for relaxing in front of an open fire. Training or meeting facilities are available and the former chapel provides an excellent function room.

The centre is ideally suited to walkers and cyclists. The Snowdon Sherpa bus provides access to all the footpaths up Snowdon and the Welsh Highland Railway passes the front gate. Mountain bike hire is available on site with Beddgelert Forest Trailquest just down the road. An exciting range of adventure days and weekends are also run from Plas-y-Nant using a local licensed activity provider.

www.plasynant.com

CONTACT Tony. Tel (01286) 650227.
Email: mail@plasynant.com
OPENING SEASON All year
OPENING HOURS Not routinely manned between 10.00 & 16.00
NUMBER OF BEDS 36: (14 rooms) (twin, double and family) some en-suite. Dogs welcome by prior arrangement.
BOOKING REQUIREMENTS Please check availability in advance. Payment for first night required as deposit.
PRICE PER NIGHT From £15per person B&B.

PUBLIC TRANSPORT
Train Station Bangor. National Express, Caernarfon. S4 bus from Caernarfon to entrance. Plas-y-Nant halt on WHLR from 2004.

DIRECTIONS
Plas-y-Nant is between Caernarfon and Beddgelert on the A4085 at the south end of Betws Garmon (GR.SH550563)

P 5m

BRYN DINAS BUNKHOUSE

Bryn Dinas
Nant Gwynant
Caernarfon LL55 4NH

Bryn Dinas Bunkhouse/Hostel is located in the magnificent Gwynant Valley right at the foot of Snowdon on the south side. The village of Nant Gwynant is situated between the idyllic twin lakes of Llyn Gwynant and Llyn Dinas and is only three miles from the picturesque village of Beddgelert. There is a good selection of pubs, cafés and restaurants in Beddgelert.

The accommodation is fully fitted for self-catering, although full-catering can be arranged. Breakfast, packed lunches and evening meals available with advance notice. There are two grades of accommodation. The Farmhouse (graded WTB 2* bunkhouse) has twenty-five bunk beds arranged dormitory style in six bedrooms, and the Cabins have twenty-nine bunk beds in twelve separate wooden cabins in the centre grounds. Please write/ring for a leaflet. New for 2005 - Brand new self-contained log cabins available.

www.bryndinasbunkhouse.co.uk

CONTACT Brenton/Hayley Tel: (01766) 890234,
Email: wrdy1@yahoo.com
OPENING SEASON Open all year
OPENING HOURS Totally flexible
NUMBER OF BEDS 54: 1 x 8 : 2 x 6 : 3 x 4 : 9 x 2 : 4 x 1.
BOOKING REQUIREMENTS Recommended (with deposit)
PRICE PER NIGHT From £12.50. per person.

PUBLIC TRANSPORT
Nearest train stations are at Porthmadog and Betws-y-Coed. The Snowdon Link runs from Porthmadog to Betws-y-Coed and stops outside hostel.

DIRECTIONS
GR 625 503. Turn left off the A5 at Capel Curig on to the A4086. At the Pen-y-Gwryd Hotel turn left onto the A498. Descend into the Gwynant valley and into Nant Gwynant. Pass the car park at base of Watkin Path. Bryn Dinas 300 yds on right, past the old post office.

See page 215 for colour photo

SNOWDON LODGE
CAFE LAWRENCE

Lawrence House, Tremadog
Nr Porthmadog
Snowdonia LL49 9PS

Snowdon Lodge is a WTB 4* hostel, and a grade 2 listed building, famous as the house in which Lawrence of Arabia was born in 1888 and recently totally modernised to provide the ultimate in clean, comfortable and secure accommodation for individuals and groups. Choice of dormitories or private rooms, with heating and personal lockers in every bedroom. Licensed bar, large dining room and café, a fully equipped kitchen, lounge/TV room with real log fires and a private car park leading to extensive woodland walks.

Ideally positioned just 6 miles from Snowdon, yet only 2 miles from beautiful sandy beaches, and only a few minutes' walk from the train station, National Express coaches, and many pubs and restaurants. Within a mile are the Ffestiniog and Welsh Highland railways, the famous Tremadog rocks for climbers, and virtually every other outdoor activity one could wish for. Guided outdoor activities arranged on request. Mountain bike hire available. Snowdon Lodge is the perfect base from which to explore Snowdonia and the Lleyn Peninsula.

www.snowdonlodge.co.uk

CONTACT Carl or Anja. Tel: (01766) 515354, Fax: (01766) 515364, Email: info@snowdonlodge.co.uk
OPENING SEASON All year. booking is essential in winter months.
OPENING HOURS No restrictions
NUMBER OF BEDS 48
BOOKING REQUIREMENTS Essential. Deposit for first night's accommodation payable by credit card.
PRICE PER NIGHT From £13.50 including light breakfast and linen.

PUBLIC TRANSPORT
Half mile from Porthmadog train station and 250 yards from National Express coach stop.

DIRECTIONS
Half a mile from Porthmadog on Caernarfon road (A487).

STONE BARN AND STUDIO

Tyddyn Morthwyl
Criccieth
Gwynedd
LL52 0NF

The Stone Barn and Studio are converted farm buildings at Tyddyn Morthwyl Farm and Caravan Park near Criccieth on the fringe of Snowdonia. The farm provides a good centre for climbing and walking in Snowdonia and the Lleyn Peninsula. Tremadog Rocks (an all year rock climbing venue) is only 7 miles away. Canoeing and wind surfing nearby.

The Barn has an alpine style sleeping platform. Hot showers and toilets are shared with the caravan park. There is a wood burning stove for heating and clothes drying (wood provided free) and a kitchen area with fridge and running water. The Studio is a small stone building with two single beds and washbasin. Several pubs in the locality serve good bar meals.

There is also a static caravan to let.

CONTACT Mrs Trumper, Tel: (01766) 522115
Email: trumper@henstabl147freeserve.co.uk
OPENING SEASON All year
OPENING HOURS Flexible
NUMBER OF BEDS 12
BOOKING REQUIREMENTS 48 hrs advanced booking required, with one night's fee as deposit.
PRICE PER NIGHT £6 per person in the Stone Barn including wood (discount for groups). £8 per night the Studio.

PUBLIC TRANSPORT
Criccieth has a train station and National Express coach service. The hostel is 1¼ miles from Criccieth and a taxi service is available.

DIRECTIONS
1¼ miles from Criccieth on B4411 Caernarfon road.

1m

BUDGET ACCOMMODATION

11, Marine Terrace
Criccieth
Gwynedd
LL52 0EF

Budget Accommodation is in a large Victorian residence located on the seafront close to Criccieth Castle with beautiful views of Harlech and the Lleyn Peninsula. The beach is great for fishing, swimming, paddling or simply for skimming stones. The house is close to the Snowdonia National Park and is an area ideal for watersports, climbing and walking. The Sustrans cycle route passes in front of the house.

The accommodation comprises twin rooms with hot and cold water. Sheets, duvets and towels plus tea and coffee making facilities are provided free of charge. There is a dining room with cutlery, crockery, toaster, kettle and microwave for making drinks and snacks and a continental breakfast can be provided if requested for an extra £1.50 per person. Cycles can be housed in the back-yard.

Smoking is not allowed anywhere in the accommodation.

CONTACT Bob or Sue, Tel: (01766) 523098
OPENING SEASON April to October inclusive
OPENING HOURS 8.00 am - 12 midnight
NUMBER OF BEDS 6: 3 x 2
BOOKING REQUIREMENTS Advanced booking advisable with 50% deposit.
PRICE PER NIGHT £12 per person, £6.00 for child sharing.

PUBLIC TRANSPORT
Criccieth village has a train station and National Express coach service.

DIRECTIONS
Turn off A497 at the centre of Criccieth and go over the level crossing. Follow the road, bearing right. Turn right at 'T' junction opposite Cadwaladers Ice Cream Parlour, past Castle and down onto the lower sea front, we are number 11.

NEFYN BACKPACKERS

St David's Road
Nefyn

Nefyn Backpackers is a large Victorian house located at the end of Nefyn village on the Lleyn Peninsula. The beach, which has 'blue flag' status is about 5 minutes' walk away and is ideal for sailing, canoeing, swimming, paddling and fishing.

Nefyn is also at the start of 'The Rivals' range of hills and is ideal for hill and coastal walking. A golf course can be found in the next village, Morfa Nefyn, also the famous Ty Coch Inn, the only pub in Wales which is on the beach. There are shops and pubs within walking distance of Nefyn Backpackers.

The accommodation comprises a dining room and common room with woodburning stove, 2 bedrooms with bedding provided, tea and coffee, and all kitchen facilities. Nefyn Backpackers provide storage for bikes at the rear of the premises.

CONTACT Gary Tel: Mobile 07762 603740
OPENING SEASON All year
OPENING HOURS All day
NUMBER OF BEDS 6: 1 x 3 : 1 x double and single
BOOKING REQUIREMENTS One week's notice required for all stays.
PRICE PER NIGHT £11pp. Discount for 7 days or more.

PUBLIC TRANSPORT
Nearest train and bus station, Pwllheli, good bus service to Nefyn approx cost £1.50.

DIRECTIONS
Nefyn is on the B4417. Nefyn Backpackers is situated at the end of Nefyn village.

P 5m

'SGUBOR UNNOS' BUNKHOUSE AND HOVERCRAFTS

Fferm Tanrallt Farm
Llangian, Abersoch
Gwynedd LL53 7LN

Croeso – Welcome 'Sgubor Unnos provides luxury bunkhouse accommodation on a Welsh speaking, traditionally run, family farm in the village of Llangian, one mile from Abersoch, famous for its watersports and surfing beaches, Hell's Mouth and Porth Ceiriad. The only accommodation of its kind on the Lleyn Peninsula it is centrally located, the ideal centre for outdoor activities, walking, surfing, cycling, golf, fishing, sailing etc. (the farm also offers hovercraft cruising – a new experience in outdoor activities). Situated a few miles from Llangian at the tip of the Peninsula lies Bardsey Island where 20,000 saints are buried!! Why not pay them a visit? Trips around the island for its wildlife, heritage etc., can be arranged and at certain times accommodation on the island itself. The modern bunkhouse offers 3 bedrooms ideal for a midweek or weekend break for individuals or groups of up to 14. Fully equipped kitchen/lounge, disabled facilities, covered BBQ area, secure storage, private parking, traditional village shop, Post Office and BT kiosk 500 metres away.

www.tanrallt.com

CONTACT Phil & Meinir, Tel: (01758)713527.enquiries@tanrallt.com
OPENING SEASON All year
OPENING HOURS All day
NUMBER OF BEDS 14: 2 x 4 : 1 x 6
BOOKING REQUIREMENTS Not essential but recommended.
PRICE PER NIGHT £14 (adult), £6 (under 10 years), including a light breakfast. Discount for more than 2 nights.

PUBLIC TRANSPORT
Nearest train station is Pwllheli (7 miles). Good local bus and taxi service to Llangian. Public transport details on web site.

DIRECTIONS
GR 296 288 On entering Abersoch from Pwllheli, take the right hand turning up the hill to Llangian. (Follow Brown signs) Pass the Glyn Restaurant on the left, carry on until dip in the road, turn left down the hill to Llangian. Tanrallt is the farm on your left on leaving the village.

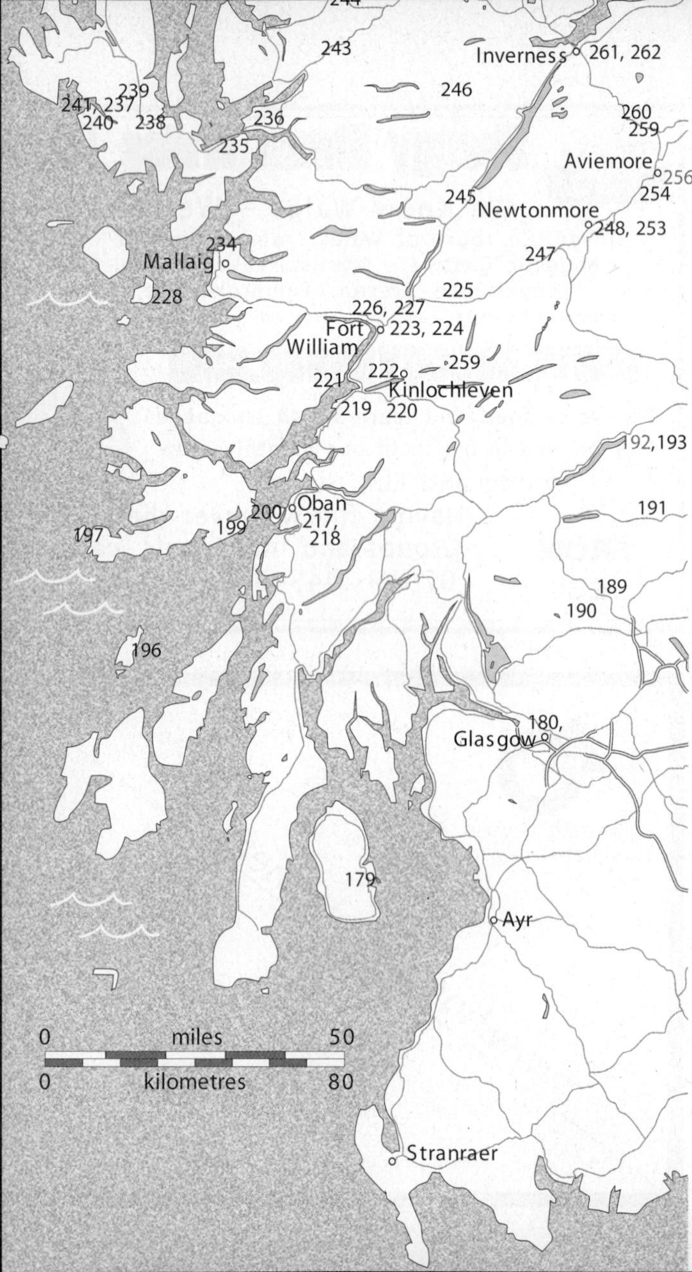

244
243
Inverness 261, 262
246
239
241, 237
240 238
236
235
260
259
Aviemore 256
254
245
Newtonmore
248, 253
234
Mallaig
247
228
225
226, 227
Fort William 223, 224
259
222
221
Kinlochleven
219 220
192, 193
198
200 Oban
217, 218
199
191
197
189
190
196
180,
Glasgow
179
Ayr
0 miles 50
0 kilometres 80
Stranraer

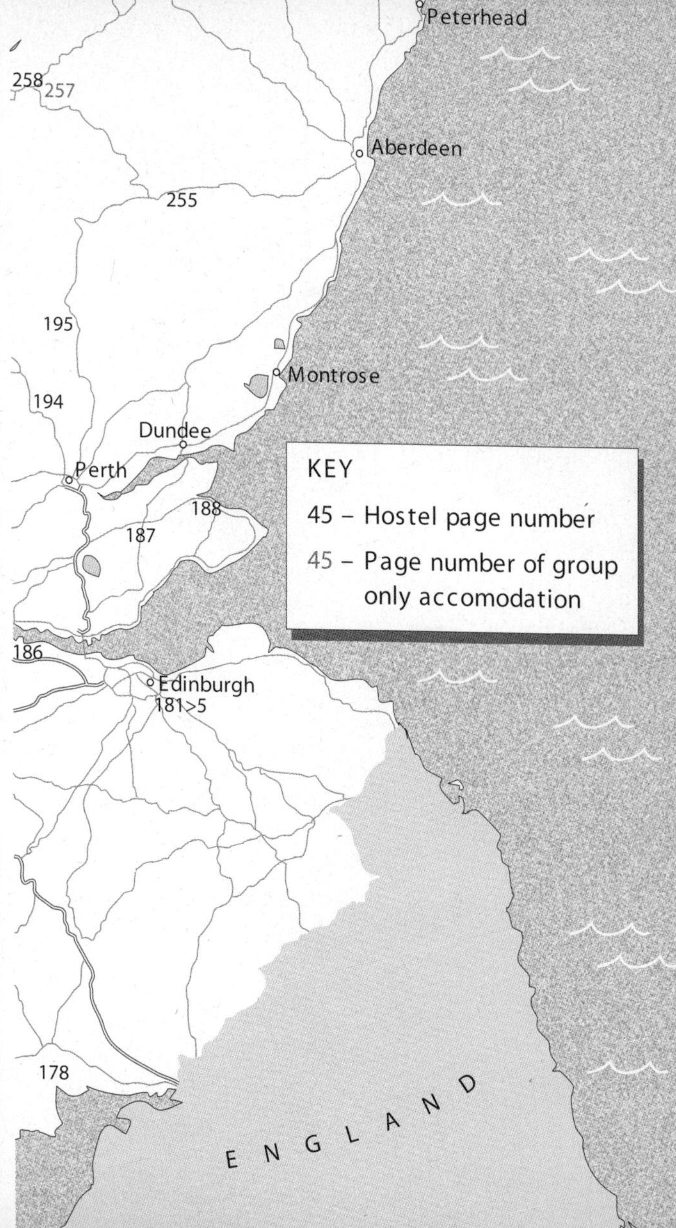
Peterhead
258
257
Aberdeen
255
195
Montrose
194
Dundee
Perth
188
187
186
Edinburgh
181>5
178
ENGLAND
KEY
45 – Hostel page number
45 – Page number of group only accomodation

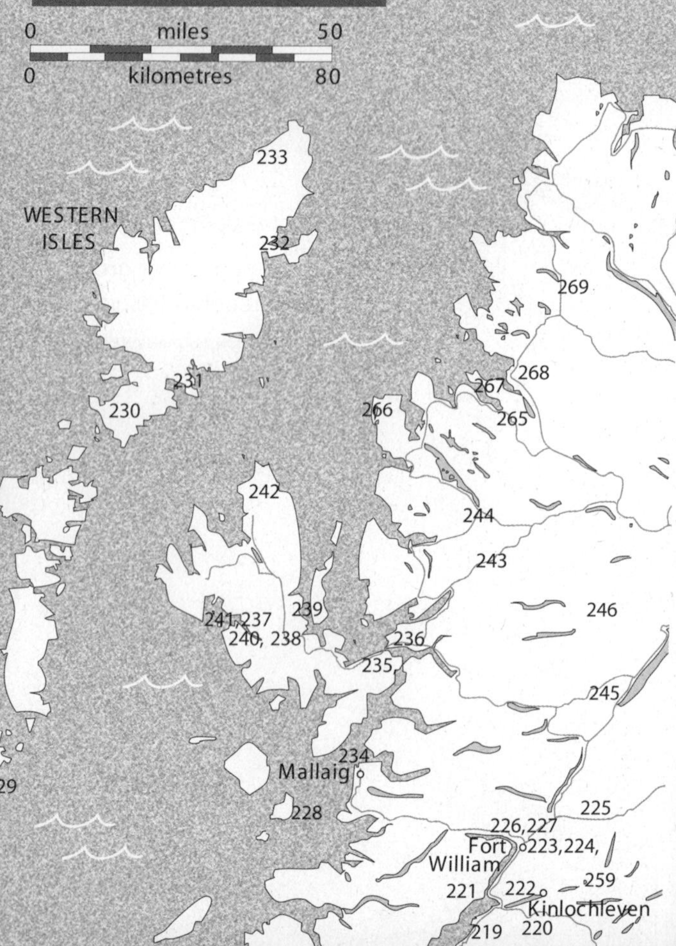
KEY
45 – Hostel page number
45 – Page number of group only accomodation
0 miles 50
0 kilometres 80
WESTERN ISLES
233
232
231
230
229
242
241,237
240, 238
239
236
235
234
Mallaig
228
226,227
Fort William
223,224,
221
222
Kinlochleven
219
220
259
225
245
246
243
244
266
267
265
268
269

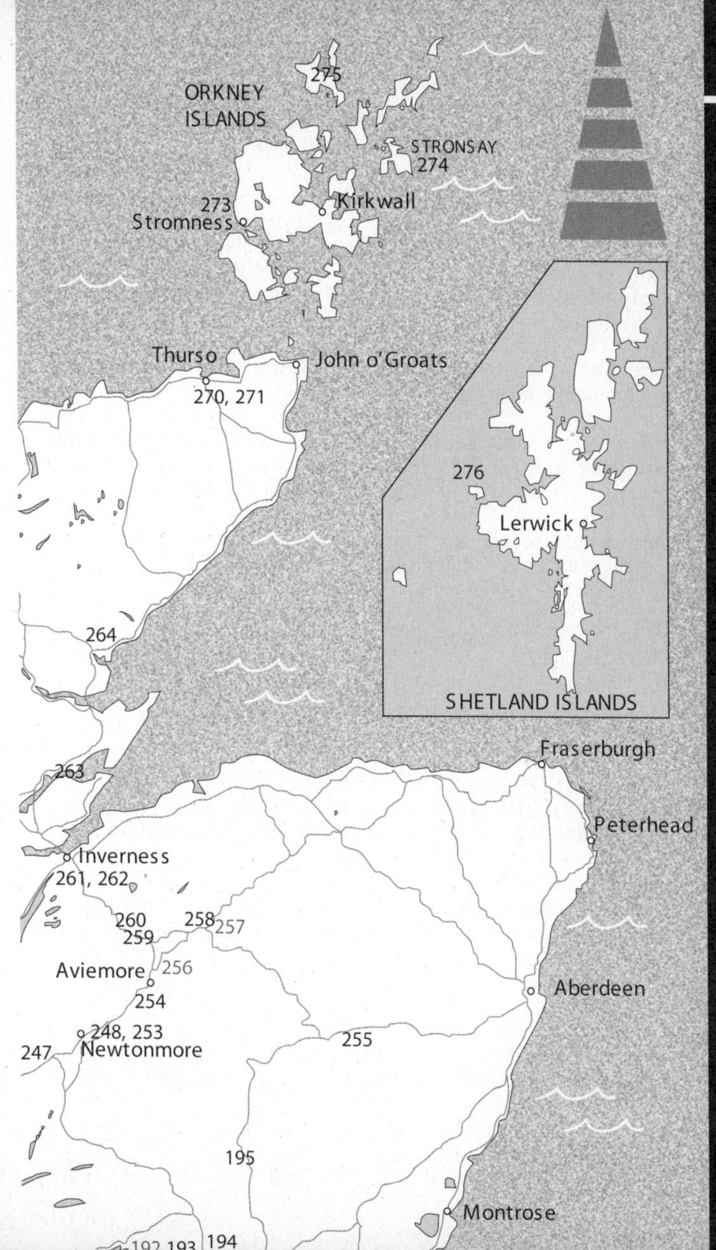
ORKNEY ISLANDS
275
STRONSAY
274
273
Stromness
Kirkwall
Thurso
John o'Groats
270, 271
276
Lerwick
SHETLAND ISLANDS
264
263
Fraserburgh
Peterhead
Inverness
261, 262
260
259
258
257
Aviemore
256
254
Aberdeen
248, 253
247
Newtonmore
255
195
Montrose
192 193 194

MARTHROWN OF MABIE LTD

Mabie Forest
Dumfries
DG2 8HB

Marthrown is set in the heart of Mabie Forest, about 6 miles west of Dumfries. We have traditional sauna, large BBQ and garden areas and plenty of room for groups. We are also an outdoor activity centre, so there is the option of trying something a little more exciting. The forest itself has newly developed mountain bike routes, ranging in length and difficulty. Bike hire is nearby as is the 7 stanes mountain bike trails.

Although we are a self-catering hostel "eating out" is less than a mile away and there is much in Dumfries and also in the nearby village of New Abbey. Marthrown is suitable for all age groups.

Facilities include secure dry store for bikes and equipment; large dining area suitable for meetings. For more info see our web site below.

www.marthrown.com

CONTACT Geoff Evans Tel (01387) 247900.
Email: Geoff@marthrown.com
OPENING SEASON All year
OPENING HOURS 24 hours
NUMBER OF BEDS 24: 1x8 1x7 1x5 1x4
BOOKING REQUIREMENTS Telephone a few days in advance.
PRICE PER NIGHT £12.50pp - £15pp (bedding included).

PUBLIC TRANSPORT
From Dumfries (Whitesands) take the bus service to Mabie Forest. (Dalbeattie via Solway Coast) It is best to arrive in daylight. 1½ mile walk from road to us.

DIRECTIONS
From Dumfries take A710 (west) to Mabie Forest passing through the village of Islesteps. Turn right past the Forest Commission Offices and follow the track, Marthrown is signposted and is exactly one mile into the forest.

H 3m

ALDERSYDE BUNKHOUSE

Lamlash
Arran
KA27 8LS

Aldersyde Bunkhouse is a purpose built bunkhouse on the beautiful Island of Arran (Scotland in miniature).

Lamlash is a haven for golfers, there are 3x18 hole, 1x12 hole and 3x9 hole golf courses all very reasonably priced. If walking or climbing is your choice Arran is ideal with various types of walks and climbs to suit all, with lovely coastal and forestry walks and Goatfell at 874 metres.

Both loch and sea fishing are available with boats for hire or organised trips. Bird life is plentiful and varied. We are a short sail from the Holy Island which has been bought by Same Ling as a retreat, visitors are welcomed. The 'Waverley', the only remaining sea going paddle steamer in the world, calls at Arran weekly during the summer for trips on the Clyde. Arran offers a unique geology formation and is well used by universities in that capacity. Brodick Castle and gardens are well worth a visit. There are standing stones at various sites, the most popular are at Machrie Moor. Crafts are part of island life and are varied, with visitor participation welcomed. Food is to suit all tastes and of a very high standard. A distillery and brewery are also very interesting.

CONTACT Tel: (01770) 600959
Email: jpricelamlash@hotmail.com
OPENING SEASON All year
OPENING HOURS All day
NUMBER OF BEDS 21: 1 x 11 : 1 x 3 : 1 x 7
BOOKING REQUIREMENTS Advisable
PRICE PER NIGHT £10 pp - group reduction and for length of stay

PUBLIC TRANSPORT
Bus meets the Ferry at Ardrossan.

DIRECTIONS
Due south from the Ferry at Ardrossan. The Hostel is in Lamlash behind the Aldersyde Hotel.

3m

 See page 212 for colour photo

CAIRNCROSS HOUSE UNIVERSITY OF GLASGOW

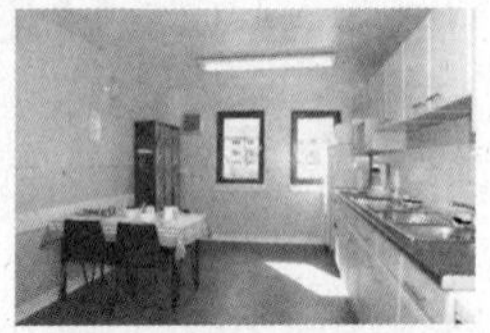

20 Kelvinhaugh Place
Glasgow G3 8NH

Cairncross House is in an excellent location within walking distance of the trendy West End and City Centre and is close to public transport. The West End is great for pubs and restaurants and has lots of good value places to eat. Nearby you will find some of Glasgow's top visitor attractions: Art Gallery and Museum, Transport Museum, University of Glasgow and its Visitor Centre, Hunterian Museum and Art Gallery (with a replica of the home of Charles Rennie Mackintosh, one of the best Mackintosh attractions in Glasgow). The City Centre offers all that you would expect - great shopping, clubs and pubs. Have fun!

The Hostel offers great value for money and is part of the University of Glasgow's student residence. It is modern and well equipped with bed linen, wash hand basin in room, use of cooking facilities, showers, free laundry facilities and common room.

CONTACT Tel: 0141 330 4116/2318 or 0141) 221 9334
OPENING SEASON June to September
OPENING HOURS 8.00 am - 10.00 pm
NUMBER OF BEDS 242
BOOKING REQUIREMENTS Advised but not essential
PRICE PER NIGHT From £14.50 per person

PUBLIC TRANSPORT
Buchanan Street Bus Station, Central Station and Queen Street Station are all 2 miles away. The nearest underground station is Kelvinhall (half mile). From George Square take buses 6 or 16 and disembark at the stop nearest to Kelvinhaugh/Radnor Street (ask driver).

DIRECTIONS
From George St take St Vincent St which becomes Argyle St after 1 mile. Through traffic lights take third left into Kelvinhaugh St, Cairncross House is on the right. From M8 J19 take A814 to Finnieston. Turn right into Finnieston St. Continue to traffic lights and turn left into Argyle St. Kelvinhaugh St is third on the left.

WESTEND HOSTEL

3 Clifton Terrace
Edinburgh
EH12 5DR

Westend Hostel is a lively hostel with a relaxed atmosphere, located in Edinburgh's historic West End, directly opposite Haymarket Rail Station and within walking distance of Princes Street and the sights, scenery and nightlife.

The hostel is freshly refurbished throughout in the colour scheme of blue and white, it is bright clean and spacious, and offers modern standards at a budget price. We provide free fresh linen and duvets, free hot showers (24 hours), continental breakfast, free tea and coffee facilities, room cleaning on daily basis, 24 hour access, secure entry, laundry (wash & dry for £2) and tour booking facility. The popular communal lounge, with satelite TV, pool table, and a well stocked bar is an ideal place to meet fellow backpackers. There is a self-catering kitchen and a choice of restaurants catering for all tastes and budgets in the immediate locality.

www.edinburghcitycentrehostels.co.uk

CONTACT Reception, Tel: (0131) 313 1031, Fax: (0131) 313 1131
Email: reservations@edinburghcitycentrehostels.co.uk
OPENING SEASON All Year
OPENING HOURS 24 Hours
NUMBER OF BEDS 95: 2x16, 1x 4, 2x12, 1x 8, 1x6, 1x5, 2x2/3
BOOKING REQUIREMENTS Advisable, phone with credit card.
PRICE PER NIGHT From £12pp in dorm, From £30 for a double room and from £45 for a triple room.

PUBLIC TRANSPORT
Waverly train station is 15 minutes' walk from the hostel. If approaching from Glasgow get off at Haymarket station which is opposite the hostel. See the Scotrail website for timetables. Airports at Edinburgh and Glasgow (50 miles away) have car hire.

DIRECTIONS
Directly opposite Haymaket Train Station. Car parking is available in the streets surrounding the hostel or at station car park.

EDINBURGH BACKPACKERS HOSTEL

65 Cockburn Street
Edinburgh EH1 1BU

The Edinburgh Backpackers Hostel has it all. Location, friendly staff, comfortable beds, affordable prices, a lively international atmosphere and did we mention location. Situated in an 18th-century building in the heart of the Historic Old Town on Edinburgh's funkiest street, our hostel is located 50 metres from the Royal Mile and less than 2 minutes' walk from the train station and airport shuttle bus. Perfectly positioned to explore the city's attractions and wild nightlife (there's no curfew either).
Our Dorm rooms are bright, clean and spacious. We also have a large number of other private rooms housed in self-catering apartments in two separate buildings on the same street. These tend to be a bit quieter and are quite popular with couples or small groups. The hostel features large self-catering kitchen, poolroom, and chill out room with Sky TV. Attached is the SX café/bar where you can have relaxing drinks or use the internet. It has a wide range of food and drinks and guests receive a 15% discount.

www.hoppo.com

CONTACT Tel: (0131) 220 1717. Advance bookings (0131) 220 2200 Email : info@hoppo.com
OPENING SEASON All year
OPENING HOURS 24 hours
NUMBER OF BEDS 153: 1x16-2x14-8x8-2qds-3trple-6 twin-7 dble.
BOOKING REQUIREMENTS Advisable in summer. No under 16's.
PRICE PER NIGHT From £13pp. Private room £19.75pp. Free ½ hour internet for anyone showing the Independent Hostel Guide when checking in. For 'Specials' see web site.

PUBLIC TRANSPORT
Airport transfer & Waverley train station 2 minutes' walk from hostel. Bus station with Citylink and local buses 5 minutes' walk from hostel.

DIRECTIONS
From Waverley Bridge go towards Old Town. On the other side of roundabout is Cockburn St. We are on top left next to Café.

BRODIES 2

93 High Street
The Royal Mile
Edinburgh
EH1 1SG

Brodies 2, rated four-stars by the Scottish Tourist Board, is a spacious and modern hostel offering double, triple and quad rooms, as well as comfortable dormitories. Our generous lounge, dining and kitchen areas offer ample space to relax, chill out and mix with other guests. We also have free internet access, free tea & coffee, laundry service, lockers for hire, CCTV-monitoring, and 24 hour access.

Smack in the middle of the Royal Mile, Brodies 2 is perfectly located and offers great facilities & a warm welcome. Lets Go 2004 says "the best value on the Royal Mile" and gives us their 'Thumbs Up' award.

www.brodieshostels.co.uk

CONTACT Receptionist, Tel: (0131) 556 2223,
Email: brodies2@brodieshostels.co.uk
OPENING SEASON All Year
OPENING HOURS Reception: 7am-midnight. Hostel: 24 hrs
NUMBER OF BEDS 74 = 2 x 2, 2 x3, 3 x 4, 3 x 6, 3 x 8, 1x10
BOOKING REQUIREMENTS Not essential but recommended in summer. Credit card required as guarantee.
PRICE PER NIGHT Dorm: £9.90 to £19.90 pp. Private rooms: £35 to £88 per room. Depending on room size & season.

PUBLIC TRANSPORT
Train: Edinburgh Waverley Station less than 5 mins' walk. **Bus:** St Andrews Bus Station, 5 to 10 mins' walk. **Air:** Edinburgh airport is 8 miles west of the city and has a shuttle bus to train station costing £5. A taxi direct from airport costs approximately £13 to £15.

DIRECTIONS
Brodies 2 is right on the Royal Mile in the centre of the Old Town between Jeffrey St and North Bridge (green & orange door just by the main parking bay).

P 1m

COWGATE TOURIST HOSTEL

94-116 Cowgate
Edinburgh
EH1 1JN

The Cowgate Tourist hostel is the perfect choice for the 21st century traveller, holidaymaker or group outing. Our unique layout ensures the perfect balance of privacy and social atmosphere. We have 11 separate apartments available for private hire (perfect for small or large groups, stag/hen parties and school groups) or individual bookings. With beds available in twin rooms or 4 & 6 bed dorms. All fully refurbished with modern fitted kitchens including fridge, freezer, oven, microwave, shower and toilet facilities. Located in the heart of Edinburgh Old Town just 10 minutes from the train station and 5 minutes from the world famous Edinburgh Castle.

www.hostelsaccommodation.com

CONTACT Tel: (0131) 226 2153, Fax: (0131) 226 7355,
Email: info@cowgatehostel.com
OPENING SEASON All year
OPENING HOURS 8am - 11pm
NUMBER OF BEDS 50 (winter) 120 (summer)
BOOKING REQUIREMENTS Booking is a must during summer months. Booking for groups essential with 25% deposit.
PRICE PER NIGHT From £11 pp. Weekly rates available off peak. Student discount available.

PUBLIC TRANSPORT:
Edinburgh Waverley Train Station is 5 minutes' walk from the hostel. Edinburgh Bus Station is 10 minutes walk from the hostel. The Airport bus runs every 10 minutes from the Airport to Waverly Train Station.

DIRECTIONS:
From Waverley station (Waverley Bridge exit) turn left down Waverley Bridge, roundabout go straight across to Cockburn Street. Follow the road around to the left and up hill. At end of the street cross the road and continue down Blair street, at the end of Blair street turn right, the hostel is about 100m on the left, opposite the 3 Sisters Pub.

CALEDONIAN BACKPACKERS

3 Queensferry Street
Edinburgh, EH2 4PA

Great panoramic views of Edinburgh Castle and a city centre location at the west end of Princes Street, only 10 minutes' walk from the bus and train stations with an airport bus stop just around the corner.
Caledonian Backpackers is one of the few hostels to provide LOCKABLE spacious dorms and private rooms, we also provide FREE sheets and duvets. Facilities include smoking and non-smoking TV rooms and well equipped kitchens as well as Internet Kiosks, free lock-up and a 24 hour laundry. We have our own large licensed bar with pool tables and live music on Saturday nights. Our bar is one of Edinburgh's live music venues hosting many newly signed bands on UK tours. With no curfews or lock-outs and a 24-hour reception guests can come and go as they please. Daily rates are from £11 with special weekly rates from only £55. *In the interest of security all guests must present a passport or drivers licence to check in.*

www.caledonianbackpackers.com

CONTACT Tel: (0131) 476 7224 Fax/Tel: (0131) 226 2939
Email : info@caledonianbackpackers.com
OPENING SEASON All year
OPENING HOURS 24 hours
NUMBER OF BEDS 280
BOOKING REQUIREMENTS Debit & Credit Card reservations only. Group booking conditions apply. Email for details.
PRICE PER NIGHT From £11 per person.

PUBLIC TRANSPORT
Waverley train station & St Andrews bus station both approx 500m from hostel. Airport bus drop-off at Shadwick Place 15m from Hostel.

DIRECTIONS
By bus/rail, walk down Princes St. with Castle on your left, at the junction look for Abbey National Bank, above is the hostel entrance, on the right. By car entering Edinburgh from west drive into Princes St, left into South Charlotte St, left again onto Charlotte Square and left again into Hope St, which leads onto Queensferry. Hostel is on the corner.

LAETARE INTERNATIONAL CENTRE

Blackness Road
Linlithgow
West Lothian
EH49 7JA

Laetare is in the heart of the Royal & Ancient Burgh of Linlithgow, the birth place of Mary Queen of Scots - on the shores of Linlithgow Loch in the shadow of the Palace. Easy access by rail and road, Edinburgh Airport is only 20 minutes away. Excellent free car parking facilities. Our helpful and friendly staff are flexible and will cater for special diets. There is a bright modern functional kitchen for self-catering guests, also a TV room/lounge area. Disabled facilities are available.

Nearby you will find Annet House local history museum, Beecraigs Country Park which offers a variety of activites ie walking, mountain biking, fishing, archery, barbecue area etc. Linlithgow Leisure Centre on town bus route, offers leisure pool, fitness suite, five-a-side football (both indoor and out).

www.laetare.org.uk

CONTACT Catherine or Patricia, Tel: (01506) 842214.
Fax : (01506) 670627. Email:- info@laetare.org.uk
OPENING SEASON All year
OPENING HOURS 8.30am - 3.30pm.
NUMBER OF BEDS 71: 3 x 4 : 4 x 3 : 21 x 2 : 5 x 1.
BOOKING REQUIREMENTS Booking essential one month, deposit required.
PRICE PER NIGHT s/c £7.50pp b/b £11 pp. h/b £16pp.

PUBLIC TRANSPORT
Linlithgow train station is 5 minutes' walk away. Bus is within 5 minutes' walk.

DIRECTIONS
By car exit M9 at junction 3. Follow sign to Linlithgow (¾ mile), you will find us opposite shopping centre in the grounds of Catholic Church.

THE BURGH LODGE

Back Wynd
Falkland
Fife
KY15 7BX

Feel good in Fife! The charming historic village of Falkland has pubs, peaks, paths and a splendid Renaissance Palace formerly frequented by Mary Queen of Scots. Falkland offers a rural getaway for travellers tired of the city, yet is within an hour of Edinburgh, St Andrews, Stirling, Perth and Dundee. On the Kingdom of Fife Millennium Cycleways route it is an ideal place to explore the surrounding countryside.

The Burgh Lodge has a 4 star rating from Visit Scotland. It's clean spacious and centrally located with free parking nearby. Expect a genuine welcome, free tea/coffee and comfy sofas in front of a log fire. Step outside and walk up East Lomond for an inspiring view. Fully equipped kitchen, but if booked in advance for groups of 6 or more we can supply meals. Leader accommodation is available for groups. Burgh Lodge has disabled suites and family rooms.

www.burghlodge.co.uk

CONTACT Tel (01337) 857710, Fax (01337) 858861
Email: burgh.lodge@btconnect.com
OPENING SEASON All year
OPENING HOURS 7am - 10 pm (late keys available)
NUMBER OF BEDS : 35: 2 x 2 : 1 x 3 : 5 x 4 : 1 x 8
BOOKING REQUIREMENTS Booking is recommended.
PRICE PER NIGHT £12. pp **Special rates in Winter.**

PUBLIC TRANSPORT
Nearest train station is Ladybank 3 miles away. Regular buses from Glenrothes, Perth and Dundee.

DIRECTIONS
From North, On M90 exit at Junction 9 (Bridge of Earn), follow signs to Gateside, Strathmiglo and Falkland. **From South,** On M90 exit Junction 8, signposted St Andrews and Falkland Palace. **On entering village** go past palace on right and immediately turn left at Bank of Scotland. The Burgh Lodge on left at entrance to free carpark.

ST ANDREWS TOURIST HOSTEL

Inchape House, St Marys Place
St Andrews
KY16 9QP

Providing high quality budget accommodation in one of Scotland's most beautiful seaside towns. No trip to Scotland would be complete without visiting this historic town founded over 1500 years ago Attractions include - St Andrews Cathedral, Holy Trinity church, the Sea Life Centre and of course the world famous Golf Course, making it ideal for those golfing enthusiasts. Our modern lively hostel benefits from a newly fitted self-catering kitchen, a large lounge and dining area, with satellite TV, Video, internet access and is just a 10 minute walk from the beach and golf course. The hostel sleeps 44 in 8 bed dorm rooms and a private family room for up to 5 people. As with all our hostels our friendly staff will be on hand throughout your stay to ensure your comfort and enjoyment.

www.hostelsaccommodation.com

CONTACT Tel: (01334) 479 911, Fax: (01334) 479 988,
Email: info@standrewshostel.com
OPENING SEASON All year
OPENING HOURS 8am-11pm summer (8am-3pm, 6pm-10pm winter
NUMBER OF BEDS 44
BOOKING REQUIREMENTS Advance booking advisable during the summer and major golfing events. Booking for groups essential with 25% deposit
PRICE PER NIGHT From £12pp. Weekly rates available off peak. Student discount available.

PUBLIC TRANSPORT
Only 5 minutes' walk from the bus station. Regular bus'es run to Leuchars train station 10 minutes journey from the city.

DIRECTIONS
From the bus station turn right onto City Road then left at the church onto St Marys Place. The hostel is 100 metres on the right above the Grill House restaurant.

1m

TROSSACHS BACKPACKERS

Invertrossachs Road
Callander
Perthshire FK17 8HW

Trossachs Backpackers has been purpose-built on its own 8 acre site, set amidst beautiful scenery (on Sustrans route 7c) just outside the bustling tourist town of Callander. The Hostel, which is the only one in the Trossachs area, opened in August 1997 and is finished to a very high standard, hence its nickname "*Posh*tel" The rooms are all en-suite and are either 8,4 or single. The 4 bed family rooms have their own private kitchen/dining facilities and can be used as twin rooms on request. There is a spacious Dining/Common Room, well equipped kitchen, a laundry and drying room. A large Meeting/ Recreation Room is also available and may be booked separately for conferences, parties, etc. We have an on-site Cycling Centre, which also sells basic provisions. Other activities available locally include Hill Walking, Pony Trekking, Canoe Hire/Instruction, Fishing, Sailing and much much more. Find more information on:-

www.scottish-hostel.co.uk

CONTACT Mark or Janet, Tel/Fax: (01877) 331200,
Email: mark@scottish-hostel.co.uk
OPENING SEASON All year
OPENING HOURS 24 hours, (Reception 08.00 to 23.00)
NUMBER OF BEDS 30
BOOKING REQUIREMENTS Booking advised for weekends. Groups must pre book (deposit required).
PRICE PER NIGHT £13.50 to £18.50 including linen & continental breakfast. Group and family discounts on request.

PUBLIC TRANSPORT
Nearest train station is at Stirling (15 miles). Nearest Citylink coach stop is at Callander (1½ miles). Pick up from Callander can usually be arranged.

DIRECTIONS
GR 606 072. The hostel is situated one mile up Invertrossachs Rd from its junction with the A81 (Glasgow Rd) in Callander.

SCOTTISH CENTRES

Dounans Centre, Aberfoyle
Stirling
FK8 3UT

Dounans is set in the Queen Elizabeth Forest Park, in the Loch Lomond and Trossachs National Park and sits on the Rob Roy Way. Accommodation is in cedar wood building in dormitories. Single rooms are available for group leaders. Ideal for groups (from 8 persons upwards) of all types to take part in a range of outdoor activities. Alternatively use Dounans as a base for your own programme or training or simply explore the local environment. All bedding provided but you will need a towel. Meals are provided (including packed lunch if going off site). Bed only can be offered but please note that there are no self-catering facilities. Outdoor and environmental activities are available, led by qualified instructors. We are licensed with AALA to run activities at all our Centres.

Dounans is one of 4 centres operated by Scottish Centres; the others are **Belmont Centre**, Meigle, Perthshire, **Broomlee Centre**, West Linton Borders and **Loaningdale Centre** Biggar. We look forward to welcoming your group to one of our Centres. Although primarily for groups, individuals are welcome to enquire regarding availability particularly for weekends and outwith school term time.

www.scottish-centres.org.uk

CONTACT Bookings Office Tel: (01899) 221115. Fax: (01899) 220644
Email : enquiries@scottish-centres.org.uk
OPENING SEASON All year – closed for Christmas & New Year
OPENING HOURS 24 hrs. Bookings between 9am & 5pm.
NUMBER OF BEDS 240
BOOKING REQUIREMENTS In advance with payment
PRICE PER NIGHT £14.50 (self-catering), £57.58 for fully catered weekend without activities.

DIRECTIONS
From Aberfoyle, Dounans is in Queen Elizabeth Forest Park. Entrance at Health Centre.

PUBLIC TRANSPORT
Train Station Stirling or Glasgow. Bus from Stirling or Glasgow to Aberfoyle (both infrequent). Short walk to Dounans.

BRAINCROFT LODGE

Braincroft
By Crieff/Comrie
Perthshire PH7 4JZ

Braincroft Lodge is a place where you really can get away from it all and be only an hour from Glasgow or Edinburgh! The accommodation is in a lovely old Scottish farmstead set amongst the rugged hills and glens of the Southern Highlands. Converted to offer modern self-catering to suit all pockets, we offer superb facilities, a relaxed atmosphere and the ultimate peaceful location for exploring Scotland's great outdoors.

The surrounding mountains and valleys offer loads of things to see and do including adventure sports like mountain biking or rafting, distilleries, exploring abandoned castles, quiet glens, standing stones, waterfalls, Loch Lomond National Park at Loch Earn, swimming or fishing on our own lock, the list goes on..! We're locals and we'd love to help you get off the beaten track and find all the best bits of our area.

www.scottishlodge.com

CONTACT Tel: (01764) 670140, Fax: (01764) 679691, Email: braincroft@scottishlodge.com
OPENING SEASON All year
OPENING HOURS All day - no curfew
NUMBER OF BEDS 56
BOOKING REQUIREMENTS Recommended
PRICE PER NIGHT £11pp - £16pp en-suite B & B. Group and child rates available.

PUBLIC TRANSPORT
Nearest train stations: Stirling, Dunblane and Perth. Pick ups by arrangement. Buses from Perth No 15 direct every hour. Ask for Braincroft Lodge. Buses from Stirling/Dunblane No 47 to Crieff then change for No 15 (direction Comrie). Buses from Oban/the west Citylink Perth-Oban service, summer only.

DIRECTIONS
Situated just off the A85 between Crieff (5 miles) and Comrie (2 miles).

DUNOLLY ADVENTURE OUTDOORS

Taybridge Drive
Aberfeldy
Perthshire
PH15 2BP

Dunolly House comprises two units, the first is a 45-bed Victorian house, the other is a smaller 15-bed cottage. All rooms are fully carpeted and centrally heated with modern pine beds (linen and duvets provided). The complex can be taken together or as separate units for groups only, with catering or self-catering.

We have a fantastic range of activities on site which can be booked by groups. They include White Water Rafting, Gorge Ascent, Archery, Mountain Biking, Hill Walking, Nature Trails, Orienteering and High Rope Challenge and Climbing Wall. We have our own qualified instructors and we are licensed to run activities for children under the regulations of the Adventure Activities Licensing Authority. Come and enjoy !!

www.dunollyadventures.co.uk

CONTACT Booking Office Tel: (01887) 820298
Email info@dunollyadventures.co.uk
OPENING SEASON All year
OPENING HOURS 24 hours
NUMBER OF BEDS 60
BOOKING REQUIREMENTS Booking is essential
PRICE PER NIGHT from £8.50.

PUBLIC TRANSPORT
Nearest train station is in Pitlochry (14 miles away). Citylink coaches stop at Ballinluig (11 miles away) and Pitlochry.

DIRECTIONS
Turn off the A9 road at Ballinluig. Travel for 5 miles. Turn right at the T junction. Travel 6 miles until Aberfeldy. Continue through the main street and we are the last house on the right as you exit Aberfeldy.

See page 206 for colour photo

ADVENTURER'S ESCAPE

Weem
Aberfeldy, Perthshire
PH15 2LD

Wade House and the Bunkhouse are at the foot of a south facing slope with beautiful walks and climbs in Tayside (Weem) Forest Park. Built in the 1700s Wade House is a listed building where General Wade stayed while building his roads. The adjoining old barn has been converted to a 4* luxury bunkhouse, with underfloor heating and log fired stoves.

Ideally situated on cycle route number 7 and the Rob Roy Way, superb mountain biking is available from the bunkhouse. The Adventurer's Escape is close to the River Tay for kayaking and canoeing. Guiding and or instruction available for climbing, mountain biking, hill walking, open canoeing and white water kayaking. Whitewater rafting and canyoning also available, equipment can be rented. Both buildings have self-catering facilities or if you wish excellent bar meals are available next door at the Weem Hotel. Midge free and sheltered sunny front garden and courtyard.

www.adventurers-escape.co.uk
www.national-kayak-school.com

CONTACT Stuart Wagstaff, Tel: (01887) 820498. 07774644660
Email: info@adventurers-escape.co.uk
OPENING SEASON All year
OPENING HOURS Flexible but generally all day
NUMBER OF BEDS Wade House **9:** 1 x 5 : 1 x 4
New Bunkhouse **22/27:** 3x4/5 : 1 x 2/3 : 1 x 8/9
BOOKING REQUIREMENTS Advisable, book by phone or email
PRICE PER NIGHT from £13 per person. Long stay rates available.

PUBLIC TRANSPORT
Buses from Aberfeldy connect to train stations at Pitlochry & Perth.

DIRECTIONS
North from traffic lights in Aberfeldy, over General Wade's bridge over the River Tay for 1km, the Adventurer's Escape is next to the Weem Hotel on the B846.

P 1m

See page 212 for colour photo

WESTER CAPUTH INDEPENDENT HOSTEL

Caputh, By Dunkeld
Perthshire
PH1 4JH

Wester Caputh Hostel, an intimate relaxed place, sits by the River Tay in beautiful rural Perthshire. Near to Dunkeld, at the heart of Scotland, it is just over an hours' travel from Edinburgh and Glasgow. There are quiet roads for cycling and excellent woodland and river walks. Close to the hostel are prehistoric, Pictish and Roman sites. The river offers some of the best rafting, canoeing and fishing in the country. Dunkeld is an unspoilt town of antiquity with places to eat and drink and plenty to see and do. We offer very comfortable bunk-bedded and twin-bedded accommodation. The hostel kitchen is equipped for serious cooking. One of the social rooms has many instruments, games and books. Music and good conversation are here to be enjoyed - or simply the deep peace of green Perthshire.

www.westercaputh.co.uk

CONTACT Tel/Fax: (01738) 710449, Email: info@westercaputh.co.uk
OPENING SEASON All year
OPENING HOURS All day, no curfew
NUMBER OF BEDS 22: 4 x 2 : 2 x 4 : 1 x 6.
BOOKING REQUIREMENTS Booking advisable
PRICE PER NIGHT From £12 to £15pp.

PUBLIC TRANSPORT
Nearest train station and Citylink stop are in Birnam, 5 miles from the hostel. Stagecoach operate a bus service from Perth (Mill Street); ask for Caputh Village. Local taxi service available.

DIRECTIONS
From north: From A9 take A923 to Dunkeld. Immediately after crossing Dunkeld bridge turn right onto A984 to Caputh (4.5 miles). After church on right turn right (onto B9099) then 1st right at foot of hill. 2nd house on right (long white building). **From south**: From A9 take B9099 through Luncarty, Stanley and Murthly. Cross river and into Caputh. Turn left at foot of hill (signposted Dunkeld). 2nd house on right.

GULABIN LODGE

Spittal of Glenshee
By Blairgowrie
PH10 7QE

Gulabin Lodge is beautifully situated in the heart of Glenshee at the foot of Beinn Gulabin offering the nearest accommodation to the Glenshee ski slopes. We offer roller, nordic, alpine and telemark skiing and snowboarding. We also have a dry ski slope where lessons are available. Gulabin is an ideal base for climbing, walking or mountain biking - whether you are a beginner or an expert. Also on your visit you can try some of the other activities available which include hang-gliding, paragliding, orienteering, survival or canoeing. There is a nine-hole golf course and pony trekking nearby. Five minutes' walk from the hostel is the Spittal of Glenshee Hotel, which with its friendly bar, can provide meals and usually has entertainment on Saturday evenings.
The lodge offers comfortable, reasonably priced accommodation for individuals, families and groups. There are free hot showers, all rooms are equipped with wash basins and linen. We offer packages to suit all types of groups. Ski, Snowboard & Nordic hire available.

www.cairnwellmountainsports.co.uk

CONTACT Manager 0870 4430253,
Email: info@cairnwellmountainsports.co.uk
OPENING SEASON All year
OPENING HOURS 24 hours
NUMBER OF BEDS 30:- 2 x 2 : 1 x 8 : 2 x 5 : 1 x 4 + 1 x 5 occasional
BOOKING REQUIREMENTS Booking advisable with 50% deposit
PRICE PER NIGHT £11pp to £15pp B&B, family rooms £40. Reduced rates for group of over 10.

PUBLIC TRANSPORT
Train and bus stations at:- Pitlochry (22 miles), Blairgowrie (20 miles), Glasgow (100 miles), Edinburgh (70 miles).

DIRECTIONS
Gulabin Lodge is on the A93 road at Spittal of Glenshee - 20 miles from Blairgowrie and 19 miles to Braemar. Transport can be arranged.

COLONSAY KEEPER'S LODGE

Colonsay Estate
Isle of Colonsay
Argyll, PA61 7YU

The Lodge is located on a peaceful and idyllic Inner Hebridean island to the south of Mull which boasts magnificent sandy beaches ancient forests and beautiful lochs. The place is teeming with wildlife which includes dolphins, seals, otters and many rare species of birds. There are ancient standing stones and a 14th-century priory with exceptional carved Celtic tombstones and the famous Colonsay House gardens and café are open to visitors to enjoy twice a week. We offer for hire mountain bikes to tour the area and tennis racquets to use on the free courts. The pub, cafés, shop and village hall, where there are regular Ceilidhs, are all within three miles. Fresh lobster, crab and langoustines can be bought from the fishing boats in the harbour and don't forget the best oysters in the world are grown on Colonsay! The lodge is a refurbished former gamekeeper's house and bothies. It is centrally heated and has large twin and family rooms plus three dormitories. It has a huge dining/cooking/sitting area and a separate sitting room with a log fire. Bed linen provided.

www.colonsay.org.uk

CONTACT Rhona Grant, Tel: (01951) 200312
Email: Colonsaycottages@dial.pipex.com
OPENING SEASON All year
OPENING HOURS 24 hours
NUMBER OF BEDS 16 6 x 2 : 1 x 4.
BOOKING REQUIREMENTS Required 24 hours in advance.
PRICE PER NIGHT £14pp twin, £10pp bothy, £12pp 4 bed dorms.

PUBLIC TRANSPORT
The train and coach station is in Oban approx 3 hours from Glasgow. Ferry to Colonsay takes 2¼ hours.

DIRECTIONS
Ferry departs Oban 5 times a week April to October, Sun, Mon, Wed, Thurs, Fri (rest of year Mon, Wed, Fri) and Port Askaig Islay on Weds. Transport for hostellers can be arranged if required.

IONA HOSTEL

Iona
Argyll
PA76 6SW

Tucked into the rocky outcrops at the north end of the island, Iona Hostel has spectacular views to Staffa and the Treshnish Isles, and beyond Rhum to the Black Cuillins of Skye.

The hostel is situated on the working croft of Lagandorain (the hollow of the otter). This land has been worked for countless generations, creating the familiar Hebridean patchwork of wildflower meadow, crops and grazing land, home to an amazing variety of plants and birds. We offer quiet sanctuary for those that seek it, while being in easy reach of island activities.

Iona Hostel is new, well-reviewed and recommended. Whether travelling on your own, with friends, or as part of one of our many visiting groups, Iona Hostel offers you a warm welcome - with the best views and duck eggs this side of heaven. 4 star STB.

www.ionahostel.co.uk

CONTACT Tel: (01681) 700781. Email: info@ionahostel.co.uk
OPENING SEASON All year
OPENING HOURS closed 2-4pm for cleaning - no curfew
NUMBER OF BEDS 21: 1 x 2 : 2 x 4 : 1 x 5 : 1 x 6.
BOOKING REQUIREMENTS Is strongly advised 33.3% deposit.
PRICE PER NIGHT £15.00 adult £10.50 under16s (bedding and light breakfast included). We regret no dogs are allowed.

PUBLIC TRANSPORT
Caledonian Macbrayne ferry service from Oban or Mull. Tel 08705 650000. For bus transport on Mull 01546 604695. Taxi service on Iona 0781 032 5990.

DIRECTIONS
You cannot bring your car onto Iona, but there is free parking in Fionnphort on Mull at the Columba Centre. Iona Hostel is the last building at the north end of the Island, 2 km from the Pier and up beyond the Abbey.

MILLHOUSE HOSTEL

Cornaigmore
Isle of Tiree
Inner Hebrides
PA77 6XA

Tiree is an idyllic Hebridean Island, perfect for outdoor pursuits, wildlife enthusiasts, and those yet to experience total tranquillity stunning white beaches and crystal clear seas. A warm welcome and excellent facilities await you at Millhouse. Bikes are for hire to explore the island, visit the thatched cottage and lighthouse museums, find the standing stones, wonder at the machair flowers or watch the seals. Watersports take place on adjacent Loch Bhasapol, and the secluded Cornaig beach is a ten minute walk away. There is a resident RSPB warden on the island and a bird hide near the hostel. For walkers, Millhouse is on the Tiree Pilgrimage route linking the ancient chapels and monuments around the island. STB 4* Hostel

www.tireemillhouse.co.uk

CONTACT Judith Boyd, Tel: (01879) 220435
Email: tireemillhouse@yahoo.co.uk
OPENING SEASON All Year
OPENING HOURS All day. Quiet after 11.30pm. Check out 10am
NUMBER OF BEDS 16/18 : 2 x 2/3 : 2 x 6. *Opening May 2005*: 3 family rooms 12 beds: 3 x 4
BOOKING REQUIREMENTS Advisable. Please check vacancies before boarding the ferry
PRICE PER NIGHT Twin £12-15pp. Dorms £12pp. Family £40-48 per room

PUBLIC TRANSPORT
Train or bus from major towns to Oban, then ferry from Oban to Tiree (Caledonian MacBrayne) OR Plane from Glasgow to Tiree (BA).

DIRECTIONS
From Ferry turn right at T junction, then left at next fork. Continue for 4 miles to Millhouse Hostel.

SHIELING HOLIDAYS

Craignure
Isle of Mull
PA65 6AY

We're right on the sea, with views to Ben Nevis. There are regular sightings of seals and otters, and sometimes of porpoises, dolphins and eagles. Stroll to the ferry, pub, bistro, shops, and miniature steam railway. Walk to Torosay and Duart Castles. Catch the bus for Tobermory; for Iona (where Columba brought Christianity to Scotland) and for Staffa (home of puffins, and inspiration for Mendelssohn's overture "Fingal's Cave").

Your accommodation is in Shielings, unique carpeted cottage tents, made by us on Mull, which are clean, bright and spacious, and have real beds for 2, 4, or 6. There are super showers, and communal Shielings with woodburner, TV, payphone and launderette. Our campsite is rated " 5 stars, exceptional, World Class" by the Scottish Tourist Board.

www.shielingholidays.co.uk

CONTACT David Gracie, Tel: (01680) 812496
Email: you can email us from our website
OPENING SEASON April to October
OPENING HOURS 24 hours (Reception 0800 - 2000)
NUMBER OF BEDS 18: 6 x 2 : 1 x 6.
BOOKING REQUIREMENTS Booking advisable. Phone bookings held to 6pm
PRICE PER NIGHT £10

PUBLIC TRANSPORT
From Glasgow, rail (08457 484950) or bus (08705 505050) at 12.00, ferry (01680 812343) at 16.00 from Oban, arrive Mull 16.40; back by 11.00 ferry, arrive Glasgow 15.45. From Edinburgh, 0900 bus, 1400 ferry; back 1300 ferry, arrive Edinburgh 18.15. Please check times before travel.

DIRECTIONS
GR 724 369 From ferry, left on the A849 to Iona. After 400 metres, left opposite church past old pier to reception - 800 metres in all.

KERRERA BUNKHOUSE

Lower Gylen
Isle of Kerrera By Oban
Argyll, PA34 4SX

The Bunkhouse, a cosy, well equipped converted stable is open all year. Tea garden and Café next door (Easter/September) serving home grown food. Amidst spectacular scenery on wild, unspoilt south coast, the bunkhouse has a peaceful, isolated location whilst being within easy reach of Oban's amenities (diving centre, bike hire, distillery, cinema etc). Short walk to Gylen Castle, secluded bays with stunning views down Firth of Lorne & Argyll islands. Kerrera is an almost car free zone, you are guaranteed a safe, peaceful walk. There is abundant wildlife: otters, sea mammals, birds, wild flowers, waterfalls, hidden caves and a secret loch. Accommodation consists of 2 separate compartments (double bunks) two sleeping platforms (one double, and one single). There is a comfortable social area, with games & stereo system, we have pure spring water on tap. People of all ages are welcome, as are dogs, as we are surrounded by a sheep farm, dogs must be kept under control at all times.

www.kerrerabunkhouse.co.uk

CONTACT Andy Crabb & Jo Heritage Tel: (01631) 570223.
E-mail: info@kerrerabunkhouse.co.uk
OPENING SEASON All year
OPENING HOURS 10am-6pm. 5pm winter. no curfew
NUMBER OF BEDS 7 : 3x2 compartments 1x1.
BOOKING REQUIREMENTS Booking advisable due to ferry restrictions. Groups by arrangement. Food by arrangement.
PRICE PER NIGHT £10pp - Sole use £50 per night.

PUBLIC TRANSPORT
The ferry is a 3km walk from centre of Oban on coastal road to Gallanach. Summer bus service. Taxi fare is £4/5. City-link coaches to Oban from Glasgow and Fort William. Last ferry 6pm sum, 5pm win.

DIRECTIONS
From ferry follow track 200m to road junction, keep left, stay on track, pass 3 dwellings. Bunkhouse 4th. (45 min walk). Transportation of gear from ferry via prior arrangement. Ferry tel 01631 563665.

Pg 74: Thorpe Farm Bunkhouse

Pg 239: Portree Independent Hostel

Pg 29: Ocean Backpackers

Pg 33, 52: Piccadilly Backpackers Hostel

Pg 286: Par Four Hostel

Pg 299: Omagh Independent Hostel

Pg 240: Waterfront Bunkhouse

Pg 229: Am Bothan

Pg 253 Craigower Lodge

Pg 13: The Old Chapel Backpackers

Pg 264: Sleeperzzz

Pg 224: Aite Cruinnichidh

Pg 192: Adventurer's escape

Pg 275: Bis Geos Hostel and Cottages

Pg 86: Whitby Backpackers at Harbour Grange

Pg 27: Torquay Backpackers

Pg 314: Wombats Munich

Pg 152: Braich Goch Bunkhouse and Inn

Pg 155: Cornerstone Quest Adventure Centre

Pg 91: Timberlodge

Pg 25: Dartmoor Expedition Centre

Pg 143: Tycanol Farm

Pg 149: Maesnant Centre

Pg 231: Laxdale Bunkhouse
Pg 180: Cairncross House

Pg 242: Dun Flodigarry Hostel
Pg 193: Wester Caputh Hostel

Pg 343: Mountain Hostel Gimmelwald

Pg 148: Maes-y-Mor

Pg 313: Jugendgastehaus
Pg 128 : Cardiff Backpacker

Pg 311: Generator Berlin
Pg 234: Dun caan hostel

JEREMY INGLIS HOSTEL

21 Airds Crescent
Oban
Argyll
PA34 5SJ

Jeremy Inglis Hostel is only 150 yards from the station and the bus terminus in Oban.

Prices include a continental breakfast with muesli, toast and home made jams, marmalade and Vegemite, etc. Tea and coffee are available at any time.

The rooms are mostly double and family size so you have some privacy, all linen is included in the price.

Kitchen facilities are provided and the hostel is heated by meter. Smoking is not allowed in the rooms.

Please phone for bookings (01631) 565933

CONTACT Jeremy Inglis, or Katrin Tel: (01631) 565933
OPENING SEASON All year. possibly closed December
OPENING HOURS No curfew, access with key.
NUMBER OF BEDS 12 to 14
BOOKING REQUIREMENTS Booking preferred. Deposit in certain circumstances.
PRICE PER NIGHT From £7.50-£8 per person (in a shared room), including continental breakfast. Single room (when available) £13-£14 per person.

PUBLIC TRANSPORT
Nearest train and Citylink drop off 150 metres from hostel. Ferries to Islands 250 metres. For ferry enquiries phone (01631) 566688.

DIRECTIONS
The Hostel is in Airds Crescent, one of the streets off Argyll Square. The Hostel is on the second floor, pink door.

    3m

CORRAN HOUSE

1 Victoria Crescent
Oban
Argyll
PA34 5PN

'Corran House' is part of a Victorian terrace with magnificent seascapes across the bay to the Isle of Kerrera and the hills of Mull. There is a warm welcome for visitors together with reasonably priced accommodation suitable for singles, couples, families and groups. The house has a large self-catering kitchen, spacious TV lounge, comfortable, commodious, well appointed guest rooms and backpacker 4 bedded dormitories with king size bunks - most rooms have en-suite facilities. Corran House is well situated for exploring Argyll and visiting the inner Hebrides as it is only a short walk along the sea front to the bus, train and ferry terminals. Downstairs from the house is Markie Dan's bar with a beer garden, patio and spectacular views over the waterfront. The pub offers great highland hospitality, tasty meals, live entertainment, wide screen Sky TV, pool table and a late licence all year round to enable the discerning drinker to sample the best range of malt whiskies on the west coast. Scottish Tourist Board 4 star rated.

www.corranhouse.co.uk

CONTACT Tel: (01631) 56 6040, Fax: (01631) 56 6854, Email: enquiries@corranhouse.co.uk
OPENING SEASON All year
OPENING HOURS Reception 10am-9pm (later arrivals should tel)
NUMBER OF BEDS 36 : 7x4 : 1x2 : 1x6. plus Guest rooms : 11.
BOOKING REQUIREMENTS Advisable, can use Credit card.
PRICE PER NIGHT Bunks £12 & £14. Guest rooms from £20 single.

PUBLIC TRANSPORT
Oban train, bus and ferry terminals are about 900m from the house.

DIRECTIONS
Corran House is on the waterfront to the west of the town centre. From the Tourist Information and all the Oban transport terminals, with the sea on your left, walk along George Street past the Columba Hotel into Corran Esplanade. Follow the seafront for 300 metres and Corron house is on right, besides Markie Dans Alehouse at carpark.

GLENCOE FARM BUNKHOUSE

Glencoe
Argyll
PH49 4HX

UNDER NEW MANAGEMENT ~ Glencoe Bunkhouse offers dormitory accommodation with a large well equipped kitchen, showers, hot and cold water. We cater for small or large groups as well as individuals.

The bunkhouse is situated in the heart of a beautiful and historic Glen. There are lots of walks, scrambles and forest trails. Glencoe offers a watersports centre and the nearby town of Kinlochleven has a new indoor ice climbing wall. Winter sports include skiing, snowboarding and climbing. On site facilities include, pay phone, mini shop, barbeque area, internet access (reasonable rates), cycle hire, free cycle for grocery shopping in village and washing and drying facilities.

www.glencoehostel.co.uk

CONTACT Paul or Penny. Tel: (01855) 811906
Email: penpaulbrown@btinternet.com
OPENING SEASON All year
OPENING HOURS 24 hours
NUMBER OF BEDS 54: 1x24 : 1x12 : 3x6
BOOKING REQUIREMENTS Booking advised in summer months. One month in advance 20% deposit.
PRICE PER NIGHT from £8 per person

PUBLIC TRANSPORT
Nearest train station 15miles. Nearest Citylink drop off 1.5miles.

DIRECTIONS
GR 116 577. On old road parallel to A82 1½ miles south of Glencoe Village, adjacent to youth hostel. Follow signs for youth hostel, Red Squirrel camp site and Glencoe Farm and Bunkhouse.

INCHREE HOSTEL

Onich
Nr. Fort William
Highlands
PH33 6SE

Inchree is perfectly located for West Highland touring and walking, being midway between Ben Nevis and Glencoe mountains. The Corran Ferry, which provides access to the beautiful Ardnamurchan Peninsula, is just 500 metres away. You can explore forest, waterfall, beach and hill walks from the door.

All accommodation is self-catering, with dorm and family en-suite rooms available in our hostel, and double and twins in separate chalets. Larger groups can book a bunkhouse for exclusive use. At the end of your day relax in our on-site Bar and Bistro, which serves good food, highland ales and malt whiskies. Group and club functions catered for. Other facilities include efficient drying rooms, barbecue area and climbing wall. Walking and touring guides provided.

www.hostel-scotland.com (Regularly updated)

CONTACT David Heron, Tel/Fax: (01855) 821287
Email: enquiry@hostel-scotland.com.
OPENING SEASON All year
OPENING HOURS All day and evening
NUMBER OF BEDS Hostel **22 beds** (2 x 8 : 1 x 6), Each Chalet (3x2), Group Bunkhouse **19 bunks**
BOOKING REQUIREMENTS Pre-booking recommended but not essential. All major credit and debit cards accepted.
PRICE PER NIGHT Hostel £11 to £13. Contact for chalet and bunkhouse rates.

PUBLIC TRANSPORT
Glasgow to Fort William Citylink coachstop at Inchree. Walk up lane for 500m to hostel entrance.

DIRECTIONS
Situated in Onich village, 5 miles north of Glencoe, 8 miles south of Fort William. Turn off A82 (Signposted Inchree) up minor road for 500 metres.

BLACKWATER HOSTEL & CAMPSITE

Lab Road, Kinlochleven
Argyll PH50 4SG

Blackwater Hostel is in the centre of the scenic village of Kinlochleven surrounded by the Mamore mountains midway between Glencoe and Ben Nevis. An ideal stopover for families, cyclists, walkers, climbers and those who enjoy the outdoors. There are high and low-level, half-hour to full-day walks, all with great views, or if you prefer there is a regular bus service from the village to Glencoe, Ballachulish and Fort William. Water sports are available nearby. Europe's first indoor 14 metre ice/climbing wall opened in December 2003 and is only 200 metres from our hostel. The hostel offers very comfortable, high-quality **STB 4 star** bunkhouse accommodation. All rooms have en-suite facilities, TV and central heating. Facilities include self-catering kitchens, lounge, dining conference area, drying room. There are supermarkets, pubs & restaurants within two minutes' walking distance. Campsite has drying room, shower block & covered potwashing/cooking area.

www.blackwaterhostel.co.uk

CONTACT Caroline, Tel: (01855) 831253,
Email: black.water@virgin.net
OPENING SEASON All year
OPENING HOURS 24 hours
NUMBER OF BEDS 39 - 2,3,4,8 bedded rooms
BOOKING REQUIREMENTS Essential
PRICE PER NIGHT £12pp including bed linen

PUBLIC TRANSPORT
The nearest train station is Fort William and National Express travels from Glasgow to Glencoe and Fort William. Regular bus service to Kinlochleven all day from Glencoe, Ballachulish and Fort William.

DIRECTIONS
GR 188 618. OS sheet 41. From A82 Glasgow to Fort William road - turn at Glencoe right to Kinlochleven. The hostel is situated near the centre of Kinlochleven. Just past the Co-op you will see our large sign with an arrow to point you in the direction of the Hostel.

BANK STREET LODGE

Bank Street
Fort William
PH33 6AY

Bank Street Lodge is situated 100 metres from Fort William High Street which has numerous shops, pubs, restaurants, banks etc. There is a fully equipped kitchen with cooker, fridge, microwave and cutlery and crockery is provided. Our commonroom/lounge has a TV, it also provides tables and chairs for eating self prepared meals, and a snack vending machine. All bedding is provided, we also have en-suite rooms available (twins, doubles and family).

The Stables Restaurant, at the front of the building, can provide breakfast by prior arrangement and also serves fine food for lunches and dinners - treat yourself.

Fort William is an ideal base from which to enjoy walking, climbing, cycling or mountain biking. The new world-renowned Nevis Range mountain bike trails and ski centre are only a short distance from the town centre.

www.bankstreetlodge.co.uk

CONTACT Kenny/John/Linda Tel: (01397) 700070
Email: bankstreetlodge@btinternet.com
OPENING SEASON All year
OPENING HOURS Reception manned 24 hours
NUMBER OF BEDS 44: 7 x 4 : 3 x 3 : 1 x 7 :
BOOKING REQUIREMENTS Booking is essential. Deposit required for long stays or groups.
PRICE PER NIGHT £12.50 (£11.60 pppn for groups of 12 or more).

PUBLIC TRANSPORT
Train and Bus stations at Fort William, 500 metres from Lodge.

DIRECTIONS
Head for Town Centre via the underpass, turn left after Tesco supermarket on Bank Street, then head up the hill for 150 metres, we are above the Stables Restaurant. Car parking is available.

CALLUNA

Heathercroft
Fort William
Inverness-shire
PH33 6RE

Situated within fifteen minutes' walk of Fort William High Street this accommodation is ideal for short or long stays. **Free transport from the town centre is available if we are at home, just give us a call**. The modern accommodation consists of one flat and two new apartments. Bedding is supplied, along with spacious kitchen and comfortable lounge. Very efficient drying rooms. On the spot advice about Ben Nevis from Alan Kimber (Mountain Guide) who owns and runs Calluna with his wife Sue. Calluna is well known for peace and quiet and fine views over Loch Linnhe to the hills of Ardgour. A popular base for climbing and canoeing groups, families and individual globe trotters. Plenty of parking for mini-buses and trailers. For accommodation and mountaineering courses see:-

www.fortwilliamholiday.co.uk

CONTACT Alan or Sue, Tel: (01397) 700451 Fax 01397 700489
Email: info@fortwilliamholiday.co.uk
OPENING SEASON All year
OPENING HOURS 24 hours (keys supplied)
NUMBER OF BEDS 22:- 5 twins 5 x 2, 3 x 4
BOOKING REQUIREMENTS Phone up beforehand
PRICE PER NIGHT £10.50 - £12.00 per person

PUBLIC TRANSPORT
Fort William train and coach stations are 20 minutes' walk from the hostel. Citylink and local bus services operate from the coach station. Alan & Sue offer a free lift from the station when convenient.

DIRECTIONS
By Vehicle: From roundabout (West End Hotel) go uphill on Lundavra Rd and take third on left (Connochie Rd) between four-storey flats. Follow Connochie Rd and do not take any right turns. You should arrive at our back door! **On Foot:** Ask for directions to the West End Hotel which is five minutes from the Tourist Office and follow the route above (15/20 minutes on foot). Phone if unsure !

P 3m

See page 206 for colour photo

ÀITE CRUINNICHIDH

1 Achluachrach
By Roy Bridge
Near Fort William
Inverness-shire, PH31 4AW

Àite Cruinnichidh, 15 miles north east of Fort William, occupies a unique sheltered spot adjacent to the Monessie Gorge; explore remote glens, mountain passes and lochs. Numerous easy walks within minutes of the hostel and seven magnificent canoeing rivers within 20 miles. The location is also ideal for climbing (rock & ice), mountain biking, skiing or just relaxing. A warm, peaceful, friendly, country hostel in a converted barn. Àite Cruinnichidh has been renovated to high standards and sleeps 32 in five rooms of four, one of six, one twin and one double/family room en-suite. All bedding supplied. A fully equipped kitchen/dining room, sitting room, excellent showers. **Additional facilities**:- sauna suite, garden, seminar room, dark room, bike hire, use of maps, advice on walking/ cycling routes. Groups and individuals welcome. Less abled guests are welcome, please enquire.

www.highland-hostel.co.uk

CONTACT Gavin or Nicola Tel:(01397) 712315 Fax: (01397) 712013
Email: gavin@highland-hostel.co.uk
OPENING SEASON All year
OPENING HOURS 24 hours
NUMBER OF BEDS 32: 1 x 6 : 5 x 4 : 1 twin : 1 family/double en-suite.
BOOKING REQUIREMENTS Booking advised, 50% deposit.
PRICE PER NIGHT £10 per person, discounts for groups

PUBLIC TRANSPORT
Roy Bridge train station is 2 miles from hostel and Citylink coaches drop off all year at Spean Bridge, 5 miles away. Pick up from local transport available.

DIRECTIONS
From Fort William follow A82 for 10 miles to Spean Bridge, turn right onto A86 for 3 miles to Roy Bridge. Pass though village and continue for 2 miles. The hostel is 100 metres on the right after passing Glenspean Lodge Hotel on left.

FARR COTTAGE LODGE & ACTIVITY CENTRE

Farr Cottage, Corpach
Fort William PH33 7LR

Farr Cottage is situated in Corpach, just 3 miles from Fort William town centre, with a breath-taking view of Ben Nevis and across Loch Linnhe, in the outdoor pursuits capital of Scotland.

We specialise in Scottish History, Kilt and Whisky evenings and there is a full range of in-house facilities including; satellite television, video lounge, licensed bar, self-catering facilities, email, laundry and drying facilities, central heating and hot showers. We also organise outdoor pursuits which comprise, white water rafting, canyoning, climbing, abseiling, skiing, snowboarding, fishing, golf and many many more! We can provide evening meals, breakfast, picnic lunches and we will ensure you have the break or holiday of a lifetime with us. Our professional team are geared to meet your needs and requirements. *The FULL Scottish Experience!!*

www.farr-cottage.com

CONTACT Stuart Tel: (01397) 772315, Fax: (01397) 772247, Email: mail@farrcottage.com
OPENING SEASON All year
OPENING HOURS 24 hours a day
NUMBER OF BEDS 30: in cottage 2 x 2 : 2 x 8 : 1 x 10. **18: in lodge** 1 x 2 : 1 x 4 : 2 x 6. Both buildings fully self contained.
BOOKING REQUIREMENTS Advance booking advised
PRICE PER NIGHT £12.50pp, £13pp or £16pp. Group rates available.

PUBLIC TRANSPORT
Corpach train station is 200m from the hostel. The nearest Citylink service is three miles away at Fort William. Taxi fare from Fort William centre is approximately £4.

DIRECTIONS
Follow the A82 north from Fort William centre towards Inverness for 1½ miles. Turn left at the A830 to Mallaig. Follow this road for 1½ miles into Corpach. We are on the right. Look for the flags.

P 1m

THE SMIDDY BUNKHOUSE

Snowgoose Mountain Centre
Station Road, Corpach
Fort William
Inverness-shire
PH33 7JH

The Smiddy Bunkhouses are alpine style hostels overlooking the south west end of the Caledonian Canal, providing top class self-catering accommodation with a pine clad interior to give a cosy atmosphere. There are fully fitted kitchens (food available from local shop), with 2 excellent drying rooms, bunkrooms of 4, 6, or 8 with all bedding provided. Comfortable sitting/dining areas and full meeting/ lecture room facilities. The location of the hostels is ideal for many outdoor activities. Advice/instruction and courses available from resident qualified and AALA licensed instructors. Ben Nevis and Glencoe provide year round mountaineering opportunities, with ski-ing in winter The area is a canoe sport mecca with good rough terrain routes for mountain bikes. The hostels are at the real start of the Great Glen cycle and walking route, two miles from the end of the West Highland Way.

www.highland-mountain-guides.co.uk

CONTACT John or Tina, Tel: (01397) 772467,
Email: info@highland-mountain-guides.co.uk
OPENING SEASON All year
OPENING HOURS All day (with key). Key deposit required.
NUMBER OF BEDS 12 + 14
BOOKING REQUIREMENTS Please telephone to pre-book.
PRICE PER NIGHT From £10 to £13.50 per person (inc bedding).

PUBLIC TRANSPORT
The hostel is two minutes' walk from Corpach Railway Station, three miles from Fort William on the Mallaig line.

DIRECTIONS
Take A82 north out of Fort William, towards Inverness, then A830 towards Mallaig and follow for 2½ miles to Corpach. Turn left immediately opposite "Key" stores, signposted 'Caledonian Canal' and 'Snowgoose Mountain Centre'. The hostel is 30yds on the left.

THE GLEBE BARN

Isle of Eigg
PH42 4RL

A new conversion of an 19th-century building, the Glebe Barn has charm and character whilst providing comfortable accommodation with magnificent views. You can enjoy breathtaking scenery along numerous walks; study fascinating geological formations, or explore varied natural habitats with incredible varieties of plant and animal species. Relax on beautiful sandy beaches, listen to the famous singing sands and watch the eagles soar above the spectacular Sgurr of Eigg. Just a mile away there is a well-stocked shop and café/ restaurant with regular traditional music sessions. Facilities at the Barn include a well-equipped kitchen, spacious lounge/dining room (polished maple floor, log fire), a combination of twin, triple, family and dormitory rooms, each with wash hand basins (linen provided), central heating, hot showers plus laundry facilities.

www.glebebarn.co.uk

CONTACT Karen or Simon, Tel: (01687) 482417,
Email: simon@glebebarn.co.uk
OPENING SEASON Individuals April to October, Groups all year
OPENING HOURS All day
NUMBER OF BEDS 24: 1 x 2 : 3 x 3 : 1 x 5 : 1 x 8.
BOOKING REQUIREMENTS Booking essential prior to boarding ferry. Deposit required for advance bookings.
PRICE PER NIGHT £10-£12pp (£24/£26 twin room). Group bookings for 3 nights or more £9pp

PUBLIC TRANSPORT
Fort William is the nearest National Express Coach stop. The early train from Fort William to Arisaig and Mallaig meets the ferry. Daily summer sailings from Arisaig or Mallaig.

DIRECTIONS
NO CAR FERRY - We generally meet visitors at the pier. Follow tarmac road around the shore and up hill until you cross a small stone bridge over a burn. Continue up hill and take first track on right. Taxi/ minibus service available on request.

DUNARD HOSTEL

Dunard, Castlebay
Isle of Barra
Western Isles
HS9 5XD

Dunard is a warm friendly, family run hostel on the beautiful island of Barra in Scotland's Outer Hebrides. The hostel has a cosy living room with a lovely open fire, hot showers and spacious kitchen. There are bunk, twin, double and family bedrooms. Situated in Castlebay the hostel has views over the castle to beaches and islands beyond. We are close to the ferry terminal, a handful of shops, and bars which often fill with live music. During the summer the island is alive for 'Feis Bharraidh' a gaelic festival of music, song and dance.

Take time and explore this truly beautiful island, stunning white beaches, quiet bays where otters hunt and seals bask on rocks, dunes and meadows carpeted in flowers, and wild windswept hills home to golden eagles. Join one of our friendly guided sea kayaking trips and paddle amongst sheltered islands for really close up wildlife encounters (no experience needed).

www.dunardhostel.co.uk

CONTACT Katie or Chris. Tel: (01871) 810 443
E-mail : info@dunardhostel.co.uk
OPENING SEASON All year, except Christmas and New Year.
OPENING HOURS 24 hours
NUMBER OF BEDS 16: 3 x 4 : 2 x 2.
BOOKING REQUIREMENTS Booking advised, especially during the summer. Booking essential for groups.
PRICE PER NIGHT £11 per person. £30 twin room. £38 family room. (sleeps 4) £130-£180 sole use. £5pp camping.

PUBLIC TRANSPORT
The hostel is a 3 minute walk from the Ferry Terminal in Castlebay. If using a local bus ask to be dropped at the hostel.

DIRECTIONS
From Ferry terminal in Castlebay head up hill, turn left and we are the third house past the old school. (200m from Terminal)

 See page 204 for colour photo

AM BOTHAN

Ferry Road
Leverburgh
Isle of Harris
HS5 3UA

Conveniently placed for the Leverburgh/ Berneray ferry this nautically-inspired facility overlooks the magical Sound of Harris and enjoys distant views of islands on the far western horizon as well as panoramic outlooks to the mountains of South Harris. The building boasts a unique and colourful decor with unexpected artefacts in every corner. In addition to an open peat-fire all rooms are centrally-heated and all bedding is provided.

There is a well-stocked shop in the village and a café, a pub and a restaurant nearby. A frequent bus service up through the islands passes the door. There is ample parking space. Wildlife and otter-watching trips are available locally (puffins arrive in May and seals breed in October) and trips to the smaller islands in the Sound of Harris can be arranged. Leverburgh is also the seafaring gateway to the fabled islands of St Kilda.

www.ambothan.com

CONTACT Ruari Beaton, Tel/Fax: (01859) 520251,
Email: ruari@ambothan.com
OPENING SEASON All year
OPENING HOURS 24 hours
NUMBER OF BEDS 18: 3x4, 1x6 + 3 futons and camping overspill.
BOOKING REQUIREMENTS Booking essential for groups. Advisable for individuals especially in summer.
PRICE PER NIGHT From £13 (adult), £10 (child). Special rates for families, groups and exclusive use.

PUBLIC TRANSPORT
A frequent bus service to Stornoway and Tarbert passes the door. The hostel is 5 minutes' walk from Leverburgh pier.

DIRECTIONS
GR NGO18863 From North or South follow the signs to Leverburgh /An T-Ob and the Tourist Board signs to Am Bothan.

ROCKVIEW BUNKHOUSE

Main Street
Tarbert
Isle of Harris
Western Isles
HS3 3DL

The Rockview Bunkhouse is ideally situated in the centre of Tarbert within five minutes' walk of all local amenities including the ferry terminal and craft shops. There is a good bus service to other areas of the Western Isles or if you prefer to be in the open air you can hire bikes in the town. Also close to local fisheries, permits available on premises.

The Bunkhouse is centrally heated throughout and offers both single and mixed dorms with bed linen (sleeping bags, liners and towels provided on request free of charge). There is a comfortable lounge to relax in with television, board games and guitar. The self-catering kitchen is equipped with cooker, microwave, cooking utensils, washing machine and tumble dryer. Showers are also available and hot water is plentiful. The Bunkhouse is suitable for groups or individuals and we look forward to welcoming you to Rockview. No animals.

CONTACT Johan or Iain Tel: (01859) 502626 or (01859) 502081.
Fax: 01859 502211. Email : imacaskill@aol.com
OPENING SEASON All year
OPENING HOURS All day
NUMBER OF BEDS 32: 1 x 12 : 1 x 20.
BOOKING REQUIREMENTS Booking advised.
PRICE PER NIGHT £10 - reduced rates for groups

PUBLIC TRANSPORT
Close to Tarbert ferry from Uig on Skye. Citylink coaches provide service from mainland cities through Skye to Uig (0990 505050). Good bus service to other areas on the Western Isles, phone (01859 502011) for details.

DIRECTIONS
In the centre of the main street of Tarbert, there is a large sign above the door.

 See page 212 for colour photo

LAXDALE BUNKHOUSE

Laxdale Holiday Park
6, Laxdale Lane
Stornoway
Isle of Lewis HS2 0DR

Laxdale Bunkhouse is contained within Laxdale Holiday Park which is a small family-run park set in peaceful tree-lined surroundings. Located 1½ miles away from the town of Stornoway, this is an ideal centre from which to tour the Islands of Lewis and Harris.

Built in 1998, the bunkhouse consists of four bedrooms with four bunks in each room and caters for backpackers, families or larger groups looking for convenient, low cost accommodation. A spacious fully equipped dining kitchen which provides two cookers, fridge and microwave. There is a comfortable TV lounge in which to relax. There is also a drying room. Toilets and showers are located within the building and are suitable for the disabled. Outside there is a covered veranda, picnic table and BBQ area.

CONTACT Tel: (01851) 706966 / (01851) 703234,
Email: info@laxdaleholidaypark.com
OPENING SEASON All year
OPENING HOURS 8am - 10pm
NUMBER OF BEDS 16: 4 x 4
BOOKING REQUIREMENTS July and August booking advisable one week in advance. Deposit secures.
PRICE PER NIGHT £11pp (high season), £10pp (low season). £150 sole use (high season), £130 sole use (low season).

PUBLIC TRANSPORT
Buses every ½ hour stop close to hostel.Taxi from town approx £2.50.

DIRECTIONS
From Stornoway Ferry Terminal take the A857. Take the second turning on the left past the hospital. Follow camping signs for one mile out of town. The Bunkhouse is located inside the holiday park. From Tarbert or Leverburgh take A859 for 40 miles to Stornoway. Turn left at the roundabout and second left after the Hospital then as above.

GALSON FARM BUNKHOUSE

Galson Farm House
South Galson
Isle of Lewis HS2 0SH

Galson Farm Bunkhouse is situated on a croft on the west coast of Lewis with stunning views overlooking the Atlantic Ocean, and is ideal for exploring the island's sandy beaches, mountains and burns, either on foot or by bicycle (cycle hire in Stornoway). The shore lies just a short walk through the croft and is ideal for fishing, bird-watching, walking and beach combing. The farm is part of a crofting village where Gaelic is the everyday language. We are twenty miles from Stornoway and eight miles from Butt of Lewis Lighthouse. The bus stops at Galson village road end.

Our fully equipped bunkhouse, set within a thick stone-walled former stable block and leading onto a cobbled yard, has one dormitory with eight bunks and two shower rooms. Bedding can be supplied if required or bring your own. There is a full kitchen/dining room so that you can self-cater or you can order meals. Come and go as you please. Shop two miles away. Booking advisable (Access/Visa) and essential for groups.

CONTACT David and Hazel Roberts, Tel/Fax: (01851) 850492,
Email: GalsonFarm@yahoo.com
OPENING SEASON All year
OPENING HOURS All day - 24 hours
NUMBER OF BEDS 8:- 1x 8
BOOKING REQUIREMENTS Always phone in advance. Bookings held till 6pm, deposit (Visa/Access) guarantees bed.
PRICE PER NIGHT £10 per person

PUBLIC TRANSPORT
The nearest ferry runs from Ullapool on the mainland to Stornoway which is 20 miles from the hostel. Local buses run from Mondays to Saturdays. Enquire at Stornoway Bus Station.

DIRECTIONS
GR 437 592. Follow A857 Stornoway to Ness(Nis) road for 20 miles. At Galson (Gabhsann) turn left at telephone kiosk. Bunkhouse is ¼ mile.

SHEENAS BACKPACKERS LODGE

Harbour View
Mallaig
Inverness-shire
PH41 4PU

The Backpackers Lodge in Mallaig offers a homely base from which you can explore the Inner Hebrides, the famous white sands of Morar and the remote peninsula of Knoydart. Mallaig itself is a working fishing village which makes it very exciting when the boats come in to land. Come and see the seals playing in the harbour waiting for the boats.

The hostel provides excellent budget accommodation with two rooms each with six beds, a drying room, full central heating and fully equipped kitchen/common room.

Meals are available from April to October.

CONTACT Tel: (01687) 462764
OPENING SEASON All year
OPENING HOURS 24 hour access
NUMBER OF BEDS 12: 2 x 6
BOOKING REQUIREMENTS Telephone ahead for availability.
PRICE PER NIGHT £13 per person.

PUBLIC TRANSPORT
Mallaig has a train station and services by Citylink coaches. For information on local buses phone (01967) 431272

DIRECTIONS
From railway station turn right, hostel is two buildings along.

DUN CAAN HOSTEL

The Pier Rd, Kyleakin
Isle of Skye
IV41 8PL

This warm and friendly hostel, set on the harbour front in the romantic fishing village of Kyleakin, is the ideal base for your Isle of Skye visit. Overlooking the ancient ruins of Castle Moil (once the home of a Viking princess affectionately known as Saucy Mary) and enjoying beautiful sea and mountain views from every room. We provide you with a well-equipped self-catering kitchen, free teas and coffees, hot showers, a cosy common room with TV, freshly laundered bed linen, a drying room for your wet clothing, lots of books to read, games to play and advice on what to see and do on this truly magnificent island. Also available at the hostel: laundry services, continental breakfast, bike hire and tours of the Island.

Please note that this is a non-smoking hostel.

Local facilities include a coffee shop, bars, restaurants and a general store and Post Office. Our friendly members of staff are always available with information and assistance. **Let's Go recommended.**

www.skyerover.co.uk

CONTACT Terry or Laila, Tel: (01599) 534087.
E-mail: info@skyerover.co.uk
OPENING SEASON All year (phone first in winter)
OPENING HOURS No curfew, access with key
NUMBER OF BEDS 16: 2 x 6 : 1 x 4.
BOOKING REQUIREMENTS Booking advisable in June, July and August. All major credit cards accepted. **Secure on-line booking.**
PRICE PER NIGHT £11pp (£12 July & August) including bedlinen, teas and coffees. No hidden costs.

PUBLIC TRANSPORT
Kyle of Lochalsh train arrivals connect with Skye Bridge Shuttle bus to Kyleakin(last stop Dun Caan Hostel). City Link coaches stop near to Hostel. Ferries Armadale, Kylerhea(Summer only).

DIRECTIONS
After crossing the Skye Bridge turn left at the roundabout for Kyleakin. Through village towards harbour and old ferry pier.

CUCHULAINN'S BACKPACKERS HOSTEL

Station Road, Kyle of Lochalsh
Ross-shire IV40 8AE

Centrally situated in Kyle of Lochalsh, Cuchulainn's is a cosy well equipped hostel which provides quality self-catering accommodation at an affordable price. There are showers, a fully equipped kitchen, a launderette and plenty of hot water.

Kyle of Lochalsh is at the mainland end of the controversial Skye Bridge, and close to the world famous Eilean Donan Castle. Kyle boasts a small fishing fleet, a swimming pool, a nine hole golf course, a supermarket and a wide variety of shops as well as two banks and a Post Office; all within easy reach of the hostel. Next door to the hostel is a friendly pub and restaurant which provides good home made food in cheery surroundings. Kyle is an ideal centre for hill-walkers, climbers and divers, and there is plenty of good fishing. Bike, car and boat (for parties of divers/fishermen) hire is available locally. Kyle is accessible by car, boat, train and bus and makes an ideal centre for touring Skye and Wester Ross. Boat trips available.

CONTACT Paul, Tel: (01599) 534492,
Email; cuchulainns_hostel@hotmail.com
OPENING SEASON All year round
OPENING HOURS All day - no curfew.
NUMBER OF BEDS 12: 1 x 2 : 1 x 4 : 1 x 6
BOOKING REQUIREMENTS Phone bookings held until 6pm. Credit/Debit card details or advance payment guarantees bed.
PRICE PER NIGHT £10 per person. Twin £12.50 per person.

PUBLIC TRANSPORT
Kyle of Lochalsh train station is 150m from the hostel. The Citylink bus stops 50m from the hostel. Buses to main places of interest in Skye pass through Kyle. Phone Citylink Highland County Skye Line (01478 612622).

DIRECTIONS
Entering Kyle on the A87 travelling north, it is the first building on the right after the railway station.

SKYEWALKER INDEPENDENT HOSTEL

Old School, Portnalong
Isle of Skye, IV47 8SL

Situated close to the Cuillin hills on the beautiful Minginish Peninsula the old village school has been tastefully converted to very high standards of comfort and has all the normal features and more! The hostel is centrally heated throughout and provides plenty of hot water and more than adequate shower and toilet facilities. The village Post Office is situated in the hostel reception and there is a well stocked shop within the licensed café in the hostel grounds. The pub is 5 minutes' walk away, and beaches and beautiful walks are nearby. All necessary bed linen is included in the price. There are no hidden charges! The perfect base for outdoor activities with hill, moors and water combining into spectacular scenery - and a hot shower and comfy bed to finish the day. Café on site.

http://freespace.virgin.net/skyewalker.hostel/index.htm

CONTACT Trevor or June, Tel: Freephone (0800) 0277 059, Fax: (01478) 640420, Email: skyewalker.hostel@virgin.net
OPENING SEASON All year
OPENING HOURS 24 hour access
NUMBER OF BEDS 36
BOOKING REQUIREMENTS In peak season booking 4 weeks in advance is advised (deposit required)
PRICE PER NIGHT From £8 per person.

PUBLIC TRANSPORT
Two local buses run each weekday. Running from Portree via Sligachan to Portnalong (hostel) and back. Citylink coaches (from the mainland and north Skye) drop off at Sligachan. We will provide free transport from/to Sligachan outside of bus hours.

DIRECTIONS
GR 348 348. From Sligachan take A863 then B8009 through Carbost and Fernilea to Portnalong. At the bus stop turn left onto Fiskavaig Road, 500m to hostel.

SLIGACHAN BUNKHOUSE

Sligachan
Isle of Skye
IV47 8SW

Sligachan Bunkhouse overlooks the 'Black Cuillins' and is an ideal base for exploring the magnificent mountains of Skye. Several routes up the peaks pass the Bunkhouse and the path to 'Loch Coruisk' can be seen from the verandah. The Bunkhouse is surrounded by peaceful mountain scenery on a track easily accessible by car. It is only a 5 minute walk from the bus stop at Sligachan, which sees a regular bus service from the mainland and Portree. The Sligachan Hotel can be seen from the Bunkhouse, about a 5 minute walk, and will provide a hot meal from breakfast through to dinner. The bar is a great place to relax after a long day's trekking and has a great display of malt whiskies and we make our own real ale at the Cuillin Brewery.

The Bunkhouse has 4 bedrooms, full kitchen facilities and a lounge with open fire.

www.sligachan.co.uk

CONTACT Catriona Coghill, Tel: (01478) 650204
Email: selfcatering@sligachan.co.uk
OPENING SEASON Feb 14th until Jan 6th
OPENING HOURS All day
NUMBER OF BEDS 20
BOOKING REQUIREMENTS Booking essential for large groups. Deposit required.
PRICE PER NIGHT £10pp. Block bookings £180 per night

PUBLIC TRANSPORT
Train - 1) Fort William to Mallaig, crossing by ferry to Armadale, buses to Sligachan (30m). 2) Inverness to Kyle of Lochalsh, catch bus over Skye Bridge to Kyleakin connect with bus to Sligachan.

DIRECTIONS
Inverness: A82 Invermoriston take A887 then A87 to Kyle of Lochalsh, cross Skye Bridge, continue on A87. Fort William: A830 to Mallaig, cross to Skye on ferry, take A851 to Broadford connect A87.

See page 201 for colour photo

PORTREE INDEPENDENT HOSTEL

The Old Post Office
The Green, Portree
Isle of Skye IV51 9BT

Centrally situated in Portree, the capital of Skye, this hostel provides quality inexpensive self-catering accommodation with a fully equipped kitchen/dining area (continental breakfast is available on request).

Originally the island's main post office it has been converted to an independent hostel sleeping 60 in small family rooms and dormitories. All bedding is provided free. There is also a well-equipped launderette on site. Only 50 metres from the bus terminus it is an ideal base for touring the island.

Within easy walking distance there is a wide variety of shops, pubs, eating places, three national banks and post office. From the hostel there are pleasant coastal and woodland walks. Bike and car hire are available locally. Portree holds an annual Folk Festival in July and the Highland Games are in August.

CONTACT The manager, Tel: (01478) 613737. Fax: (01478) 613758.
Email: skyehostel@yahoo.co.uk
OPENING SEASON All year
OPENING HOURS No curfew
NUMBER OF BEDS 61
BOOKING REQUIREMENTS Phone booking held to 6pm. Advance payment guarantees bed. Visa/Mastercard/Switch accepted.
PRICE PER NIGHT £11.00 to £12.00 per person.

PUBLIC TRANSPORT
Cross island buses from the mainland to Uig pass through Portree.

DIRECTIONS
Situated 50 metres from the main square in the town. Approaching Portree on the A850/A87 road from the mainland the hostel is between the long stay car park and the town centre.

 See page 204 for colour photo

WATERFRONT BUNKHOUSE

The Old Inn
Carbost
Isle of Skye
IV47 8SR

Waterfront Bunkhouse has been purpose built to provide a high degree of style and comfort. Standing as it does, twenty feet from the edge of Loch Harport, the accommodations command breathtaking views of the Cuillins. The bunkhouse offers opportunities as a base for the hill walkers or the sightseeing tourist with spectacular scenery and abundant wildlife in the surrounding hills and glens.

The hostel sleeps 24 and consists of dormitory type rooms 2 x 6 bed rooms and 3 x 4 bed rooms. One of the rooms is en-suite (the crows nest). Upstairs there is the kitchen and common room with a balcony overlooking the loch again with spectacular views. Full laundry facilities are available as are shower facilities which are also open to visiting yachtsmen. The waterfront bunkhouse is about 40 mins from Broadford 25 mins from Portree.

www.carbost.f9.co.uk

CONTACT Angus or Spencer, Tel: 01478 640205, Fax: 01478 640325, Email: waterfront@oldinn.f9.co.uk ,
OPENING SEASON All Year (please ring for availability).
OPENING HOURS 24 Hours
NUMBER OF BEDS 24: 2 x 6 bed & 3 x 4 bed
BOOKING REQUIREMENTS In peak season booking 4 weeks or more in advance is advised (deposit required).
PRICE PER NIGHT £12.00 per night (£11.00 if staying 3 nights or more)

PUBLIC TRANSPORT
The nearest train station is Kyle of Lochalsh. City Citylink coaches (from the mainland and north Skye) drop off at Sligachan. Two local buses run each weekday, from Portree via Sligachan to Fiskavaig.

DIRECTIONS
From Sligachan take the A863 for 4 miles then left onto B8009 for 4 miles to Carbost. The Waterfront Bunkhouse is in the centre of the village next to the Old Inn public house and opposite the school.

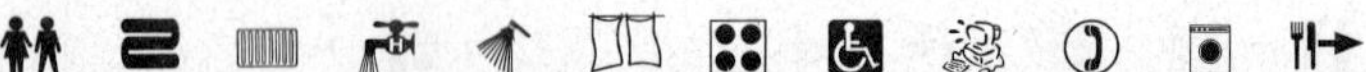

CROFT BUNKHOUSE AND BOTHIES

Portnalong
Isle of Skye, IV47 8SL

Originally converted from barns, the Bunkhouse & Bothies comprise 5 fully independent accommodation units on a 13-acre croft on the west coast of Skye. Advice on walks and tours, free map loan, pub 500 yds.

Bunkhouse - sleeps 12, built-in bunk beds, hot showers, fully equipped kitchen, washing machine, drying room & large common room with table tennis table etc

Bothy - sleeps 6 in first floor dormitory with views over crofts to Portnalong harbour. Ground floor fully equipped kitchen/living room, toilet & hot shower, drying room. A popular family unit.

Bothy Beag - sleeps 4 in a compact self-contained unit, 2 built in bunk beds in fully equipped kitchen/living room, shower and toilet.

Cabin - sleeps 2 in a small self-contained kitchen/living room with bunk bed, en-suite toilet facilities. Fine views over crofts to the sea.

But&Ben - sleeps 4, barn to cottage conversion, all facilities.

www.skye-hostels.com

CONTACT Dave Tel/Fax: (01478) 640254,
Email: skyehostel@lineone.net

OPENING SEASON All year

OPENING HOURS No curfew

NUMBER OF BEDS Bunkhouse 12, Bothies 6,4 and 2, But&Ben 4.

BOOKING REQUIREMENTS Phone bookings held to 6pm. Advance payment guarantees bed (Visa/Access accepted).

PRICE PER NIGHT £8 to £9 per person. Camping £3 to £5.

PUBLIC TRANSPORT

Citylink coaches from mainland pass through Sligachan. Two buses daily (weekdays only) from Portree via Sligachan to Portnalong.

DIRECTIONS

GR 348 353. From Sligachan take the A863 for 4 miles then left onto B8009 for 6 miles through Carbost and Fernilea to Portnalong. Follow signs for Croft Bunkhouse & Little Gallery, it is 500yds past the pub.

 See page 212 for colour photo

DUN FLODIGARRY HOSTEL

Flodigarry By Staffin
Isle of Skye
IV51 9HZ

The hostel is set in the beautiful Trotternish peninsula of North Skye. The area is famous for the distinctive cliffs and rock formations of the Quiraing and enjoys spectacular views of both the Western Isles and Wester Ross. Hiking, hill walking, rock climbing and enjoying the stunning scenery are popular pursuits. Many of the trails are accessible right from the hostel. There are boat trips, sea kayaking and pony trekking available in the area. Whilst out and about you may see, among other wildlife, otters, whales and golden eagles.

The hostel is centrally heated and fully equipped with all bedding and sheets provided. Phone the hostel for travel information outwith the public bus service times. There is a hotel with bar and restaurant 100 metres from our door. Groups are welcome, there is a camping area.

www.hostel-scotland.co.uk

We are members of Independent Backpackers Hostels Scotland.

CONTACT Tel: (01470) 552212.
Email: hostel.flodigarry@btopenworld.com
OPENING SEASON All year, but phone from November to March,as we may be closed.
OPENING HOURS All day
NUMBER OF BEDS 40: 3 x 2 : 3 x 6 : 2 x 8.
BOOKING REQUIREMENTS Booking is essential for groups and suggested for individuals during the summer.
PRICE PER NIGHT £10pp - £15pp. Cash or cheque with bank card, sorry we do not accept credit cards.

PUBLIC TRANSPORT
Buses come from Portree daily, except Sunday and stop 100 metres from the hostel.

DIRECTIONS
GR464 720. 34 kilometres north of Portree, 5 kilometres north of Staffin on coast road. Adjacent to the Flodigarry Hotel. Landranger map 23.

GERRY'S ACHNASHELLACH HOSTEL

Craig, Achnashellach
Strathcarron, Wester-Ross
Scotland IV54 8YU

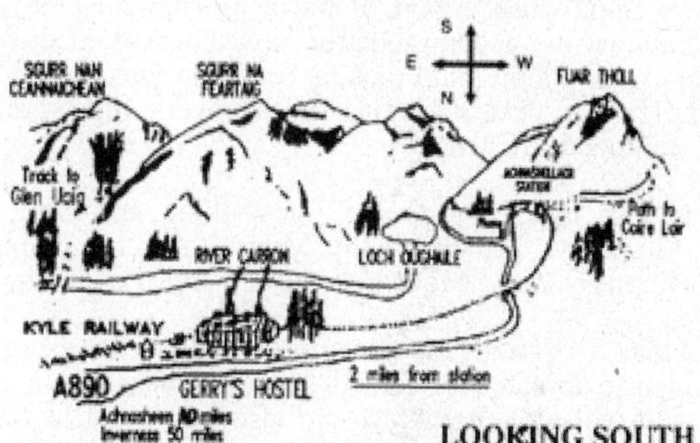

LOOKING SOUTH

Gerry's Hostel is situated in an excellent mountaineering and wilderness area on the most scenic railway in Britain. The hostel has a common room with log fire, library and stereo. Come and go as you please. No smoking inside or out.

Accommodation for non-smokers.
www.gerryshostel-achnashellach.co.uk

CONTACT Gerry, Tel: (01520) 766232,
OPENING SEASON All Year (check by phone)
OPENING HOURS Booking in times 5pm to 8.30pm. Later by prior arrangement only.
NUMBER OF BEDS 20: 1 x 10 : 2 x 5
BOOKING REQUIREMENTS Prepay to secure bed, or phone.
PRICE PER NIGHT From £10pp, discount for long stay large groups.

PUBLIC TRANSPORT
Achnashellach Station is 4km west of the hostel. Nearest Citylink coaches drop off at Kyle of Lochalsh.

DIRECTIONS
GR 037 493. 95 miles north of Fort William, 50 miles west of Inverness on A890.

KINLOCHEWE BUNKHOUSE

Kinlochewe by Achnasheen
Wester Ross
IV22 2PA

Kinlochewe Bunkhouse is part of the Kinlochewe Hotel. Following some alterations, the accommodation now consists of one dormitory with 12 bunks and individual lockers for each bunk (padlocks are not provided). There is central heating, hot showers, toilets, drying room and well equipped kitchen.

The Bunkhouse is ideally placed for walking and climbing in the Torridon Mountains and the many Munros that they have to offer, indeed there are over 20 Munros within 20 miles of Kinlochewe.

The Hotel Bar is open all the year round, and serves excellent home-made food at affordable prices. (It also has a selection of 50 malt Whiskys and real ale). Breakfast can also be served in the Hotel by prior arrangement. Sleeping bags and towels are not provided. For cyclists we are able to provide secure housing for bicycles.

www.Kinlochewehotel.co.uk

CONTACT Roderick McCall, Tel: (01445) 760253.
Email: kinlochewehotel@tinyworld.co.uk
OPENING SEASON All year
OPENING HOURS 8am - midnight
NUMBER OF BEDS 12
BOOKING REQUIREMENTS Booking essential for groups, deposit required. Advisable for individuals but not essential.
PRICE PER NIGHT £10 per person.

PUBLIC TRANSPORT
Nearest train station is in Achnasheen (10 miles away). Trains run three times a day, postbus meets the lunchtime train and also comes to Kinlochewe. Tuesdays, Thursdays & Fridays the 5pm Westerbus from Inverness to Gairloch stops outside the hostel around 6.45pm.

DIRECTIONS
Kinlochewe is situated at the junction of the A832 Garve to Gairloch road and the A896 north from Torridon.

MORAG'S LODGE

Bunoich Brae
Fort Augustus
Inverness-shire PH32 4DG

Morag's Lodge is set in wooded grounds just minutes' walk from the village of Fort Augustus. The village, situated at the southern end of Loch Ness, is ideally located for hill walking, cycling and kayaking. There are many other outdoor activities available locally including a golf course. The hostel offers the best quality budget accommodation for backpackers. Rooms hold a maximum of six people in huge comfy beds and most have en-suite facilities. There is a double and a twin available. You can relax in the sun lounge (with television and a selection of videos) or enjoy a drink beside the open fire in the bar. A drying room is also available. There is a well equipped self-catering kitchen and large dining room, however breakfast and dinner are provided on request (for a modest charge). Adequate parking is available in the hostel grounds.

The hostel graded 4 star by Visit Scotland.

www.moragslodge.com

CONTACT Liz or Rebecca Tel: (01320) 366289.
Email : lizpp@radicaltravel.com
OPENING SEASON All year
OPENING HOURS All day, check in from 5pm
NUMBER OF BEDS 50: 7x6 : 1x4 : 2x2
BOOKING REQUIREMENTS Booking recommended. No advance booking in July/August. Credit card details or cheque required to confirm any advance bookings.
PRICE PER NIGHT £13pp bunk. £18pp double or twin.

PUBLIC TRANSPORT
Bus stop for Fort William and Inverness 300m from Lodge.

DIRECTIONS
From Inverness, arrive at Fort Augustus, turn first right up Bunoich Brae. Morag's Lodge 100m on left. From Fort William, go through village past petrol station and car park, next left up Bunoich Brae.

P 1m

GLEN AFFRIC BACKPACKERS

Cannich By Beauly
Inverness-shire
IV4 7LT

Glen Affric Backpackers offers A high standard of accommodation at a budget price. The bedrooms accommodate one or two people in single beds. We also have larger rooms with four beds which are ideal for families. All bedding is provided in price. The hostel has two common rooms each with log burning fires and an ample supply of wood. One common room has a television and a large assortment of reading matter. The other common room is a peaceful reading/ study area with comfy chairs and a small kitchen area. We have a large dining/kitchen area fully equipped with cookers, fridges and microwave. A chest freezer is also available. There are ample toilet and shower facilities with constant hot water.

The hostel is situated in the village of Cannich which is an ideal base for touring the Highlands. We are surrounded by beautiful scenery with an abundance of walks in the locality.

CONTACT Kath Gregory, Tel: (01456) 415263
Email: Rob@Cannich.freeserve.co.uk
OPENING SEASON All year (except Xmas and New Year)
OPENING HOURS Access 24 hrs, service between 9am-10pm
NUMBER OF BEDS 70
BOOKING REQUIREMENTS Groups should book in advance with 10% deposit.
PRICE PER NIGHT £10 per person.

PUBLIC TRANSPORT
Nearest train station at Inverness, 26 miles away. Nearest Citylink drop off at Drumnadrochit, 14 miles. Regular bus service (Highland Buses) from Inverness, passes hostel three times a day.

DIRECTIONS
By car:- take A82 out of Inverness to Drumnadrochit, then A831 for Cannich. Upon entering Cannich look for hostel sign on left.

POTTERY BUNKHOUSE

Caoldair Pottery, Laggan Bridge
Inverness-shire
PH20 1BT

The Pottery Bunkhouse is situated within the new Cairngorm National Park, in the valley of the river Spey looking onto the Monadhliath mountains to the North. See it to believe it! Laggan is a working Highland village with a reputation for adventurous rural initiatives, such as the **Laggan Forestry Project, which now boasts a full-on mountain biking course.** It provides an ideal base for day trips to many places including Loch Ness, or for local exploration of the Monadhliath mountains, Strathmashie forest, Loch Laggan, Creag Meagaidh Nature Reserve, the Corrieyairack Pass, Ben Alder and many tracks and paths.

The Bunkhouse is a purpose built timber building nestling at the rear of the Caoldair pottery and coffee shop. The facilities include two en-suite family rooms and three bunkrooms, disabled shower/toilet, lounge and TV room, kitchen, drying room, central heating throughout, **newly installed HOT-TUB SPA.** The on-site coffee shop provides excellent home-baking with a range of clothing and artefacts for purchase (summer season only). The nearest building is the pub (400m) which provides meals and a lively local bar.

www.potterybunkhouse.co.uk

CONTACT Lynda, Tel: (01528) 544231,
Email: lynda@potterybunkhouse.co.uk
OPENING SEASON All year
OPENING HOURS All day. No curfew
NUMBER OF BEDS 34
BOOKING REQUIREMENTS Please telephone to check availability especially for weekends and group bookings.
PRICE PER NIGHT £10.00pp or £12.00 pp with linen.

PUBLIC TRANSPORT
Nearest trains and Citylink coaches are in Newtonmore (7 miles).

DIRECTIONS
You will find us on the A889, 8 miles from the A9 at Dalwhinnie heading west to Fort William and Skye.

NEWTONMORE HOSTEL

Craigellachie House
Main Street, Newtonmore
Inverness-shire
PH20 1DA

Newtonmore, a traditional village in the Cairngorms National Park, is a great base for outdoor activities, relaxing or touring. The village has shops, a petrol station and several hotels which serve good value food and drink. See where Monarch of the Glen is filmed, visit the Highland Folk Museum, the MacPherson Museum and Waltzing Waters! Walk, climb, ski, canoe, windsurf, cycle, fish, golf, birdwatch or sail.

Our purpose built hostel has showers, brilliant drying room, well equipped kitchen, central heating and lounge/dining area with wood burning stove. **No meters. Smoking is not allowed anywhere in the hostel.** Smokers may light up outside.

Inverness 46 miles, Fort William 50 miles, Glasgow/Edinburgh 110 miles. *Come and stay in our hostel, the area is unique. You'll love it.*

www.HighlandHostel.co.uk

CONTACT Kathryn or Peter, Tel: (01540) 673360, pete@HighlandHostel.co.uk
OPENING SEASON All year
OPENING HOURS All day, no curfew
NUMBER OF BEDS 14: 1 x 2 : 2 x 6
BOOKING REQUIREMENTS Phone to check availability, 20% deposit or credit card details.
PRICE PER NIGHT £10.00 pp sharing, £12 pp private (min2), £140 - sole use.

PUBLIC TRANSPORT
Newtonmore train station ½ mile from hostel (we'll collect from there or Kingussie Station). Buses from Inverness and Perth stop close by (08705 50 50 50).

DIRECTIONS
GR 713 990. The hostel is behind Craigellachie House in the centre of the village at the junction of the A86 and B9150. Look for blue signs.

P AM 1m

CRAIGOWER LODGE

Golf Course Road, Newtonmore
Inverness-shire PH20 1AT

Craigower Lodge is situated in its own quiet grounds in the highland village of Newtonmore within the Cairngorms National Park. We have excellent transport links by road, rail and flights to Inverness. Our central Highlands location makes Craigower the ideal base for outdoor activities. Within easy reach of Craigower we have the rivers Spey, Findhorn, Roy and Spean. For the Mountaineer we are halfway between The Northern Corries and Creag Meagaidh. Hillwalkers have an abundance of Munros nearby, for skiers and snowboarders, Cairngorm Mountain is nearby and Nevis Range within an hour. For the cyclist we have Sustrans route 7 coming through the village and the all new Wolftrax downhill trails at Laggan are a must. We welcome individuals, families, groups and clubs to this magnificent part of Scotland where we can quite literally say "it's all on our doorstep". The Lodge is extensively renovated to STB 3* hostel status and provides self-catering and catered accommodation for up to 68 people. Instruction, guiding and activity breaks available all year. We look forward to welcoming you to Craigower Lodge.

www.activeoutdoorpursuits.com

CONTACT Tel: (01540) 673319 - Fax: (01540) 673390
Email:- info@craigowerlodge.com
OPENING SEASON All year
OPENING HOURS 8 till late
NUMBER OF BEDS 68
BOOKING REQUIREMENTS Booking essential, by phone or email
PRICE PER NIGHT £12.00 per person

PUBLIC TRANSPORT
Newtonmore Train Station ¼ mile. For info. 08457 484950. Buses from Inverness, Glasgow and Edinburgh. For info. 08705 505050. Private transport available to groups to and from most parts of Scotland. **Tours available.**

DIRECTIONS
From the main street in Newtonmore, turn into Curleys Lane next to the Co-op, take 1st right after 50m and follow lane around for 50m.

P H 1m

GLEN FESHIE HOSTEL

Balachroick House
Kincraig, Inverness-shire
PH21 1NH

Set in beautiful Glen Feshie with immediate access to the Cairngorm National Nature Reserve, this hostel is ideally placed for walking, climbing and cycling. In winter Glen Feshie is the perfect base to try cross-country ski touring. Both Nordic skiing equipment and mountain bikes can be hired from the hostel. Watersports and pony trekking are nearby for those with transport.

The hostel has three bunkrooms each with four beds, and a double room (duvets and linen provided). Hot showers, and good drying facilities are available. The kitchen is fully equipped for self-catering and there is a wood burning stove in the common room/dining area. Porridge provided free for breakfast, other meals including vegetarian/vegan meals can be provided with notice. There is a small store selling essentials, homemade bread, free range eggs and other goodies.

CONTACT Jean Hamilton, Tel: (01540) 651323
Email: glenfeshiehostel@totalise.co.uk
OPENING SEASON All year
OPENING HOURS All day - 24 hours
NUMBER OF BEDS 14: 3 x 4 : 1 x 2.
BOOKING REQUIREMENTS Booking advised at weekends.
PRICE PER NIGHT £9.50 per person (including porridge for breakfast), £32 for family bunkroom (4/5 beds), £108 whole hostel.

PUBLIC TRANSPORT
Train stations at Kingussie (15km) and Aviemore (15km). Citylink buses stop at Kingussie and Aviemore and also limited number stopping at Kincraig (7km from hostel). Hostel can collect from buses and trains if contacted in advance.

DIRECTIONS
GR 849 009. From Kingussie take B9152 to Kincraig. Turn right at Kincraig, down unclassified road, after 2km turn left onto the B970 towards Feshiebridge. After crossing the River Feshie in 1.5km, turn right onto a road signposted Achlean and hostel, follow for 4km.

BLUE MOUNTAIN LODGE

Anderson Road
BALLATER
Aberdeenshire AB35 5QW

In the Cairngorm National Park is the delightful town of Ballater, eastern gateway to the Scottish highlands. On the edge of town, The School-House offers excellent accommodation to individuals and groups of up to 24, with facilities for 6 disabled guests. The owners, Alan and Cathy Low have renovated this Victorian building to the highest standard to provide quality facilities at affordable prices. There are 3 dormitories, each with 3 bunk beds designed to allow easy conversion to double or family rooms. All dormitories have bathrooms and there's social space, a drying room and cycle shed. Breakfast is included in the overnight price and evening meals and tasty packed lunches are available.

The garden supplies vegetables and outdoor eating areas. There are classroom facilities and the School-House runs a range of walking, relaxation and language programmes. A relaxed atmosphere and warm welcome awaits all School-House guests and as Cathy is a well-known storyteller, there's often a bedtime story for those who want one! Royal Deeside has much to offer, including Munros, riverside and forest walks, snow sports, whisky and castles.

CONTACT Alan or Cathy Low Tel: (013397) 56333,
Email: schoolhouseballater@btinternet.com
OPENING SEASON All year
OPENING HOURS All day
NUMBER OF BEDS 18: 24 possible (3 rooms with 6 or 8 people)
BOOKING REQUIREMENTS Booking advised, essential for groups
PRICE PER NIGHT From £10 per person, includes breakfast.

PUBLIC TRANSPORT
From Aberdeen Bus Station (bus enquiries (01224) 212266).

DIRECTIONS
From Aberdeen follow the A93 to Ballater (43 miles). **From Inverness** follow Grantown-on-Spey then A939 to Ballater (70 miles). **From Perth** follow A93 to Blairgowrie, then continue to Ballater (65 miles).

P

NETHY STATION

Nethy Bridge
PH25 3DS

GROUPS ONLY

Sharing a car park with the *Speyside Way* and just yards from the river, this converted station offers all that a group could expect from a bunkhouse. It is well-equipped, fully centrally heated and has two public areas.

Most rooms have triple bunks. One of the 2-bunk rooms and the store room only have outside access. Whether you self-cater or we cook for you as a group you will have access to the kitchen at all times. We never ask groups to share the building so you may eat, sleep, walk, ski, board, hike, ride, fish etc...whatever you like at your own convenience!

The station is only 200 yards from the centre of *Nethy Bridge* with its shop, butcher, pubs and Interpretive Centre and half-way between two wintersports areas.
Dogs are welcome but please do not let them sleep on the beds.

www.nethy.org

CONTACT Patricia or Richard, Tel: (01479) 821370
Email: info@nethy.org
OPENING SEASON All year
OPENING HOURS Any time
NUMBER OF BEDS: 22: 2 x 9 : 2 x 2.
BOOKING REQUIREMENTS Essential (with deposit)
PRICE PER NIGHT from £9pp electricity included. Minimum of 6 .

PUBLIC TRANSPORT
Take train or Citylink coach to Aviemore. Local buses are available from Aviemore to Nethy Bridge Post Office. Phone (01479) 811566 for information.

DIRECTIONS
GR 002 207. Hostel is adjacent to the Speyside Way. From the B970, with post office on your right, go over the bridge and turn left immediately. Past the butcher turn second right.

5m

BALLINDALLOCH HOSTEL

SpeysideWay
Ballindalloch
AB37 9AB

The old Railway Station at Ballindalloch at the junction of the Rivers Spey and Avon provides an excellent base for white water canoeing, walking and cycling, with the Speyside Way passing the door and access to the river just 100 yards away. The hostel sleeps 16 people in rooms of 2 x 4, 1 x 6, and 1 x 2, with 2 shower/bath rooms. There is a large lounge with a wood burning stove, a large kitchen and drying area with the entrance area designed as a drying room. This is a non-smoking hostel for self-catering only. Metered electricity. The Post Office, shop and petrol are available 1 mile away.

In Winter the Hostel is available for lets with skiing at the Lecht just 16 miles away

CONTACT Tel: (01540) 651272. E-mail; office@lochinsh.com
OPENING SEASON All year
OPENING HOURS After 4pm
NUMBER OF BEDS 16
BOOKING REQUIREMENTS Booking required with 25% deposit. Full payment 4 weeks prior to arrival plus £100 security deposit held against breakage or damage and refunded 1 week after departure less electricity.
PRICE PER NIGHT £8 per night (minimum 6 persons).

PUBLIC TRANSPORT
Nearest railway station is Aviemore. Bus sevice to Grantown. Buses pass Cragganmore road end.

DIRECTIONS
From the South and North travel to Grantown on Spey taking A95 towards Elgin and follow for approx 12 miles. As you drop down towards the Avon River turn left at sign for Cragganmore and Speyside Way. Hostel is opposite telephone kiosk.

From North East take road to Aberlour and follow A95 towards Grantown for 12 miles. Half mile after the Ballindalloch Post Office turn right at sign for Cragganmore, then as above.

ARDENBEG BUNKHOUSE AND OUTDOOR CENTRE

Grant Road, Grantown-on-Spey
Moray
PH26 3LD

Ardenbeg Bunkhouse and Outdoor Centre is based in Grantown-on-Spey, part of the beautiful Cairngorms National Park and ideal for many activities available in this lovely holiday area, during both winter and summer.
The Bunkhouse sleeps up to 24 people in rooms of 4, 6, 6, and 8. Each room has its own toilet and shower room and access to the drying room. There are two fully equipped self-catering kitchens with dining areas, televisions, microwaves and boogie boxes. There is plenty of off road parking and an extensive enclosed garden with play equpment and 2 BBQ's. We offer optional instruction and equipment hire for paddling, climbing and mountain routes. We can also provide weather forecasts and avalanche reports to allow you to enjoy a full day of activities.

www.ardenbeg.co.uk

CONTACT Rebecca Tel: (01479) 872824
Email : enquiries@ardenbeg.co.uk
OPENING SEASON All year round
OPENING HOURS All day
NUMBER OF BEDS 24 : 1x4 : 2x6 : 1x8
BOOKING REQUIREMENTS Book in advance to avoid disappointment. No under 16s without adults.
PRICE PER NIGHT £12 per person

PUBLIC TRANSPORT
Nearest train station Aviemore. Nearest airport Inverness. Good bus services from both places to Grantown Square. Ardenbeg is 2 minutes' walk.

DIRECTIONS
From the A9 approach Grantown on the A95 passing Dulnain Bridge. At first roundabout turn left into Grantown, just before traffic lights turn left into Chapel Rd, turn right at the end of the road into Grant Rd, Ardenbeg is on the left.

CARRBRIDGE BUNKHOUSE

Dalrachney House
Carrbridge
Inverness-shire
PH23 3AX

Carrbridge Bunkhouse is a cosy wood panelled cabin with a turf roof situated next to the River Dulnain. The village sits nestled in the glorious Spey Valley - famous for its year round attractions and activities to suit all including ski school and ski hire, home of Landmark Centre, golf, pony trekking and an indoor swimming pool with sauna and steam room. In the winter the best of Scottish skiing and climbing is to be found on the snow covered mighty Cairngorms and in the summer every kind of watersport can be enjoyed within this area of unsurpassed beauty.

The Bunkhouse has a fully equipped kitchen/dining room with wood burning stove, toilets and showers, sauna, drying room and ample parking. The village is nearby for provisions and a variety of eating places.

www. carrbridge-bunkhouse.co.uk

CONTACT Tom/Allyson, Tel: (01479) 841250,
Email: jonesbunk@aol.com
OPENING SEASON All year
OPENING HOURS 24 hours
NUMBER OF BEDS 18:- 2 x 2 1 x 4 1 x 10
BOOKING REQUIREMENTS Booking recommended.
PRICE PER NIGHT £7.50pp, group discounts.

PUBLIC TRANSPORT
Bus and train service in village. Citylink coach services from London to Edinburgh and Glasgow to Inverness stop at Carrbridge.

DIRECTIONS
GR 896 229 A short walk from the village on the road to Inverness or follow the riverside footpath to Dalrachney House.

SLOCHD MHOR LODGE

Slochd
Carrbridge
Inverness-shire
PH23 3AY

Slochd Mhor Lodge is perfectly situated in the spectacular Strathspey in the Cairngorm National Park and halfway between the villages of Carrbridge and Tomatin. The Lodge is on an 'off road' section of the No 7 Sustrans cycle route and surrounded by hills and forests. This is also perfect walking country and in winter there are nordic ski trails from the doorstep. All other outdoor pursuits are within easy reach.

Slochd Mhor Lodge offers a genuine welcome in warm cosy surroundings. Fully equipped kitchen with wood burning stove and a spacious dining area together with large lounge/lecture room with woodburner. Other facilities include a drying room and laundry facilites, some en-suite rooms, a room suitable for wheel-chair user, an on-site cycle shop/workshop, MT bike hire, and in winter nordic ski hire. We have basic provisions for sale and there is an outside seating and BBQ area. Ample parking.

www.slochd.co.uk

CONTACT Liz or Ian Tel: (01479) 841666
Email: slochd666@aol.com
OPENING SEASON All year
OPENING HOURS 24 hours
NUMBER OF BEDS 30: 1x12 : 1x8 : 2x4 : 1x2
BOOKING REQUIREMENTS Booking recommended
PRICE PER NIGHT £11.50pp. Sole use & group discounts available.

PUBLIC TRANSPORT
Nearest bus and train station; Carrbridge (4miles). City Link London/ Edinburgh and Glasgow/Inverness stop at Carrbridge.

DIRECTIONS
Coming from south on A9, after mileage board marked 'Inverness 23' travel 1½ miles north, take first opening on left marked 'Slochd'. We are first opening on right (¼ mile).

EASTGATE BACKPACKERS

38 Eastgate, Inverness
IV2 3NA

Eastgate Hostel is a perfect base for backpackers, walkers and cyclists to explore the Highland capital and surrounding area. Loch Ness is only a short drive away, as is Urquhart Castle and Culloden battlefield. Day trips to Skye, Orkney and the north are all possible, tours available to Culloden & Loch Ness at discounted rates using our own tour bus. Inverness boasts an excellent choice of pubs, clubs and restaurants to suit all tastes, while a large modern shopping centre is located directly opposite us. We are a 5 minute walk from the train and bus stations. Find us on the second floor, opposite the "Eastgate Shopping Centre". Enjoy your stay in a cosy, relaxed atmosphere with friendly staff, who will advise you on travel arrangements, bookings etc. Make full use of all our facilities: large kitchen, lounge/dining room, beer garden, barbecue, ample showers, 2 twin rooms, 1 quad room, 5 six-bedded rooms, free tea and coffee, no curfew, cycle hire, internet access. Book-a-bed-ahead service. Children and groups **most** welcome. Book early for twin rooms. A'visit Scotland' 3* hostel.

www.Eastgatebackpackers.com

CONTACT Tel/Fax (01463) 718756,
Email: info@eastgatebackpackers.com
OPENING SEASON All year
OPENING HOURS Reception 8am-11pm. No curfew.
NUMBER OF BEDS 47
BOOKING REQUIREMENTS Booking required 2/3 weeks in advance in summer. 20% deposit for group bookings.
PRICE PER NIGHT from £10. Winter weekly rates. Discount for ISIC, ISE, VIP Backpackers, Young Scot and Citylink cards.

PUBLIC TRANSPORT
Inverness has a train station and is served by Citylink.

DIRECTIONS
Turn left outside train/bus stn, cross at traffic lights next to taxi rank. Walk to High St, turn left, in 50m you will see Eastgate Shopping Centre. We are opposite on the right. Enter next to Chinese takeaway.

INVERNESS TOURIST HOSTEL

24 Rose Street
Inverness
IV1 1NQ

Situated in the beautiful city of Inverness - one of the fastest growing cities in Europe and the capital of the Scottish Highlands, our newest hostel offers top quality traveller and tourist accommodation for individuals as well as small and large groups. We are fully equipped with a modern shared kitchen, lounge/dining area with wide-screen plasma TV and DVD player, internet access and complimentary tea & coffee.

Our friendly staff will be happy to arrange highland tours for you with a selection of the best tour operators in Scotland or offer help and advice in planning trips of your own.

The Inverness Tourist Hostel is the ideal location for exploring the wilds of Scotland or enjoying a relaxed city break with interesting people from around the world.

www.hostelsaccommodation.com

CONTACT Reception, Tel: (01463) 241 962 , Fax: (01463) 241 574, Email: info@invernesshostel.com
OPENING SEASON All Year
OPENING HOURS 8am - 11pm
NUMBER OF BEDS 60
BOOKING REQUIREMENTS Advance booking advisable during the summer. Booking for groups essential with 25% deposit.
PRICE PER NIGHT From £11 per person. Weekly rates available off peak. Student discount available.

PUBLIC TRANSPORT
The hostel is directly beside the main bus terminal and just 5 minutes from the train station.

DIRECTIONS
From Inverness train station turn right onto Academy Street, down two blocks and take 2nd right. The hostel is next to the bus station.

1m

BALINTRAID BACKPACKERS

Balintraid House
Balintraid
by Invergordon
Ross-shire, IV18 OLY

Balintraid Backpackers is a rambling house in a beautiful location looking directly out onto historic Cromarty Firth. It offers a comfortable alternative to staying in Inverness when driving North or West, or an ideal location to base your Highland holiday. Locally you can see dolphins, seals, swans and migrating birds in the firth. Take a short drive to Shin Falls or Rogie Falls and see salmon leaping up the waterfalls. Explore the Pictish Trail, sample whisky at nearby Glenmorangie Distillery and maybe catch sight of that elusive haggis on 'dem hills as you enjoy walks to the Fyrish monument, Ben Wyvis and numerous others. Discover original Caledonian forests at Glen Affric. Visit a castle or two. Relax to traditional feis music at local venues and hotels. Facilities include a well-equipped kitchen, centrally heated, warm duvets and comfy beds, internet access, table tennis and badminton, piano and small library. Camping okay in grounds. Free range eggs available, and tea/coffee.

www.balintraidbackpackers.co.uk

CONTACT Petria, Tel: (01349) 854446,
Email: petria@balintraid.fsworld.co.uk
OPENING SEASON All Year
OPENING HOURS 24 Hours
NUMBER OF BEDS 10: flexible, single/double/family/group dorm.
BOOKING REQUIREMENTS Advisable, groups require deposit.
PRICE PER NIGHT £10 per adult, £5 per child

PUBLIC TRANSPORT
Citylink/Stagecoach stop at house. Trains from Inverness (Thurso/Wick) will stop at Invergordon. Phone for pick up, 3 miles away.

DIRECTIONS
26 miles north of Inverness. Turn off A9 for Invergordon and follow coastal road (B817) northwards for 2 miles, passing through small village of Saltburn. After the last house there are two big fields then a clump of trees. Balintraid signposted into the trees.

 See page 205 for colour photo

SLEEPERZZZ.COM

Rogart Station
Sutherland
IV28 3XA

Stay on a first class train in Rogart in the heart of the Highlands halfway between Inverness and John O'Groats. The two railway carriages have been tastefully converted, with many original features. Each sleeps 8, with two beds per room, and has a kitchen, dining room, sitting room and two showers and toilets. They are heated and non-smoking. All bedding is included. We also have a cosy showman's wagon which sleeps two.

Three trains per day in each direction serve this small crofting community which has a shop, post office and pub with restaurant. Glenmorangie and Clynelish distilleries, Dunrobin Castle and Helmsdale's Heritage Centre are easy to reach by train or car. See the silver salmon leap at Lairg and the seabirds and seals in Loch Fleet. Or just enjoy the peace of Rogart. The climate is good and the midges are less prevalent than in the west! Families welcome. Free use of bikes for guests.

www.sleeperzzz.com

CONTACT Kate or Frank, Tel: (01408) 641343. Mob 07833 641226
Email: kate@sleeperzzz.com
OPENING SEASON All year
OPENING HOURS 24 hours
NUMBER OF BEDS 22: 8 x 2 : 1 x 4 : 1 x 2.
BOOKING REQUIREMENTS Booking is not essential.
PRICE PER NIGHT £10 per person, (10% discount for rail users and cyclists).

PUBLIC TRANSPORT
Wick to Inverness trains stop at the door.

DIRECTIONS
We are at the railway station, 4 miles from the A9 trunk road, 54 miles north of Inverness.

SÀIL MHÓR CROFT

Camusnagaul
Dundonnell
Ross-shire IV23 2QT

Sàil Mhór Croft is a small rural hostel which is situated at Dundonnell on the shores of Little Loch Broom. The mountain range of An Teàllach, which has the reputation of being one of the finest ridge walks in Great Britain, is right on our doorstep and the area is a haven for walkers of all experience as well as for photographers. Whether you wish to climb the summits, walk along the loch side, visit a beautiful sandy beach or just soak up the tranquillity of the area, you know the scenery cannot be beaten anywhere in the country.

The hostel offers accommodation for up to 16 persons in three dorms which are fitted with anti-midge screens. Guests have a choice of using our self-catering facilities or we can provide a full breakfast. It is advisable to ring in advance in order to book yourself a bed, the next self-catering hostel is many miles away.

www.sailmhor.co.uk

CONTACT Dave or Lynda, Tel: (01854) 633224,
Email: sailmhor@btopenworld.com
OPENING SEASON All year, except Xmas and New Year
OPENING HOURS Flexible
NUMBER OF BEDS 16:- 2 x 4 : 1 x 8
BOOKING REQUIREMENTS Always phone in advance. Groups should book as soon as possible.
PRICE PER NIGHT £10per person, self-catering. Sole use £130.

PUBLIC TRANSPORT
Unfortunately we are situated in an area of outstanding beauty which is not served well by public transport. Nearest train station is Inverness (60 miles). Nearest City Link bus drop off is Braemore Junction (15 miles). Wester bus passes the hostel 3 times a week; Mon, Wed and Sat., it also provides a service between Gairloch and Ullapool on Thursday afternoon. New to the area is a daily - return 'summer only' service between Inverness - Ullapool and Gairloch.

DIRECTIONS
GR 064 893 (sheet 19) 1½ miles west of Dundonnell Hotel on A832.

RUA REIDH LIGHTHOUSE

Melvaig
Gairloch
IV21 2EA

Perched on the cliff tops 12 miles north of Gairloch, Rua Reidh Lighthouse must have one of the most dramatic settings of all the Scottish Hostels. The lighthouse still beams out its light over the Minch to the Outer Isles and Skye, but since its automation the adjoining house, no longer needed for keepers, has been converted into a comfortable independent hostel.

The centrally heated house has two sitting rooms with log fires, a self-catering kitchen, a drying room, three private rooms and four dorms (each sleeping four), some rooms with en-suite shower. Meals are available from the main dining room and guided walking and rock sports sessions are also offered. The area of the lighthouse is unspoiled and makes a perfect place to watch for whales, dolphins etc. For an *away from it all experience* travel to the 'edge of the world' and Rua Reidh Lighthouse.

CONTACT Tel: (01445) 771263,
Email: ruareidh@netcomuk.co.uk
OPENING SEASON All year (except last 3 weeks in Jan)
OPENING HOURS 9am - 11pm
NUMBER OF BEDS 24: 1 x 6 : 2 x 4 : 5 x 2.
BOOKING REQUIREMENTS Pre-booking advisable.
PRICE PER NIGHT £9.50 (small dorm) to £17.00 (private twin/double room with en-suite facilities)

PUBLIC TRANSPORT
Nearest train station Achnasheen (40 miles). Nearest Citylink coaches Inverness (80 miles). Westerbus (01445) 712255 run a daily connection between Inverness/Gairloch (12 miles from hostel).

DIRECTIONS
From Gairloch take the road signed Big Sands and Melvaig, follow this road for 12 miles to the lighthouse. The last 3 miles is a private road with speed limit of 20 mph.

BADRALLACH BOTHY, COTTAGE, B&B & CAMPING SITE

Croft No 9, Badrallach, Dundonnell
Ross-shire, IV23 2QP

On the tranquil shores of Little Loch Broom overlooking An Teallach, one of Scotland's finest mountain ranges, Badrallach Bothy and Camp Site with its welcoming traditional buildings offers a fine base for walking and climbing in the hills of Wester Ross, Caithness and Sutherland. You can fish in the rivers, hill lochs and sea, or simply watch the flora and fauna including many orchids, golden eagles, otters, porpoises, pine martens, deer and wild goats. Guests often sit around the peat stove in the gas light (there is now electric here too) and discuss life over a dram or two. Hot showers, spotless sanitary accommodation (STB graded 4 star excellent) an unbelievable price (thanks to S.N.H), and the total peace makes our Bothy and camp site (12 tents only) one that visitors return to year after year. We also have a cottage to let (STB 4 star) and offer B&B (STB 4 star) in July and August for even more luxury. Hire canoes, kites, bikes or boats.

www.badrallach.com

CONTACT Mr/Mrs Stott, Tel: (01854) 633281,
Email: michael.stott2@virgin.net
OPENING SEASON All year
OPENING HOURS All times
NUMBER OF BEDS 12 plus bedspaces (Alpine style platforms). We have had 20 at a squeeze, mats & sleeping bags required.
BOOKING REQUIREMENTS Recommended
PRICE PER NIGHT £4 per person. £1.50 per vehicle. £50 sole use.

PUBLIC TRANSPORT
Train stations, Inverness,Dingwall,Garve (30miles). Citylink Braemore Junction (12miles) on Inverness to Ullapool route. Westerbus (01445 712255) operate Mon/Wed/Sat between Inverness/Gairloch, drops at road end Dundonnell, 7 miles from hostel. Pick-up can be arranged. Ullapool/Altnaharrie foot ferry in summer (2 miles).

DIRECTIONS
GR 065 915 Located on shore of Little Loch Broom 7 miles along a single track road off the A832, one mile east of the Dundonnell Hotel.

CEILIDH PLACE BUNKHOUSE

West Argyle Street
Ullapool, IV26 2TY

The Ceilidh Place is a small complex consisting of a music venue/ performance space, restaurant, hotel, bar, bookshop, coffee room, gallery and bunkhouse. There are regular ceilidhs and concerts (sometimes jazzy/classical) at the Ceilidh Place. We also have visits from folk musicians and small touring theatre companies. The bunkhouse does not have self-catering facilities but the coffee shop is open from 8.30am to late evening, 7 days a week. It serves hot food, soups, salads, great coffee and cakes and is a super place to relax, read and write cards or memoirs.

The village of Ullapool is a small exciting port and fishing town, with ferries from the Outer Hebrides. The Ceilidh Place is in the centre of the village of Ullapool. It is also next to the camp site. The bunkhouse is much favoured by hill walkers and families as an ideal base for touring Wester Ross.

Phone Effie for more information today.

CONTACT Effie, Tel: (01854) 612103,
Email: stay@theceilidhplace.com
OPENING SEASON All year
OPENING HOURS Service 8am to midnight.
NUMBER OF BEDS 30
BOOKING REQUIREMENTS Booking is advisable in summer.
PRICE PER NIGHT £15 to £18 per person.

PUBLIC TRANSPORT
Nearest train station is Garve (33 miles). Citylink coaches from Inverness stop at Ullapool pier a short walk from the Hostel. Phone (0990 505050) for details. Also leaving from the pier are ferries to Stornoway on the Isle of Lewis.

DIRECTIONS
Turn right after the pier and first left. Check in at Ceilidh Place reception.

P

INCHNADAMPH LODGE

Inchnadamph, Assynt
Nr Lochinver, Sutherland
IV27 4HL

Situated at the heart of the dramatic Assynt mountains, Inchnadamph Lodge has been tastefully converted to provide luxury hostel accommodation at a budget price. Twin, family and dormitory (4-8 people) rooms are available and a continental-style breakfast is included. There are a self-catering kitchen, lounge and dining room (with real fires), study facilities and games room. Packed lunches are available on request and bar meals are served at the Inchnadamph Hotel. At the foot of Ben More Assynt, and overlooking Loch Assynt, you are free to explore one of the wildest areas in the Highlands. Mountains can be climbed from our door! Within walking distance are two National Nature Reserves which are home to a wide diversity of birds, plants and animals. Interesting rock formations provide excitement for geologists. Nearby lochs are popular for fly fishing. Details and photos on our website

www.inchnadamphlodge.co.uk

CONTACT Chris, Tel: (01571) 822218, Fax: (01571) 822232,
Email: info@inchnadamphlodge.co.uk
OPENING SEASON All year - phone November-March inclusive
OPENING HOURS 24 hours
NUMBER OF BEDS 38: 8x2 : 7x2 : 4x2 (dormitory) 12 (twin/double)
BOOKING REQUIREMENTS Advised, required Nov-March.
PRICE PER NIGHT £10.50-£12pp (dormitory) £16.50-£18 (twin room) inc continental breakfast and linen. Group discounts.

PUBLIC TRANSPORT
Transport is available to our door from Inverness 6 days a week, either by train to Lairg and then postbus, or by coach to Ullapool and minibus to Inchnadamph. Times vary - please call us for details.

DIRECTIONS
Inchnadamph is 25 miles north of Ullapool on the Lochinver/Durness road. The lodge is the big white building across the river from hotel.

SANDRA'S BACKPACKERS HOSTEL

24-26 Princes Street
Thurso
Caithness
KW14 7BQ

Thurso is the northern most town on the UK mainland. Caithness has a rich history which can be traced back to its Viking roots. The cliffs are spectacular and every narrow rock ledge is alive with guillemots, kittiwakes, fulmars and posing puffins. The wildlife off shore is equally fascinating where seals and porpoises haunt the surf. A great way to experience both the coast and the wildlife is to take one of the boat trips around the coast.

The Hostel has recently been upgraded and extended. Using their own backpacking experience the owners have developed a level of luxury and service which ranks it amongst the top places to stay. Bike hire is available from the Hostel, surfing, pony trekking, fishing, quad biking are all available in the area. 10% discount on food from the adjoining, family-run Snack Bar. Free transport to Scrabster for 12 noon Orkney Ferry.

www.sandras-backpackers.ukf.net

CONTACT George, Tel: (01847) 894575,
Email: Sandras-backpackers@ukf.net
OPENING SEASON All Year
OPENING HOURS 24 Hours
NUMBER OF BEDS 30: 4 x 4 - 1 x 6 - 3 x 2 (or 3) beds
BOOKING REQUIREMENTS Advisable, deposit please for groups.
PRICE PER NIGHT Dorm £10, Double/Twin £28

PUBLIC TRANSPORT
Train Station 10 minutes' walk. Bus stop 2 minutes' walk.

DIRECTIONS
From train station follow Princes Street downhill to Sandra's. Buses stop on St George Street, walk uphill (2 mins) lst right, lst left and 1st right again to Princes Street. By car or bike follow A9 to Olrig St, take junction opposite Bank onto bottom end of Princes Street.

P AM 1m

THURSO YOUTH CLUB HOSTEL

Old Mill, Millbank Rd
Thurso, KW14 8PS

Our hostel occupies a converted 200-year-old water mill and is ideally located overlooking river and park. We provide clean, comfortable accommodation in a friendly environment. A warden is on duty throughout the day to provide any assistance you may require, there is no curfew. Our facilities include a large fully-equipped kitchen, dining area, games room, TV & video lounge, secure cycle storage and private parking. Thurso, the largest town on the north coast of Scotland, is on Route 1 of the National Cycle Network leading to John O'Groats. We provide the perfect base for exploring the surrounding area and a convenient stopover for all travel connections. The Orkney Islands ferry sails from nearby Scrabster. This area has many archaeological sites and the outdoor activities available include fly fishing, surfing, horse riding, bird watching, swimming, sea angling, cycling and golf. **www.tyc-hostel.com**

CONTACT Allan Hourston, Tel: (01847) 892964
Email: t.y.c.hostel@btinternet.com
OPENING SEASON July and August (all year for groups)
OPENING HOURS All day, no curfew
NUMBER OF BEDS 22: 1 x 4 : 1 x 8 : 1 x 10
BOOKING REQUIREMENTS Booking essential for large groups.
PRICE PER NIGHT £9 (includes continental breakfast and use of internet and laundry facilities). Discount for groups of 10+

PUBLIC TRANSPORT
Thurso train station, Citylink bus stops, local buses to Wick, John O'Groats & Scrabster & post bus connections to Tongue & Durness are all 5 minutes' walk from hostel.

DIRECTIONS
By foot:- From T. Info Centre, follow river past road traffic bridge to foot bridge, cross the river, the hostel is in front of you. From railway station, turn right, Lovers Lane, at bottom turn left, walk 25m, turn right, cross the foot bridge. **By car**:- Millbank Road is at east end of road bridge, turn down where theatre is signposted.

P AM 1m

ORKNEY ISLANDS

Summer passenger Ferry from
JOHN O'GROATS

MV Pentland Venture Every Day 1 May to 30 September 2005.

Every day	Dep John O'Groats				Dep Burwick (Orkney)			
1 May-31 May	9am			6pm	9.45pm			7pm
1 June-2 Sept	9am	10.30am	4pm	6pm	9.45pm	11.30am	5.15pm	7pm
3 Sept-30 Sept	9am			4.30pm	9.45pm			5.30pm

Special off peak return to Kirkwall.

£24

Depart John O'Groats mid afternoon.
Return from Orkney any morning.
(Free transfer for ferry meets afternoon train approx 2.45pm at Thurso Rail Station every day).

OR, Travel to & from Orkney direct from
INVERNESS
on
The Orkney Bus

Special return fare £42

Every Day	Dep Inverness (Northbound)	Arrive Kirkwall	Dep Kirkwall (Southbound)	Arrive Inverness
1 May-31May	2.20pm	7.30pm	9.0am	1.45pm
1 June-2 Sept	7.30am	12.05pm	9.0am	1.45pm
	2.20pm	7.30pm	*4.15pm	9.00pm

JOHN O'GROATS FERRIES, Ferry Office

John O'Groats, Caithness, KW1 4YR.

Tel (01955) 611353 FAX (01955) 611301

www.jogferry.co.uk Freephone 0800 7317872

* Telephone (01955) 611 353 to book 7.30am from Inverness and 4.15pm from Kirkwall

BROWNS

Stromness
Orkney
KW16 3BS

independent backpackers hostels · scotland ·

This family run accommodation is ideally situated in the centre of a small fishing town, **Stromness**. It makes an excellent base for the tourist - a few minutes' walk from the ferry terminal and bus stops. There is a bus service to Kirkwall every few hours Monday to Saturday. Bus tours also run every day and cycles are available for hire to visit the various sites of interest - **Skara Brae, Maeshowe, Standing Stones** etc. Ferries run to the smaller islands daily.
In summer there is daylight all evening and one can stroll through our peaceful town and along the shore to watch the seals. Our kitchen/common room looks onto the street and has one big table where everybody gathers around to chat often into the late evening. There are pubs and restaurants all nearby, some evenings they have locals singing and playing in them. There is a provisions shop and bakehouse across the street that opens at 7.30am selling new bread and rolls for your breakfast.

CONTACT : Sylvia Brown, Tel: (01856) 850661
OPENING SEASON All year
OPENING HOURS All day. No curfew, keys provided with a deposit.
NUMBER OF BEDS 12: 3 x 1 : 3 x 2 : 1 x 3.
BOOKING REQUIREMENTS Booking advisable during March to October. Pre-paid booking secure (sae for receipt). Tel bookings kept only for limited time.
PRICE PER NIGHT From £10.00 per person (inc linen).

PUBLIC TRANSPORT
Train or bus to Thurso, bus 2 miles to Scrabster then boat to Stromness. Alternatively from Gills Bay to St Margarets Hope by boat or John O'Groats by boat to Burwick then bus to Stromness via Kirkwall.

DIRECTIONS
Browns accommodation is near to the harbour in Stromness, just 5 minutes along street.

STRONSAY FISHMART

Whitehall Village
Stronsay
Orkney
KW17 2AR

This family run hostel is ideally situated in the small fishing village of Whitehall, built on the sea front it is only 100yds from the ferry terminal. Some rooms overlook the harbour where you can see seals and other wildlife from the comfort of your room. Stronsay Fishmart Hostel has three bedrooms and a self-catering kitchen with dining area.

The Fishmart also includes a café and a heritage centre showing the history of Stronsay and its key position in the herring trade. The village includes a pub, shop and post office. Taxis are available to allow you to explore the many walks and beaches on the island. Stronsay has the most diverse bird population in Orkney and also one of the largest seal populations.

under 16's must be accommpanied by an adult

CONTACT Madeleine or Clive. Tel: (01857) 616386
Email:- Stronsayfishmart@yahoo.co.uk
OPENING SEASON All year
OPENING HOURS All day, no curfew, keys provided
NUMBER OF BEDS 10: 2 x 4 : 1 x 2
BOOKING REQUIREMENTS Not essential but recommended in high season
PRICE PER NIGHT £10 bedding required - £13 with bedding supplied. Breakfast available from café by arrangement

PUBLIC TRANSPORT
Daily Ferry and Air service to Orkney mainland.

DIRECTIONS
From the Ferry Terminal, The Fishmart is at the end of the pier on your right.

See page 207 for colour photo

BIS GEOS HOSTEL AND COTTAGES

Westray
Orkney
KW17 2DW

Traditional Orkney croft re-built to an exceptional standard situated above Westray's western cliffs, commanding a breathtaking view of Rousay, Orkney Mainland and Hoy silhouetted on the Southern horizon. The hostel has 12 bunks in 2 & 4 bed apartments, a large kitchen with modern appliances. Under floor heating, and a cosy conservatory.

Also available two cottages, "Family Cottage" 2 bedrooms sleeps 4-5 and "Peedie" small studio/cottage sleeps 2. Both are traditional cottages with open fires, modern appliances and underfloor heating. "Family Cottage" has a sauna and spa bath whilst "Peedie" has a cosy box bed.

An almost certain cure for stress!.
www.bis-geos.co.uk

CONTACT Alena Tulloch, Tel: (01857) 677420. Email via website
OPENING SEASON All year round
OPENING HOURS Open 24 hours
NUMBER OF BEDS 12: in hostel 2 x 4 : 2 x 2, plus 6/7 in cottages.
BOOKING REQUIREMENTS Booking is advised as hostel is becoming very popular.
PRICE PER NIGHT £11 high season. For groups/block bookings enquire via our website. Transport available from Ferry Terminal.

PUBLIC TRANSPORT
From Scottish mainland Gills Bay or Scrabster Ferry. From Kirkwall Westray Ferry to Rapness. Contact details for all ferries are on our website.

DIRECTIONS
Bis Geos is signposted from Westray village of Pierwall on road to Noup Head. Minibus available from Ferry Terminal. See website for maps and directions.

HURDIBACK BACKPACKERS HOSTEL

Hurdiback,
Papa Stour
Shetland
ZE2 9PW

Papa Stour is a beautiful unspoilt island, with spectacular cliffs and caves, ideal for walkers, bird watchers and photographers, or just to enjoy the fresh air and peace. Spot the seals, otters and the occasional dolphin or orca, you can also fish, canoe or hire a cycle. There are long hours of daylight in the summer and in the autumn and winter you can spy the northern lights. Glimpse the untamed wildness of this remote corner of the world.

Hurdiback is a comfortable bunk house on a working croft, overlooking a picturesque bay. There are two bedrooms and a kitchen/sitting room. Equipment includes electric cooker, microwave, toaster, kettle and fridge. Heating, bed-linen and towels are included in the price, a laundry service is available and we have a store-room of basic requirements.

www.papastour.shetland.co.uk

CONTACT Martin or Fay Tel: (01595) 873229
Email: fay@hurdiback.shetland.co.uk
OPENING SEASON All Year
OPENING HOURS 9-30am to 7-00pm
NUMBER OF BEDS : 8. 2 x 4
BOOKING REQUIREMENTS Advisable, groups require deposit.
PRICE PER NIGHT £10 per person

PUBLIC TRANSPORT
Ferry departs West Burrafirth, Fri, Sat Sun 1800 hrs, Mon and Wed 0900 hrs bookings (01595) 810460. Bus departs Viking Bus Station Lerwick Fri.Sat.1700, Feeder bus from Bixter to West Burrafirth. Booking required 24 hrs in advance (01595) 860266. By Air Loganair (01595) 840246.

DIRECTIONS
Hurdiback is signposted from the Ferry and Airport.

293
Galway
Ennis
291
Limerick
290
Tralee
289
Killarney
287
Cork
286
Bantry

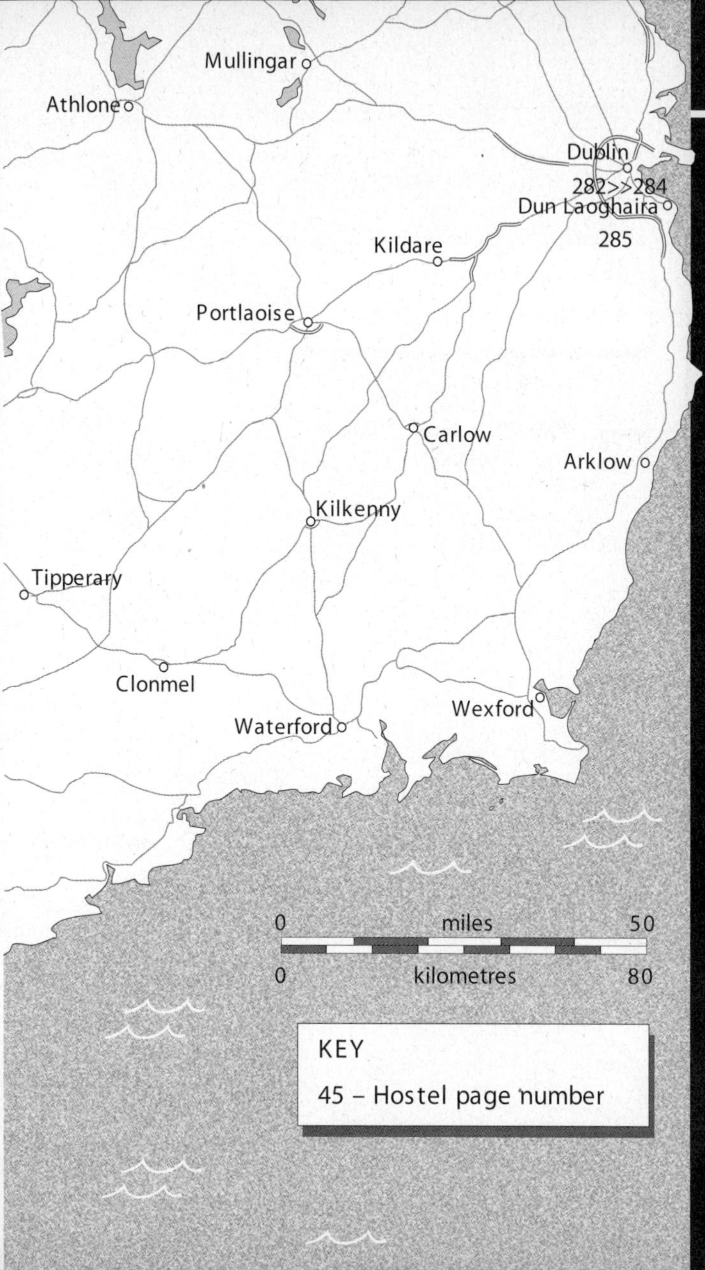

Mullingar
Athlone
Dublin
282>>284
Dun Laoghaira
285
Kildare
Portlaoise
Carlow
Arklow
Kilkenny
Tipperary
Clonmel
Wexford
Waterford

0 miles 50

0 kilometres 80

KEY

45 – Hostel page number

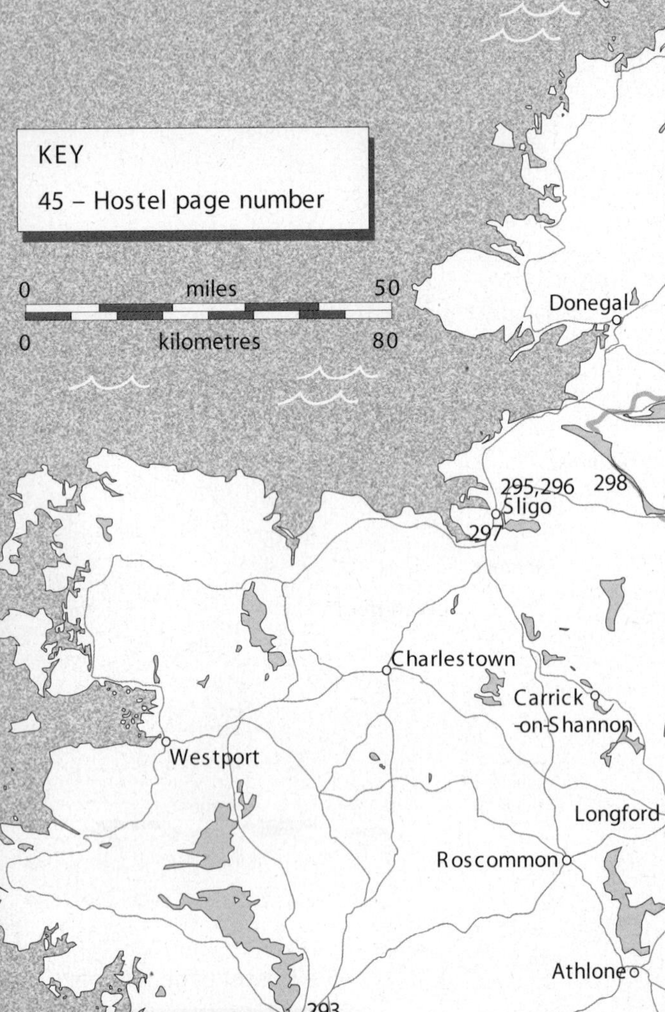
KEY
45 – Hostel page number
0 miles 50
0 kilometres 80
Donegal
295,296
Sligo
297
298
Charlestown
Carrick
-on-Shannon
Westport
294
Longford
Roscommon
Athlone
293
Galway

301
302
Coleraine
Londonderry
Ballymena
Larne
Strabane
300
299
Omagh
Cookstown
Belfast
Craigavon
Enniskillen
Armagh
303
Downpatrick
Newry
Newcastle
Belturbet
Cavan
Dundalk
Drogheda
Navan
Mullingar
282>>284
Dublin
Dun Laoghaira
Kildare
285

LITTON LANE HOSTEL

2-4 Litton Lane
Dublin 1

Litton Lane hostel is a small, cosy family run hostel located right in the middle of Dublin city centre. Beside O'Connell Street and the now famous Temple Bar, the hostel suits the traveller who wants to be in the thick of it!

The building was originally a recording studio to the likes of Van Morrison and Sinead O'Connor and has been converted to 8 and 10 bed dormitories and private rooms. Facilities include free luggage storage, internet access, free bed linen, TV lounge and a kitchen well equipped to cater for your needs. We also provide self-catering apartments next to the hostel at very competitive rates. You cannot beat Litton Lane for location in this exciting city.

www.irish-hostel.com

CONTACT Reception, Tel: (01) 872 8389
Email: litton@irish-hostel.com
OPENING SEASON All Year
OPENING HOURS 24 Hours
NUMBER OF BEDS 114 : 6 x 10, 6 x 8, 3 x 2
BOOKING REQUIREMENTS Booking in advance recommended. 10% deposit for groups.
PRICE PER NIGHT from € 15 pp for dorms. Private rooms from € 35 per person

PUBLIC TRANSPORT
Nearest train station is Connolly Station. From here walk to O'Connell Street and follow directions below. From ferry or airport take bus to O'Connell Street.

DIRECTIONS
Litton Lane is located off Batchelors Walk which runs along the River Liffy in the city centre. Coming from O'Connell Street turn right at the Halfpenny Bridge; Litton lane is then the second right.

ISAACS HOSTEL

2-5 Frenchmans Lane
Dublin 1

Isaacs Hostel is Dublin's first independent holiday hostel, situated in the city centre, five minutes from O'Connell Street Bridge, and adjacent to the City's central bus and train station. Originally a warehouse, the hostel still retains many of its original features and unique character. Accommodation is in dormitories, triple, twin/ double and single rooms with prices starting from €11.75 per person per night and includes a light breakfast. For the budget conscious traveller, Isaacs Hostel is definitely the perfect choice in Dublin. Meals are served all day in the friendly restaurant which offers good value meals. A fully equipped kitchen is also available for those who wish to cater for themselves. Facilities include Bureau de Change, free bed linen, free hot showers, bicycle storage, secure left luggage facilities, internet access and safes. Live music and BBQ's are on offer during the summer months. A visit to Dublin would not be complete without a visit to Isaacs.

Book online: www.dublinbackpacker.com

CONTACT Tel: (01) 8556215. Fax: (01) 8556574. Email: hostel@isaacs.ie
OPENING SEASON All year
OPENING HOURS 24 hours
NUMBER OF BEDS 263
BOOKING REQUIREMENTS Recommended especially in high season & weekends. Groups need a deposit. Credit cards accepted.
PRICE PER NIGHT €12pp (low season) €14pp (high season) for bunk in large dorm. €4 supplement on Friday/Saturday nights. Prices include light breakfast. Beds from €10 when you book online.

PUBLIC TRANSPORT
From Dublin Airport: take the airlink bus to Busaras (central bus station). **From Dun Laoghaire Ferryport:** take the DART into Connolly Station.

DIRECTIONS
Isaacs Hostel is one minute's walk from central bus station. From Connolly Station walk down Talbot Street take third on left for Isaacs.

JACOBS INN

21 - 28 Talbot Place
Dublin 1

Definitely the crème de la crème in budget accommodation. Jacobs Inn is situated in Dublin city centre just minutes by foot from the main bus and train stations, the shopping centre and the main visitor attractions.

All rooms are en-suite with shower. Accommodation is offered in twin, triple, family and multi-bedded rooms. Facilities include self-catering kitchen, restaurant (open all day), lift, Bureau de Change, TV Lounge with nightly video shows, left luggage facilities, internet access and key card access to all rooms. There are safes in all rooms (small charge). Linen is provided in all rooms and towels are provided in twin, triple and family rooms. Towel hire is also available.

Book online: www.dublinbackpacker.com

CONTACT Sharon, Tel: (01) 8555660, Fax: (01) 8555664.
Email: jacobs@isaacs.ie
OPENING SEASON Closed 23rd to 27th December
OPENING HOURS 24 hours
NUMBER OF BEDS 297: 4xtwin : 5xtriple : 4x4 : 2x6 : 12x8 : 15x10
BOOKING REQUIREMENTS Recommended in high season and at weekends. Deposit required for group reservations and private rooms. Credit cards accepted.
PRICE PER NIGHT €15 (low season) €17 (high season) per person, for multi-bed accommodation. €4 supplement on Friday and Saturday nights. Prices include light breakfast. Special offers from €10 when you book online.

PUBLIC TRANSPORT
From Dublin Airport: take the airlink bus to Busaras (central bus station). **From Dun Laoghaire Ferryport:** take the DART into Connolly Station.

DIRECTIONS
Jacobs Inn is adjacent to the police station opposite to bus station. From Connolly Station go down Talbot Street and take first road on the left.

GLENCREE CENTRE FOR RECONCILIATION

Glencree
Enniskerry
Co Wicklow

Glencree Centre for reconciliation is a unique organisation in Ireland dedicated to peace-building and reconciliation. Glencree Centre is located 12 miles from the centre of Dublin and 7 miles from Enniskerry Village.

This beautiful location is an ideal setting for groups or individuals looking for space and tranquillity in which to work and explore the countryside.

The Centre has shared accommodation for up to 50 people in 2,3,4 bedded rooms plus one 11 bedded dormitory. All rooms are clean and comfortable. We have 6 en-suite rooms, including one with wheelchair facilities.

www.glencree-cfr.ie

CONTACT Tel: (01) 2829711 Fax: (01) 2766085
Email : Admin@glencree-cfr.ie
OPENING SEASON January - December
OPENING HOURS 24 hours
NUMBER OF BEDS 53: 1 x 11 : 2 x 4 : 6 x 3 : 8 x 2
BOOKING REQUIREMENTS Booking is essential with a deposit of 25 %
PRICE PER NIGHT € 20 Bed and continental breakfast.

PUBLIC TRANSPORT
Nearest train station Bray Dart 9 miles, hourly bus (No.185) runs from the station to Enniskerry 6 miles from Glencree. At 9am & 6pm each day a bus will take you direct to Glencree from Bray Dart Station.

DIRECTIONS .
In Enniskerry take the road to the right of the monument, up the hill towards Glencree for 6 miles. The centre is on the left just past the German war cemetery and the youth hostel.

 See page 203 for colour photo

PAR FOUR HOSTEL

Glengarriff Road
Donemark, Bantry
Co Cork

Welcome to Par Four Hostel, this is a small hostel, family run and catering for up to 10 people, it has lovely bright rooms looking out onto gardens. There are full cooking facilities and lovely hot showers. You may rent you own self-catering unit but because of its popularity you will need to book in advance. There are views across to Bantry Bay Golf Club and the sea.

Location wise it is superb being directly off the main road yet just a short hop from Bantry which has everything you might need, including a great choice of restaurants serving excellent food and for those who enjoy the pub, there is plenty of craic and traditional music. During the summer there are festivals, horse trotting, fishing, classical music, walking weekends and golf. There is still a traditional market on Fridays where locals and visitors meet. Whether on a relaxing break or just passing through there is always a friendly welcome, *you will not miss our sign.*

www.parfourbantry.com

CONTACT Bronagh Sweeney Tel: (027) 50205
Email: Par4bantry@eircom.net
OPENING SEASON All year
OPENING HOURS All day
NUMBER OF BEDS 10: 1x4 : 2x2 : 1x2 en-suite
BOOKING REQUIREMENTS Please telephone in advance
PRICE PER NIGHT from €13pp- €18pp. 50% reduction for children. From €200 per week self-catering unit.

PUBLIC TRANSPORT
Nearest train station Cork. Bus from Bantry daily.

DIRECTIONS
Take the N71 out of Bantry approximately one mile, (pass Esso Station). Par Four is the third entrance past Bantry Pitch and Putt and opposite Golf Course.

FÁILTE HOSTEL

Shelbourne St
Kenmare
Co Kerry

Opposite the Kenmare Post Office you will find the warm and welcoming Fáilte Hostel. Our wonderfully clean and well run hostel is an ideal base from which to explore the 'Ring of Béara' and 'Ring of Kerry'.

This home from home has kitchen facilities including an Aga Cooker and hot water. Coffee - Tea - Sugar --- FREE. Those not wanting to cook will find meals available locally.

The hostel is centrally heated including the common room and also has free hot showers and drying facilities. The beds are to be found in small dormitories and private rooms, with sheets and duvets provided. To ensure a good night's sleep a 1.30am curfew is observed.

CONTACT Tel: (064) 42333 Fax : (064) 42466
Email : failtefinn@eircom.net
OPENING SEASON 1st April to 31st October
OPENING HOURS All day, 1.30am curfew
NUMBER OF BEDS 39: 3 x 2 : 2 x 4 : 1 x 5 : 2 x 6 : 1 x 8
BOOKING REQUIREMENTS Please book in writing with 33% booking fee.or Visa Credit Card: number+name+expiry date
PRICE PER NIGHT €14 (dorm) €18 to €22 (double room/twin) €15 - €19.50 (private room for 3/4/5/6)

PUBLIC TRANSPORT
Bus to Killarney daily. Bus to Sneem, Cork and Castletownbere during the summer season. For details contact Bus Eireann (064) 34777.

DIRECTIONS
The hostel is opposite the post office in Kenmare town.

MARINA INN

Strand Street
Dingle
Co. Kerry

Dingle is the best town in Ireland for traditional music which is available 363 days a year (every day except Christmas Day and Good Friday). This is a fabulous fishing village sitting on the West Coast of Ireland, (Next stop - New York) and is in one of the few native Irish speaking parts of the island.

Dingle also hosts "Fungi" the dolphin who lives in Dingle Bay alone. He has been here for 16 years and loves swimming with people in the mornings. Great spot!!!!!

The Marina Inn offers basic private room accommodation, we have four rooms (3 family and one twin) the family rooms have wash basins and views overlooking the Pier in Dingle. We offer an extensive menu of fresh seafood and are highly recommended locally for quality and value, "Best fish and chips you'll get anywhere".

CONTACT Gavin O'Grady Tel: +353 (0) 66-9151660
Email GOGRADY90@hotmail.com
OPENING SEASON April until September
OPENING HOURS All day
NUMBER OF BEDS :- **11** 3 x 3 - 1 x 2
BOOKING REQUIREMENTS Not essential
PRICE PER NIGHT from €20 pp €30 per room (2 or 3 beds).

PUBLIC TRANSPORT
Buses run every day from Tralee which links to everywhere in Ireland by bus or by train.

DIRECTIONS
Bus stops 250m from Main Pier. There is a car park by the main Pier or you can park on the street. The Marina Inn is at the top of the Pier.

MOUNT BRANDON HOSTEL

Cloghane
Castlegregory
Co Kerry

Mount Brandon Hostel is situated at the foot of Ireland's second highest mountain in one of the most unspoiled areas of Ireland. The beautiful village of Cloghane is on the Dingle Peninsula in the scenic region of Western Ireland.

Mount Brandon Hostel was originally built with the customer's needs in mind. All bedrooms are en-suite. There is a fully equipped self-catering kitchen which allows the guests to cater for themselves The hostel is built on the water's edge with panoramic views from the television lounge, the dining area and many of the bedrooms. The hostel provides a perfect base for hillwalkers and fishermen, the ideal place to relax and soak up the magnificent views and atmosphere of the area.

www.mountbrandonhostel.com

CONTACT Ingo. Tel: (066) 7138299. Email: ILockingen@aol.com
OPENING SEASON All year
OPENING HOURS All day
NUMBER OF BEDS 37: 7 x 2 : 3 x 4 : 1 x 5 : 1 x 6
BOOKING REQUIREMENTS Advisable. 2 weeks' notice with deposit
PRICE PER NIGHT Dormitory €17pp, single room €25, twin €20pp.

PUBLIC TRANSPORT
On Fridays there is a bus to and from Tralee.

DIRECTIONS
From Tralee follow the main road via Camp to Dingle, follow direction to Conor Pass, turn off at the foot of the Pass to Brandon.

JAMAICA INN

Sixmilebridge
Co Clare

Jamaica Inn is a comfortable, modern hostel located in the village of Sixmilebridge in East Clare. Nearby are signposted walking routes, numerous lakes and rivers. Visitor attractions are Bunratty Castle and Folkpark, Cragaunowen celtic site, and Quin Abbey. Ten miles away are the towns of Limerick and Ennis.

Jamaica Inn has off-street parking, a laundry and drying room, a restaurant, self-catering kitchen, a small TV room and large common room. We have dorms and private rooms. All rooms are heated and linen is provided.

www.jamaicainn.ie

CONTACT Michael McNamara, Tel: (061) 369220, Fax: (061) 369377
Email: info@jamaicainn.ie
OPENING SEASON All year
OPENING HOURS 08.30 to 22.00
NUMBER OF BEDS 62: 3 x 10 : 6 x 4 : 4 x 2.
BOOKING REQUIREMENTS Groups need to book in advance.
PRICE PER NIGHT €16 to €35.

PUBLIC TRANSPORT
3 buses daily from Limerick rail and bus stations and from Shannon Airport to Sixmilebridge. Taxi fare Shannon/Sixmilebridge €15.

DIRECTIONS
N18 & R462 from Limerick, N19 & R471 from Shannon Airport. N18 & R471 from Ennis. Hostel is in the centre of the village of Sixmilebridge and is signposted.

SLEEPZONE GALWAY CITY AND CONNEMARA

Bothar na mBan
Woodquay
Galway City
Co Galway

Sleepzone serves as the perfect gateway to the beautiful West of Ireland. We can arrange packaged or customized tours to the Aran Islands, Cliffs of Moher, The Burren and Connemara.

Sleepzone Galway City is situated in the centre of Galway City only three minutes from the bus and rail terminal and close to pubs, cafés and restaurants. The accommodation is spacious with nearly 200 beds in en-suite rooms, there is a fully equipped self-catering kitchen, TV lounge and barbecue terrace. We offer free internet access, free WiFi, 24-hour reception, bureau de change and safety deposit boxes. We ask that under 16's are accompanied by an adult/ supervisor.

Sleepzone Connemara, Leenane, Co Galway, overlooking beautiful Killary Harbour, will be opening in Spring 2005.

www.sleepzone.ie

CONTACT Ronan Garvey Tel: (91) 566999. Fax: (91) 566996
Email: info@sleepzone.ie
OPENING SEASON All Year except 3 days at Christmas
OPENING HOURS 24 Hours
NUMBER OF BEDS 196: 10,8,6,4,2(double or twin) and 1 bed dorms.
BOOKING REQUIREMENTS Credit card to reserve. Advance payment for groups.
PRICE PER NIGHT €13pp to €18pp-Dorm. €15 to €60-Room. According to season and accommodation.

PUBLIC TRANSPORT
Bus and Rail Terminals within three minutes' walk.

DIRECTIONS
From Bus and Rail Terminal go to opposite corner of Eyre Square and turn right (see Cuba Bar on your left). Take next turn left (Bothar na mBan). Sleepzone is 80 metres down on the left hand side.

INISHBOFIN ISLAND HOSTEL

Inishbofin
Co Galway

This hostel is situated in one of Irelands's most westerly islands. Inishbofin is a beautiful island with several magnificent sandy beaches which are safe for swimming. The island (population 200) has two hotels, a pub, restaurants, post office and one grocery shop. It is also well known for its excellent traditional music sessions.

The hostel itself was originally a traditional farmhouse which has been converted into a modern hostel which retains all the character and charm of the old building. Its large conservatory offers spectacular views of the Connemara Mountains and coastline. It has a cosy sitting room, complete with a stove and a good selection of books and magazines. We have family rooms to suit 3 to 8 people, private rooms and small dorms plus a self-catering kitchen.

Under 16's must be accompanied by an adult

www.inishbofin-hostel.ie

CONTACT Kieran or Theresa. Tel: (095) 45855
Email enquiries@inishbofin-hostel.ie
OPENING SEASON Easter to September inclusive
OPENING HOURS All day
NUMBER OF BEDS 38
BOOKING REQUIREMENTS Booking can be made on the day - deposit required for advance booking.
PRICE PER NIGHT Dorm €12 pp, private room €16-€18pp (sharing).Camping is allowed at €7 per night

PUBLIC TRANSPORT
Michael Nee's private bus company runs a daily service to Cleggan during the summer months, for further details contact (095) 51082. Bus Eireann has scheduled runs daily (091) 562000.

DIRECTIONS
Turn right at the end of the pier. The hostel is situated 700 metres from the pier on the road to the east village.

HARBOUR HOUSE HOSTEL

Finisklin Road
Sligo
Co Sligo

Built in the early 1800s for the city's Harbour Master, this house has been converted into clean comfortable accommodation. With most of the rooms en-suite, from spacious dorms to family, twin, double and single rooms. Custom made pine bunks with good mattresses will add to the comfort of your stay.
Harbour House is situated only ten minutes' walk from the centre of Sligo town and the main train and bus terminus for the north west of Ireland. For groups we can also arrange walking tours, golfing holidays and coarse or sea angling trips, all with the benefit of local guides. Your group can enjoy a continental breakfast or use our self-catering facilities for tea, coffee and snacks. Car/coach parking is available. We are Let's Go Ireland recommended and Irish Tourist Board approved

www.harbourhousehostel.com

CONTACT Tel: (071) 9171547 mob 0862598293
Email: harbourhouse@eircom.net
OPENING SEASON All year
OPENING HOURS Reception open until 10pm
NUMBER OF BEDS 50
BOOKING REQUIREMENTS Booking essential for groups and twin rooms. Credit card secures booking.
PRICE PER NIGHT Dorm €16pp to €18pp. Twin €20pp to €25pp

PUBLIC TRANSPORT
Sligo has trains and buses from Dublin. Buses from Belfast 3 a day, from Derry 5 a day and from Galway 6 a day. Harbour House is 10 minutes' walk from bus and train stations. Sligo Airport 5 kilometres.

DIRECTIONS
From Train/bus station, left onto Lord Edward Street, left at traffic lights to Union Street and left again at Poitin Still. Follow Finisklin Road to the junction of Ballast Quay. By car from Donegal or N Ireland (N15) turn right at end of Hughes Bridge follow Ballast Quay to the junction of Finisklin Road.

EDEN HILL HOLIDAY HOSTEL

Marymount, Pearse Road
Co Sligo

This tastefully converted Victorian house, owned for 40 years by the first cousin of W.B.Yeats, is exceptionally clean and comfortable. It sits in a quiet cul-de-sac just off the main Dublin/Donegal road. Many of the rooms have beautiful mountain views and first class customer care is our absolute priority. Situated just 10 minutes' walk from the town centre it provides a perfect base for touring this area of outstanding natural beauty. We have our own private car park and a small camp site. There is a fully equipped self-catering kitchen, large dining room and a comfy TV lounge. All bed linen is supplied and hot showers, tea, coffee, oil and condiments are included in the price. Let's Go Ireland recommended & Irish Tourist Board approved.

http://homepage.eircom.net/~edenhill

TELEPHONE/FAX CONTACT Tel: (071) 91 43204
Fax: (071) 91 54690, Email: edenhillhostel@eircom.net
OPENING SEASON 3rd January until 19th December
OPENING HOURS Reception open until 10pm. (later by arrangement) Summer closed 1-3pm. Winter closed 12-4pm
NUMBER OF BEDS 33
BOOKING REQUIREMENTS Strongly advised for private rooms. Credit card details or 50% deposit secures booking
PRICE PER NIGHT Dorms €12-€14. Private Rooms €16-€18 (Some reductions for under 14yrs. Under 2yrs free. Travel cot available.

PUBLIC TRANSPORT
Trains from Dublin. Bus/coach travel to all parts of Ireland available from Sligo. Bus stops (by request) opp. Esso station on Pearse Rd.

DIRECTIONS
By bus or car from Dublin, Mayo or Galway turn left into Marymount (estate) opposite the Innisfree 'Esso' service station. From the north by car follow signs to Dublin N4 out of the town centre and look for the 'Esso' station on your left. From Tourist Office on Temple St walk up Mail Coach Rd to the junction with Pearse Rd. We are opposite Christies supermarket. Entrance via Marymount/Ashbrook Estate.

THE GYREUM

Corlisheen
Riverstown
Co Sligo

The Gyreum is a home from home hidden in a massive timber tumulus in the heart of Western Europe's best preserved and most extensive megalithic neighbourhood. The building is directly juxtaposed with the winter and summer solstices, in alignment with the cairns of Carrowkeel, the Si Lu rock of Moytura and most impressively the summer solstice dusk behind Queen Maeve's mound atop Knocknarae - Ireland's Uluru.

The rooms are tasteful and simple - more luxurious than a hostel, less private than a guesthouse. A huge attraction is the great central hall which has extraordinary views across five counties.

The Gyreum is mostly aimed at groups wanting to do retreats, rehearsals or courses. Individuals are welcome when there is no group in sole occupancy. There is a filling organic breakfast served each morning and, if the hostel is busy, broth at midday from a great cauldron.

www.smirsh.com/gyreum

CONTACT Colum, Tel: (071) 9165994, Email: gyreum@smirsh.com
OPENING SEASON All year
OPENING HOURS All day
NUMBER OF BEDS 16: 2x5, 2x3
BOOKING REQUIREMENTS Recommended as group bookings are frequent.
PRICE PER NIGHT€20 incl breakfast, shared room. €25 small room.

PUBLIC TRANSPORT
Buses from Sligo go as far as Castlebaldwin. Nearest train station is at Ballymore.

DIRECTIONS
By car to Castlebaldwin from Dublin. Turn right to Bow and Arrow pub crossroads - go straight through next crossroads (Killadoon).

LEITRIM LAKES HOSTEL

Kiltyclogher
Co Leitrim

Spacious new 32 bed hostel. Hidden away in one of Irelands's most unspoilt counties lies the peaceful village of Kiltyclogher, situated in North Leitrim, only 20 miles from Sligo. The village is surrounded by hills and mountains, ideal for a lazy afternoon ramble or an all day hillwalking adventure. There are mountain lakes to challenge the most experienced of fishermen and there are bicycling tracks to suit young and old.

So if it is adventure you are after or if it is just to get away from it all, then come stay with us in "Kilty". The 19th-century village courthouse has been converted into a luxurious self-catering apartment for up to 8 people. We also have camping facilities. Pubs and shop are situated about 50 yds from Hostel.

No under 16s without proper supervision

CONTACT Marian Miller (Manager). Tel/Fax: (072) 54044.
Email:- llhostel@gofree.indigo.ie
OPENING SEASON All Year
OPENING HOURS Manager 9am - 5pm. otherwise use answerphone
NUMBER OF BEDS 32 in hostel
BOOKING REQUIREMENTS Recommended but not essential except for large groups.
PRICE PER NIGHT €9.50pp. For groups 15 or more €9.00 pp.Family room €13.00pp. Sharing child under 12 years €5.00.

PUBLIC TRANSPORT
Train Station Sligo (24 miles). National Express Manor Hamilton (9 miles) Ferry Belfast (95 miles)

DIRECTIONS
From Dublin-Navan-Cavan-Blacklion-Glenfarne-Kiltyclogher. Sean McDermott's monument in centre of town. Straight through to Hostel on the left. Bottom of the hill (100 metres).

See page 203 for colour photo

OMAGH INDEPENDENT HOSTEL

Glenhordial
9a Waterworks Road
Omagh, Co Tyrone BT79 7JS

We are a small family-run hostel, nestling at the edge of the Sperrin Mountains. Billy and Marella Fyffe with their children and sundry dogs etc, look forward to having you to stay. This hostel has 27 beds, the rooms are of varying sizes sleeping from 1 to 7 people. We have all the usual facilities (check out the symbol chart below), we also have a large conservatory area for relaxing in, an outdoor play area where children can play in safety, and an unbelievable panoramic view of the Northern Irish countryside!

We positively encourage families, disabled people, dog owners and any other minority group, as well as the usual mainstream folk. The hostel is convenient to the Ulster American Folk Park (4 miles), the Ulster History Park (5 miles) and we are 2 miles from the Ulster Way. Megalithic sites abound in this area. Fantastic Group rate now available - whole hostel for £100 per night for groups staying 2 or more nights.

www.omaghhostel.co.uk

CONTACT Marella and Billy, Tel/Fax UK (02882) 241973,
Email: marella@omaghhostel.co.uk
OPENING SEASON 1st March to 30 September.
OPENING HOURS All day, please arrive before 10pm.
NUMBER OF BEDS 27:- 1 x 1 2 x 2 2 x 4 2 x 7
BOOKING REQUIREMENTS Pre-booking essential for groups one month in advance, deposit required.
PRICE PER NIGHT £8 per adult, £7 under 18 years.We accept euros

PUBLIC TRANSPORT
Free pickup from Omagh bus station by arrangement.

DIRECTIONS
From Omagh take B48 towards Gortin. Turn right onto Killybrack Road before The Spar Shop. Keep on road and follow signs to hostel.

GORTIN ACCOMMODATION SUITE AND ACTIVITY CENTRE

62 Main Street, Gortin
Omagh,
Co Tyrone

Gortin Accommodation Suite is idyllically set in an area of outstanding natural beauty, close to national visitor attractions including the Ulster American Folk Park and the Ulster History Park. It provides 4 star self-catering homes and hostel accommodation of the highest standards and is located centrally in the village. Enjoy exploring the rolling hills, enchanted woodland, pine forests, lakes and tumbling rivers and streams. There is an indoor sports hall which is fully equipped for various sports. Outdoor activities such as canoeing, cycling, angling, bouldering, body boarding and climbing can be organised for a minimum group of 8 people. Prices of activities start from £20 per day. The complex also includes 5 acres of outdoor playing fields and a kids' play park. The village has a selection of bars and restaurants with live music most weekends. Bicycle hire available on site.

www.gortin.net

CONTACT Tel: UK (02881) 648346
Email: visit.gortin@virgin.net
OPENING SEASON All Year
OPENING HOURS 9am to 5pm. Warden on call after hours.
NUMBER OF BEDS 40
BOOKING REQUIREMENTS Booking advised for holiday season and at weekends. Deposit required.
PRICE PER NIGHT From £10.00 per person.

PUBLIC TRANSPORT
There is a bus stop in the village with regular buses to and from Omagh. For bus enquiries phone (02882) 242711.

DIRECTIONS
Gortin is 10 miles north of Omagh and 20 miles south of Strabane. Our hostel is part of a complex which fronts onto the main street in the centre of the village. Look out for the Pedlar's Rest restaurant and our blue and yellow signs on the main street.

P 1m

RICKS CAUSEWAY COAST HOSTEL

4 Victoria Terrace
Portstewart
BT55 7BA

Rick's hostel is situated in the town of Portstewart, only 50 metres from the ocean. It has a mix of accommodation including small dormitories, private rooms for two and family rooms. Some of the rooms are en-suite. All have central heating with duvets and all bed linen provided. There is a self-catering kitchen and it is planned soon to provide meals for those who require them. The spacious common room has an open fire, contains books, games, music, a video-recorder and is overflowing with plants.

Portstewart itself is a relaxed seaside town with a 3½ kilometre long sandy beach. It contains lively pubs and great value restaurants. There are excellent public transport connections to Belfast, Derry and Dublin. It is an ideal base from which to explore the north coast including the Giant's Causeway, Bushmills whiskey distillery, Carrick-a-rede Rope Bridge and Dunluce Castle or for trips to the glens of Antrim or Derry.

CONTACT Tel: UK (028) 708 33789, IR (048) 708 33789
Email: rick@causewaycoasthostel.fsnet.co.uk
OPENING SEASON All year
OPENING HOURS All day. No night time curfew
NUMBER OF BEDS 34
BOOKING REQUIREMENTS Recommended by phone or email
PRICE PER NIGHT £8.50pp dorm. £11.00 pp double/twin. £13.00pp en-suite

PUBLIC TRANSPORT
Nearest train station Coleraine with frequent buses to Portstewart. Direct bus links from Belfast, Derry, Dublin, The Giant's Causeway and Coleraine, all stop at Atlantic Circle Bus Stop 100 metres from Hostel.

DIRECTIONS
By car from the A2 take road signposted Portstewart Point/The Herring Pond, the hostel is 100 metres from this turn.

SHEEP ISLAND VIEW

42A Main Street
Ballintoy
Ballycastle
Co Antrim
BT54 6LX

Situated on the Causeway Coast, this family run hostel is ideally situated for exploring this beautiful area including the famous Glens of Antrim. The modern purpose built hostel offers large self-catering kitchen and communal room. Meals can be prepared for groups on request. We have rooms in a variety of sizes ~ all en-suite.

A ten-minute walk takes you to the famous rope-bridge or our picturesque harbour. The village has a shop and post office, two pubs, both with restaurants and both offering entertainment most nights of the week. Often traditional sessions are on offer with everyone welcome to join in.

www.sheepislandview.com

CONTACT Seamus or Josephine, Tel: UK (028) 20762470 or 20769391, Email: info@sheepislandview.com
OPENING SEASON All year
OPENING HOURS All day
NUMBER OF BEDS: 100 : variety of size rooms, all en-suite
BOOKING REQUIREMENTS Booking is essential in high season
PRICE PER NIGHT £11pp £8 child under 12 (under 2 free)

PUBLIC TRANSPORT
Coastal bus from Belfast, twice a day No 252. Service No 172 Coleraine/Portrush 6 times a day. Free pick up from Bushmills, Giants Causeway and Ballycastle.

DIRECTIONS
Ballintoy on main coast road (B15) between Bushmills and Ballycastle. Hostel situated on main street in centre of village.

BARHOLM

11. The Strand
Portaferry
Co Down
BT22 1PF

Barholm is a Victorian House, it can sleep up to 50 people. The house is tastefully furnished, overlooks Strangford Lough and is situated in an Area of Outstanding Natural Beauty. We can offer our guests a choice of single, double, family or group rooms at budget prices. As well as being fully equipped for self-catering we can provide meals on request. A conference room is available for seminars, functions etc and can seat up to 50 people.
Portaferry offers typical Irish charm and hospitality and natural interest, it is the home of Exploris one of Europe's finest aquaria to which our guests are offered concessionary tickets. The area around Portaferry has much to offer, attractions vary between sporting activities and exploring the wildlife of the Lough. Strangford Lough is recognised internationally for the quality of the dives available in the area, both novice and expert divers alike can enjoy diving all year round, there is a compressor available for airfills.

CONTACT - Linda Cleland Tel: UK (028) 427 29598
Email: barholm.portaferry@virgin.net
OPENING SEASON All year-Groups only from November to March
OPENING HOURS 9am-2.30 (weekends 10am to1pm + 4pm to 8pm)
NUMBER OF BEDS: 50: 3x1 : 1x3 : 2x4 : 2x9 : 3xdble,1sgle : 1xdble,2sgl. (Visitor beds can be added to all rooms except singles)
BOOKING REQUIREMENTS pre-booking advised for choice of rooms - especially groups
PRICE PER NIGHT from £13 high season, £12 low season, £10 per child (3-12). Under 3 free. Discount for long stays or groups (8 plus). Whole house from £425 low season, £475 high season.

PUBLIC TRANSPORT
No 10 bus from Belfast to Portaferry - drop off point "The Square" follow ferry signs - Barholm directly opposite ferry terminal.

DIRECTIONS
By car from Belfast follow directions to Newtownwards then sign posted to Portaferry - Barholm is opposite ferry terminal.

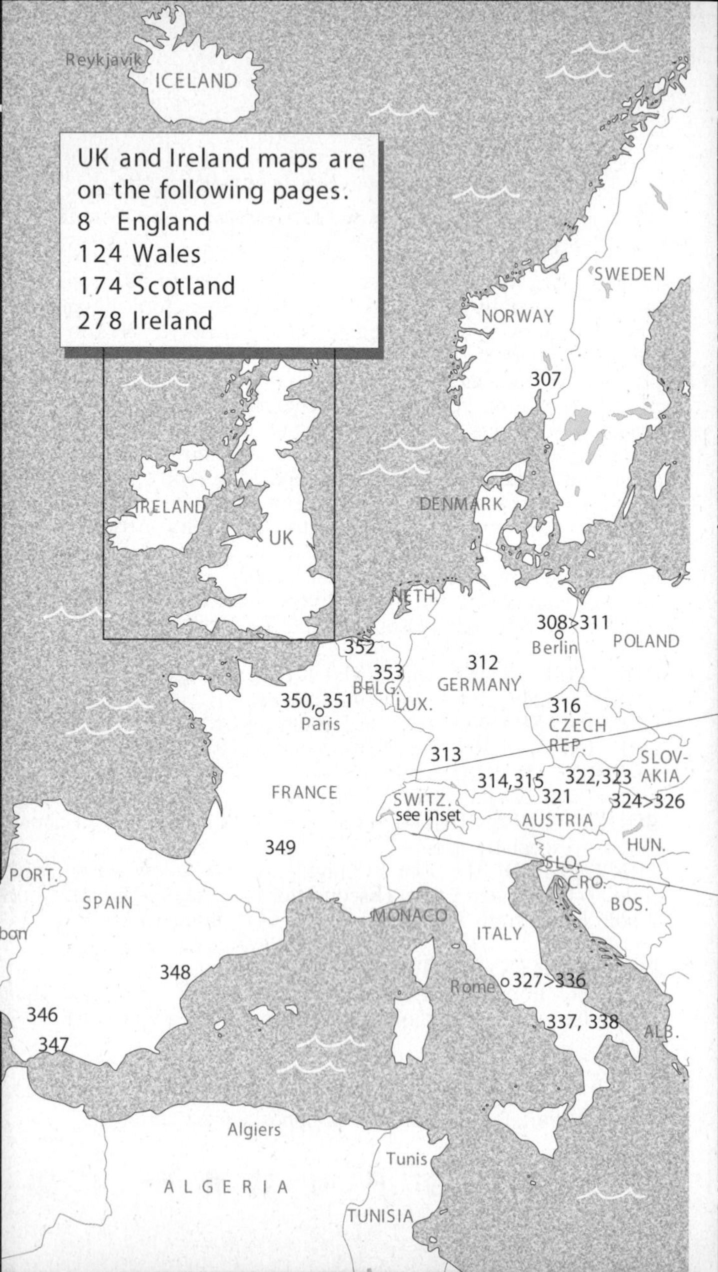

UK and Ireland maps are on the following pages.
8 England
124 Wales
174 Scotland
278 Ireland

Reykjavik
ICELAND
SWEDEN
NORWAY
307
IRELAND
UK
DENMARK
NETH.
308>311
Berlin
POLAND
352
312
353
GERMANY
BELG.
LUX.
350, 351
Paris
316
CZECH REP.
313
SLOVAKIA
314,315
322,323
321
324>326
FRANCE
SWITZ.
see inset
AUSTRIA
349
HUN.
SLO.
CRO.
PORT.
SPAIN
BOS.
MONACO
Lisbon
ITALY
348
Rome
327>336
346
337, 338
ALB.
347
Algiers
Tunis
ALGERIA
TUNISIA

KEY
45 – Hostel page number

0 miles 500
0 kilometres 800

EST.
LAT.
LITH.
306 Moscow
RUSSIA
BELARUS
KAZAKHSTAN
UKR
MOLDO
ROMANIA
345 Zurich
Bern
339
340
Geneva
341
342
343
344
FED
REP
YUG.
BULGARIA
ZER.
MAC.
IRAN
GREECE
354
TURKEY
SYRIA
IRAQ
CYPRUS
LEBANON
JORDAN

SHERSTONE HOSTEL

Gostinichny proezd 8, building 1
3rd Floor, Room #324
127106 Moscow
RUSSIA

Hostel Sherstone is located within 7 minutes' walk of Vladykino metro station (grey line) in the north eastern part of Moscow. Although it is some distance from the centre on foot, it is only 20 minutes to the Red Square by metro. Just near to the hostel are the main Botanical Gardens and Russian exhibition centre, Ostankino TV tower with charming Ostankino estate and space museum. Sherstone's friendly English speaking staff are always ready to offer advice and any information on what to see and do.

Our apartments are recently renovated and have private bathrooms, TVs, telephones and fridges. We have no curfew. We can arrange airport and train station transfers and have a guide service. (English, French and Japanese) IMPORTANT When entering Russia demand a stamped MIGRATION CARD at customs. Without it you cannot be registered or provided with accommodation in Russia.

www.hostels-trains.ru

CONTACT Tel: +7 901 7112613. Fax: +7 095 783 34 38.
Email: info@sherstone.ru
OPENING SEASON All year.
OPENING HOURS 8am till midnight
NUMBER OF BEDS 50
BOOKING REQUIREMENTS On-line booking, email or telephone.
PRICE PER NIGHT €17 - €40 per person. Discounts for Groups of 10 + and for over 10 night stays. Discount €1 for HI and Euro 26 cards. We can help you to obtain a Tourist Visa for up to 1 month.

PUBLIC TRANSPORT
Sheremetyevo Airport shuttle bus available (#517) to metro station Planernaya, and #851 to metro station Rechnoy Vokzal. Take the grey line to Vladykino which is only 7 minutes' walk from Sherstone.

DIRECTIONS
From any railway station take the brown line up to Novoslobodskaya and change to grey line to Vladykino.

ANKER HOSTEL

Storgata 55
Sofienberg
0506 Oslo
NORWAY

The Anker Hostel is a unique starting point for an adventurous visit to Oslo. You can find Grunerlokka, with numerous exotic restaurants and shops close by and Karl Johan, Oslo's steaming main street just a 10/15 minute stroll away.

The hostel offers a relaxed and international atmosphere. All rooms with showers and toilet suitable for all age groups. The 4- and 6-bedded rooms provide single gender accommodation on a shared basis. If you prefer your own room there are single and twin rooms available. Duvet and pillow are included and you can hire bed linen and towels at reception or alternatively you can bring your own. Sorry no sleeping bags are allowed. Cooking facilities are available. Bus and tram stop right outside the Anker Hostel.

www.ankerhostel.no

CONTACT Tel: +47 22 99 72 10, Fax: +47 22 99 72 20,
Email: hostel@anker.oslo.no
OPENING SEASON All year
OPENING HOURS June-August 24 hrs no curfew. September to June phone, fax or email for details
NUMBER OF BEDS 389/130 (high/low season)
BOOKING REQUIREMENTS Booking all year by telephone, fax or email. Advance booking advisable during June, July and August.
PRICE PER NIGHT (Accommodation only) NOK150 (6-bedded dorm), NOK175 (4-bedded dorm), NOK440 (twin)

PUBLIC TRANSPORT
From railway station take Tram 11,12 and 15 or bus 30, 31 and 32. Ask for Hausmannsgate stop.

DIRECTIONS
We are in walking distance from the railway station, please see our web site.

A&O HOSTEL FRIEDRICHSHAIN KREUZBERG GMBH

Boxhagener Strasse 73, 10245 Berlin
GERMANY

The A&O HOSTEL is situated in the middle of the student district of Friedrichshain surrounded by trendy bars, clubs and shops for young people. You can choose between single and double rooms, as well as multi-bedded rooms with 4, 6, 8 or 10 beds (with or without private facilities). The Hostel is equipped with billiards, table tennis, volleyball, bicycle hire, beer garden, barbecue, public TV and DSL-internet access at a good price. Car/bus parking in courtyard.

www.aohostels.com

CONTACT Reception, Tel: +49-(0)30-29 77 81-0, Call free: 0800-222 57 22 (only in Germany), Email: hostel@web.de
OPENING SEASON All Year
OPENING HOURS 24 Hours
NUMBER OF BEDS 648: 1 x 10, 35 x 8, 23 x 6, 40 x 4, 25 x 2, 10 x 1
BOOKING REQUIREMENTS Essential in May, June and Sept.
PRICE PER NIGHT From €10 per person, special prices for groups. Details on website. 10% off for backpackers organisation members.

PUBLIC TRANSPORT
Train: Station Ostbahnhof DB: S-Bahn, line S 3, 5, 7 or 75 to Station Ostkreuz. **Station Zoologischer Garten DB:** S-Bahn, line S 3, 5, 7 or 75 to Station Ostkreuz. **Bus:** Central Bus Station ZOB: Take subway line U2 until station Zoologischer Garten. Change to the S-Bahn, line S 3, 5, 7 or 75 and go on to station Ostkreuz. **Plane: Airport Tegel TXL:** Use bus X9 until station Zoologischer Garten (terminus). Change to S-Bahn, line S 3, 5, 7 or 75 and go on to station Ostkreuz. **Airport Schönefeld SXF:** S-Bahn, line S9, to station Ostkreuz.

DIRECTIONS
Car: Follow signs to Berlin Zentrum and to Alexanderplatz. Turn into Karl-Marx Allee, drive into Frankfurter Allee until Warschauer Strasse. Turn right into Warschauer Strasse and take first left Boxhagener Strasse. Hostel is 500m on left. **S-Station Ostkreuz: 3 min walk:** From exit Sonntagstraße walk on and turn right into Lenbachstraße. Go ahead to Boxhagener Straße and hostel.

A&O HOSTEL AND HOTEL MITTE GMBH

Köpenicker Strasse 127 - 129, 10179 Berlin
GERMANY

The A&O HOSTEL and HOTEL is the perfect accommodation for backpackers and groups in the geographic centre of Berlin. Open from March 2004, all rooms are high standard with private facilities. There are over 700 beds only a short walk from the River Spree and the East Side Gallery, close to the Märkisches Museum and almost as near to the famous Oranienstrasse in Kreuzberg. You can reach the city's sights quickly and simply from here by public transport.

www.aohostels.com

CONTACT Reception, Tel: +49-(0)30-80947-0, Call free: 0800-222 57 22 (only in Germany). Email:hostel@web.de
OPENING SEASON All Year
OPENING HOURS 24 Hours
NUMBER OF BEDS Hostel 712: :83 x 6, 7 x 4, 93 x 2 .
Hotel 210: 14 x 4, 7 x 2, 14 x 1
BOOKING REQUIREMENTS Essential in May, June and Sept.
PRICE PER NIGHT From €13 per person, special prices for groups. Details on website. 10% off for backpackers organisation members.

PUBLIC TRANSPORT
Train: Go to Station Ostbahnhof DB. **Bus**: Central Bus Station ZOB, Take the Subway line U2 until station Zoologischer Garten. Change to the S-Bahn, line: S 3, 5, 7 or 75 to Ostbahnhof. **Plane: Airport Tegel TXL:** Use Bus X9 to station Zoologischer Garten (terminus). Change to the S-Bahn, line S 3, 5, 7 or 75 until Ostbahnhof. **Airport Schönefeld SXF:** Take the S-Bahn line S 9 to station Ostbahnhof.

DIRECTIONS
Car: Follow signs to Berlin Zentrum and Alexanderplatz. Turn into Karl-Marx Allee until Strausberger Platz. First exit at roundabout into Lichtenberger Strasse and then Michaelkirchstrasse. Turn left on the first traffic light after river Spree into the Köpenicker Strasse. After 100 m you see the hostel on right. **From Station Ostbahnhof DB** main exit, cross the Street and go over the "Schillingbrücke" bridge. Turn right into the Köpenicker Strasse. Hostel is on left after 100 m.

A&O HOSTEL AM ZOO GMBH

Joachimstaler Strasse 1-3
10623 Berlin
GERMANY

The A&O HOSTEL am ZOO is right by the main ZOO railway station. You can't get more central. The famous shopping mile Ku´damm, the zoological garden, the Memory Church and the department store Kaufhaus des Westens can be reached in few minutes' walk. You may explore the City West conveniently by walking, by renting a bike or by booking a sightseeing tour round the city from the railway station Zoo. You will be accommodated in rooms with several beds. Many of them have private facilities, some of them have showers and lavatories on the same floor.

www.aohostels.com

CONTACT Reception, Tel: +49 (0)30-889135-0, Call free: 0800-222 57 22 (only in Germany), Email: hostel@web.de
OPENING SEASON All Year
OPENING HOURS 24 Hours
NUMBER OF BEDS 470: (10x 10, 30 x 8, 12 x 6, 11 x 4, 31 x 2, 12 x 1)
BOOKING REQUIREMENTS Essential in May, June and Sept.
PRICE PER NIGHT From €10 per person, special prices for groups on request. Visit website for detailed up-to-date prices. 10% off for members of any backpackers organisation.

PUBLIC TRANSPORT
Train: Station Ostbahnhof DB: Take the S-Bahn, any line, to station Zoologischer Garten (8 stops). **Bus: Central Bus Station ZOB:** Take the subway line U2 to station Zoologischer Garten (5 stops). **Plane: Airport Tegel TXL:** Take the bus X9 to station Zoologischer Garten (terminus). **Airport Schönefeld SXF:** Take the S-Bahn, line S9, to station Zoologischer Garten (19 stops).

DIRECTIONS
From station Zoologischer Garten (Station Zoo) 30m to walk: exit Hardenbergplatz turn right and cross Hardenbergstraße. After ca. 15m go up the stairs. There you'll find our hostel. **Car:** Follow the signs to the city part of Charlottenburg and in Charlottenburg follow the signs to Zoo. The A&O Hostel is right by the train station Zoo.

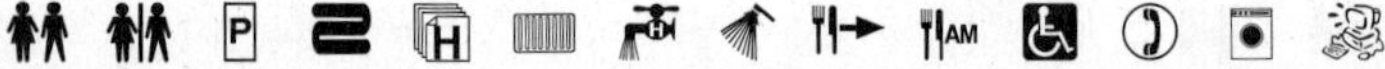

GENERATOR BERLIN

Storkower Strasse 160
10407 Berlin
GERMANY

Generator Berlin is the perfect place for all backpackers and groups in the exciting Eastern centre.

Our excellent facilities include a funky bar and beer-garden (Happy Hour daily from 5-7 pm), Internet Café, 24-hour TV-lounge and restaurant serving tasty meals from 6-10 pm. Hot showers, breakfast, bed-linen and towels are FREE!

www.generatorhostels.com

CONTACT Reception Tel: + 49 30 417 2400
Email: reservations@generatorhostels.com
OPENING SEASON All year
OPENING HOURS 24 hours
NUMBER OF BEDS **854**: 1x14 : 119x2 : 88x4 : 7x6 : 26x8
BOOKING REQUIREMENTS Booking May, June & July may be necessary.
PRICE PER NIGHT From €12 per person. (Groups 1 in 26 free)

PUBLIC TRANSPORT
Zoologischer Garten or Ostbahnhof: S-Bahn eastbound to Ostkreuz. then Ring S-Bahn northbound get off Landsberger Allee Station. The Generator is large white and blue building next to the station! **Schönefeld Airport**: S9 train to Treptower Park. Change to Ring S-Bahn northbound. Get off at Landsberger Allee. **Tegel Airport:** Bus X9 to Jungfernheide. Change to Ring S-Bahn eastbound, to Landsberger Allee S-bahn station.

DIRECTIONS
Follow signs to Berlin Zentrum, then to Alexanderplatz, pass under railway-bridge and take 2nd street right (Mollstraße). Continue on this road until you're on Landsberger Allee. After approx. 3km turn left onto Storkower Straße (behind the "Forum" on your left). The Generator is in the courtyard on your left!

PENTHOUSE BACKPACKERS

Moserstrasse 19
49074 Osnabrueck
GERMANY

Penthouse Backpackers is a homely hostel situated in the centre of Osnabrueck, close to shops and pubs. The whole area is rich in history with the Jewish museum, designed by the famous architect Daniel Libeskind, the medieval city centre and Roman battlefields. The area also caters well for nature lovers with the beautiful Teutoburg Forest where you can see the million-year-old dinosaur tracks or many romantic castles and watermills. The history of coal mining can be explored by glass-walled lift which takes you deep into the old mining shafts. Specialities are the "Maiwoche" (for 1 week in May there are free open air concerts) or the Christmas markets from 1st of December in the wonderfully lit heart of the City Centre.

The hostel has both private rooms and dormitories and a fully equipped kitchen. After a day's sightseeing or activities come back and join our other guests on the roof top terrace.

www.penthouseBP.com

CONTACT Cathy Tel:+49 541 600 9606
Email: info@penthousebp.com
OPENING SEASON All year
OPENING HOURS All day after check-in which is between 8:00 - 11:00 and 17:00 - 20:00
NUMBER OF BEDS 30
BOOKING REQUIREMENTS Call ahead/arrive at check-in hours.
PRICE PER NIGHT €14 Dorm, €17 Twin, €15 Quad, €20 En-suite.

PUBLIC TRANSPORT
Osnabrueck train station is straight ahead from the hostel only 300m.

DIRECTIONS
From the 'Hellern' Autobahn turn, take right into the town centre. Pass the Castle, City Centre and before the brick red Post Office building turn right. The hostel is the 3rd building on the left side.

See page 216 for colour photo

JUGENDGASTEHAUS

Richard Wagner Str. 2
70184 Stuttgart (Mitte)
GERMANY

The Jugendgastehaus Stuttgart half way down from Stuttgart's landmark the "television" tower, to the centre of "Benz-Town", just a few minutes away from all the highlights in the valley, is a well known place with plenty of elbowroom, multicultural atmosphere and friendly staff. We are known to have excellent prices for international groups, backpackers and for all "young and feeling young" individuals from every continent. Lounges and games rooms provide an opportunity for meeting the other guests.

We sell the "Three day Ticket" for public transport, please ask our friendly staff for details about reduced weeks for groups or families.

www.hostel-Stuttgart.de

CONTACT Tel: +49 711 241132.Fax +49 711/2 36 11 10
Email : JGH-Stuttgart@internationaler-bund.de
OPENING SEASON closed 22nd Dec to 6th Jan
OPENING HOURS 6.30 - 23.00.
NUMBER OF BEDS 110
BOOKING REQUIREMENTS Book by phone, fax or email.
PRICE PER NIGHT €16.00 to €32.00

PUBLIC TRANSPORT
Public Street cars:- Downstairs at Main Station to street cars ("U") take line #15 direction Ruhbank/Fernsehturm. 7th stop **Bubenbad** turn right twice and you are here.

DIRECTIONS
By car exit A81 Zuffenhausen/Zentrum follow signs Zentrum stay on #B27 (direction Tubingen). 1km after Hauptbahnhof turn right, drive underground, turn left Olgaeck at sign S-Ost follow rails uphill.

Highway A8 exit Flughafen or Degerloch pass the TV tower, then direction Zentrum to **Bubenbad.**

 See page 208 for colour photo

WOMBAT'S CITY HOSTEL

Senefelderstrasse 1
80336 Munich
GERMANY

With Wombat's exceptionally high standards and level of service we have created another amazing hostel in the best city centre location. We have developed a fantastic building - the new favourite of backpackers in Munich! We offer Munich's top bunks at bottom rates in bright, clean and quiet rooms in the best location you can get - a quiet side street just across the road from the main train station.

All our rooms are equipped with showers, toilets and comfortable big bunk beds. There is no age limit, no curfew, no lockout and no stupid rules. Rates include a free drink in our "womBAR", while an "all you can eat" buffet breakfast is optional and available for €4. In our spacious courtyard you can relax and use our internet surf stations for that all-important tourist information for Munich. Make Wombat's your base to explore the city of parks.

www.wombats-hostels.com

CONTACT Reception, Tel: +49 89 599 89 18 0,
Email: office@wombats-munich.de
OPENING SEASON All Year
OPENING HOURS 24 Hours
NUMBER OF BEDS 300
BOOKING REQUIREMENTS Not essential
PRICE PER NIGHT €19 - €22 in 4, 6 and 8-bed rooms; €32 in doubles

PUBLIC TRANSPORT
The hostel is in the most central location, all major sights are within easy walking distance.

DIRECTIONS
We are just across the street from the main train station.

4 YOU MUNICH HOSTEL

Hirtenstr 18, 80335
Munchen/Munich
GERMANY

4 You Munich hostel/youth hotel is 200m from the central train station, in the heart of this beautiful city and near to all the sights and places of interest.

The hostel has been ecologically built and has facilities for the disabled. Bed linen is included. So that our guests can make the most of their stay and experience all the atmosphere there is no lockout or curfew and we have a reception area which is open 24 hours a day to provide you with all the information you need. If you wish to relax after a hard day's sightseeing you can stay within the hostel which has table soccer, internet facilities, or enjoy a meal in our own restaurant. The hostel is famous for our superb breakfast buffet.

Our house also features two floors of single and double rooms. All these rooms are equipped with a private bath or shower, toilet, desk, radio/ alarm clock and telephone.

www.the4you.de

CONTACT Tel: +49 89 55 21 660, Fax: +49 89 55 21 6666,
Email:info@the4you.de
OPENING SEASON All Year
OPENING HOURS All day
NUMBER OF BEDS 200:- 2 x 12 : 10 x 2 : 12 x 6 : 2 x 8 : 2 x 4 plus hotel
BOOKING REQUIREMENTS Please phone, fax or email
PRICE PER NIGHT Hostel €17 - €37.50 Hotel €43.50 - €102. During October Fest Hostel plus €3.50 Hotel €78.50 - €140.

PUBLIC TRANSPORT
The main train station (Hauptbahnhof) is just 200m from the hostel. This is also the base for a lot of Metros, S-Bahns and Travis Busse.

DIRECTIONS
By car please ask for the City Centre. On foot we are three minutes from main station. At the end of the platform turn left and take the exit Arnulfstr. Across the road you will see a yellow hotel called Eden Wolf. We are in the street behind, 100m on your left.

ARPACAY HOSTEL

Radlicka 76
150 00 Prague 5
CZECH REPUBLIC

Arpacay hostel is a small hostel located in the centre of Prague. The hostel and its clean and comfortable rooms offer a homely and really relaxing atmosphere. At the hostel you can find indoor and terrace picnic area with beautiful Prague scenery. At reception you will find helpful staff with smile ready to help you.

You can use the laundry facilities and internet is FREE, all prices include continental breakfast, linen, towels and shower. You can choose from a wide range of rooms from doubles to apartments with private bath, toilet and kitchen or dormitory style rooms. At the hostel is NO CURFEW, you will get your own key which you keep for all your stay. The check-in time is at 12noon to 10pm. See our website for full information.

www.arpacayhostel.com

CONTACT Reception Tel.+420/251 552 297. Fax. +420/251 552 297
Email : prague@arpacayhostel.com
OPENING SEASON All year
OPENING HOURS 8am to 10pm (key is provided for stay)
NUMBER OF BEDS 44: 5x2 : 5x3 : 1x4 : 1x5 : 1x apartment for 8 : 1x apartment for 2
BOOKING REQUIREMENTS Book through website or phone for further information.
PRICE PER NIGHT 300-360 CZK Nov to Feb (€10 to €12)
430-630 CZK March to Oct (€13 to €19)

PUBLIC TRANSPORT
Main train station (15 minutes). Airport Ruzyue. (40 minutes).

DIRECTIONS
From main train station, or Centre or Old Town take tram No 14 to Krizova (stop in front of hostel). From Airport take a bus 100 to Zlicin then the underground line B to Smichovske Nadrazi, cross small bridge over railway. The hostel is 50m straight on on LH side.

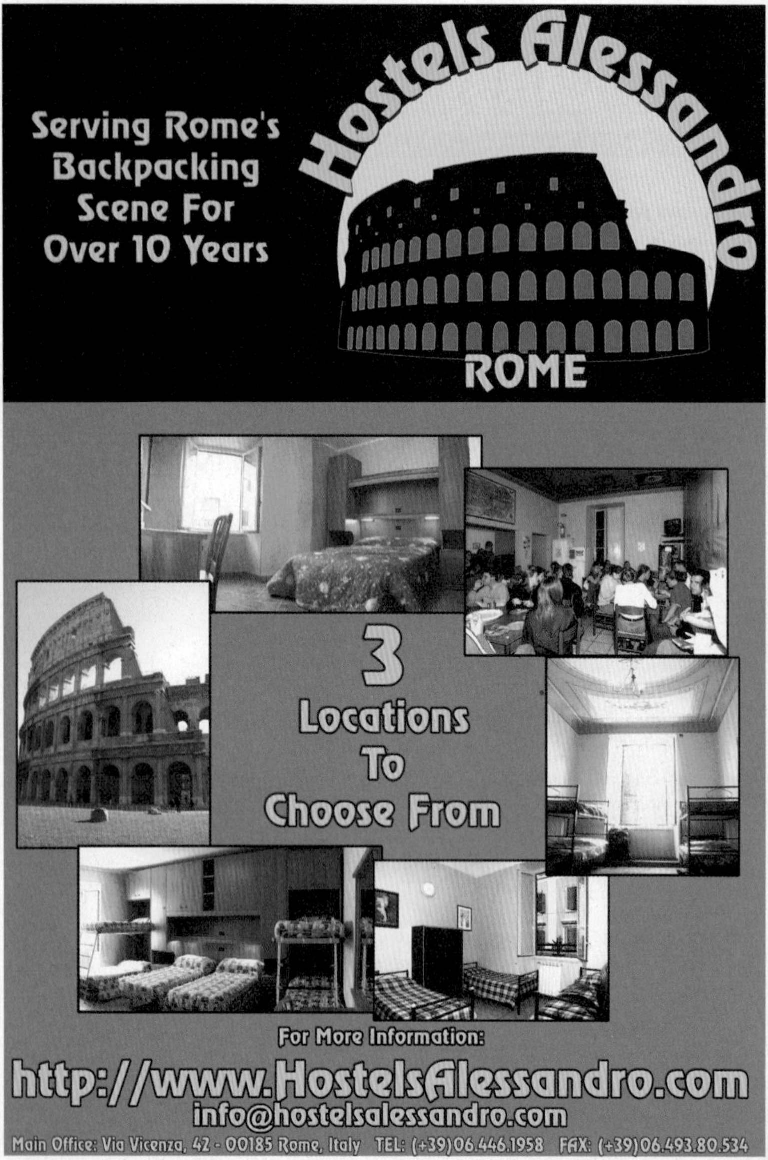
Serving Rome's Backpacking Scene For Over 10 Years
Hostels Alessandro
ROME
3 Locations To Choose From
For More Information:
http://www.HostelsAlessandro.com
info@hostelsalessandro.com
Main Office: Via Vicenza, 42 - 00185 Rome, Italy TEL: (+39)06.446.1958 FAX: (+39)06.493.80.534

YOHO INTERNATIONAL YOUTH HOTEL

A-5020 Salzburg
Paracelsusstrasse 9
AUSTRIA

The Yoho Salzburg is one of the best and most traditional youth hostels in Austria, maybe in Europe. It is one of the most popular meeting points for travellers of all countries of the world. Coming here makes you feel like coming home.

The hostel offers an excellent breakfast and the swinging bar provides excellent food, a happy hour everyday and the best music to take care of our hungry and thirsty guests. There are daily films, CNN, internet access and the friendly staff are always willing to assist. The Busabout stops directly at the Yoho and the best tour operators for sightseeing, adventure and skiing tours pick up directly from the front door.

YOHO-Salzburg is a must - easy to find - hard to leave.
www.yoho.at

CONTACT Renate or Gottfried, Tel: +43 662 879 649, Fax: +43 662 878 810, Email: office@yoho.at
OPENING SEASON All year
OPENING HOURS All day
NUMBER OF BEDS 160
BOOKING REQUIREMENTS Please ring the same day or day before your stay. You can also book by email or fax.
PRICE PER NIGHT €16 dorm to €21 twin room

PUBLIC TRANSPORT
We are near to the train station, where you will find a big poster in the Hall giving full details.

DIRECTIONS
Car: Go down from the highway at 'Salzburg Mitte' straight ahead, under the train underpass, then turn second right. Another 100 metres and you will see hostel. Train station:2 00m to the city, at train underpass turn left (Gablesberger Strasse), then as above.

 See page 214 for colour photo

WOMBATS CITY HOSTEL

Grangasse 6
A-1150 Wien/Vienna
AUSTRIA

This newly constructed hostel has a design based on a colour concept from the University of Modern Arts. Centrally located the hostel is very convenient to all parts of the city and all public transport is within easy walking distance.

The Hostel has no curfew and you will not be locked out. It has all the facilities you would expect from a backpackers' hostel, including internet corner and laundry. Accommodation is available in 4 and 6-bed dormitories and there are double rooms all with shower and toilet. The international and friendly staff are one of the best points of Wombats City Hostel. Staff from France, Ireland and Germany will help you with all aspects of your stay. You can relax and enjoy the hospitality of the WomBAR where you can drink beers from all over the world and get some snacks until 2.00 am. Enjoy your stay.

www.wombats-hostels.com

CONTACT Tel: +43 1 897 2336, Fax: + 43 1 897 2577,
Email: office@wombats-vienna.at
OPENING SEASON All year
OPENING HOURS 24 hours
NUMBER OF BEDS 296
BOOKING REQUIREMENTS Please phone, fax or email
PRICE PER NIGHT €18 - 4 & 6 bedroom, €24 - 2 bed room. All prices per person per night.

PUBLIC TRANSPORT
The major subways (U3,U6) are within easy walking distance, only 3 stops on the U3 to downtown. Take the airport shuttlebus to Westbahnhof, or from Sudbahnhof take tram 18 to Westbahnhof.

DIRECTIONS
From Westbahnhof take main exit and turn right onto Mariahilfer Strasse, follow until No 152. Turn right into Rosinagasse and go straight on till Grangasse.

HOSTEL RUTHENSTEINER

Robert Hamerlinggasse 24
1150 Vienna
AUSTRIA

Hostel Ruthensteiner is the "friendly hostel" with a great International atmosphere! Centrally located and just a 3 minute walk from the Westbahnhof Train Station with easy access to all of Vienna's major sites, Hostel Ruthensteiner is also the original independent Hostel in Central Europe so we know how to make backpackers feel right at home!
Our friendly, multilingual staff will strive to make your stay a memorable and happy one. We offer clean and bright 2, 3, 4 and 5 bedded rooms and larger dorms (most with brand-new hardwood floors), use of a self-service kitchen and barbeque in our lovely garden, free and unlimited hot showers, lockers in all rooms, laundromat, musical instruments for your free entertainment - all in a smoke-free environment. We also have internet access to connect with family and friends. Please come visit!

www.hostelruthensteiner.com

CONTACT Tel: +43 1 893 4202 or +43-1-893 2796
Email: info@hostelruthensteiner.com
OPENING SEASON All year
OPENING HOURS 24 hours, no curfew or lockout
NUMBER OF BEDS 77: 2x10 : 2x5 : 3x4 : 7x3 : 7x2.
BOOKING REQUIREMENTS Booking is advised by phone, email or through our secured website.
PRICE PER NIGHT €11.50 - €13pp large dorms, €13.50 - €19.50.pp 3-5 bedded rooms and €20-€22pp in 2-bedded rooms

PUBLIC TRANSPORT
From Westbahnhof Station exit the main entrance, turn right, turn right onto Mariahilferstrasse, 2nd left onto Haidmannsgasse, first right onto Robert Hamerlinggasse.

DIRECTIONS
The Hostel is 3 minutes' walk from Westbahnhof Train Station. Busabout pickup is one minute away on Mariahilferstrasse. Mitch's Tours to Budapest and Grape-Grazing Tours along the Danube pick up from the front door!

HOSTEL FORTUNA

H1097 Budapest
Gyáli út 3/B
HUNGARY

Hostel Fortuna bids you a warm welcome! We offer cosy surroundings, a quiet location, and a relaxed base for your exploration of the city. Our 29 en-suite rooms are of various types and prices, so you are sure to find something to suit you. The bar and reception are always open, so our multilingual staff are ready to help and advise you 24 hours a day.

www.Fortunahostel.hu

CONTACT Reception Tel: +36-1 215 0660.
Email: info@Fortunahostel.hu
OPENING SEASON All Year
OPENING HOURS 24 Hours
NUMBER OF BEDS 81: 1x1 13x2, 6x 3,7x 4, 2x4-bedded apartments.
BOOKING REQUIREMENTS Booking secured by credit card is advisable in high season and especially over New Year. A deposit is not required for less than 15-person groups.
PRICE PER NIGHT Single rooms €41 low season, €62 high season. Double rooms €50 per room low season, €70 high season.

PUBLIC TRANSPORT
Rail: Keleti station, 4km, 20 mins with tram # 24. **Bus:** Nepliget International Bus Station 0.5km. **Metro:** Nagyvarad ter, 300m, 5 minutes' walk. Journey time to town centre: 15 minutes.

DIRECTIONS
By car: Entering the city on M7 from Vienna, follow Hegyalja ut across Erzsebet bridge, turn right at crossroads, then left at large junction onto Ulloi ut. Follow road for 2km and turn right on to Vagohid utca immediately after Nagyvarad ter. On foot from Metro station: "Nagyvarad ter", exit the metro towards the exit which leads Southeast between a small park and the high-walled Hospital Entrance. After 50m, cross Vagohid utca and the hostel is 100m along on the right.

MELLOW MOOD CENTRAL HOSTEL

1052 Budapest
Bécsi utca 2
HUNGARY

Mellow Mood is a comfy and cheap new hostel, a real backpacker hostel, with 24-hour bar and reception, and it simply couldn't be more downtown! Get into the mood in the centre of Budapest!

Full details and photos on line at:

www.mellowmoodhostel.com

CONTACT Judit Ignacz, Tel: +36 1 411 1310
Email: info@mellowmoodhostel.com
OPENING SEASON All Year
OPENING HOURS 24 Hours
NUMBER OF BEDS 176=4x2, 13x4, 6x6, 10x8
BOOKING REQUIREMENTS Booking in advance is essential. We ask for credit card details to guarantee the booking, but we do not ask for deposit in advance.
PRICE PER NIGHT Double room €25 low season, €30 high season pp. In 8 bed room: €14 low season, €20 high season, pp.

PUBLIC TRANSPORT
Metro: Take any metro line to the central metro stop, where the 3 metro lines meet at Deák Ferenc tér. **Rail:** Keleti (Eastern) station 2 km (3 metro stops). **Bus:** Népliget International Station 5km (6 metro stops). **Boat:** Various Danube boat docks 0.5km.

DIRECTIONS
Enter city from Vienna, M7, Hegyalja út. Follow signs for centrum across the Danube (Erzsébet bridge). On the Pest side of bridge, take immediate right turn then 1st left, and again 1st left, then under underpass (right lane, straight on) to arrive on Bécsi utca. Hostel is red corner building 200m after underpass. **On foot from Deák Ferenc tér Metro:** Exit the metro on to the pedestrian Deák Ferenc utca (right next to Le Meridian Hotel), walk down the street, turn left onto Bécsi utca. Hostel entrance is 50m on the right side.

MARCO POLO HOSTEL

1072 Budapest
Nyár utca 6
HUNGARY

Marco Polo Hostel is a delightful centrally located property, which although officially a hostel and unclassified, offers all the facilities of a hotel. Bedrooms are spacious, clean and recently decorated in bright fresh colours. The large bar in the cellar has a wonderful ambience, its décor depicting the story of Marco Polo's travels

www.marcopolohostel.com

CONTACT Mrs Andrea Trefil, Tel: +36 1 413 2555
Email: info@marcopolohostel.com
OPENING SEASON All Year
OPENING HOURS 24 Hours
NUMBER OF BEDS 156 : 36x2 ; 6x4 ; 5x12
BOOKING REQUIREMENTS Advisable from March to October
PRICE PER NIGHT Dorms €18 pp low season, €29 pp high season. Doubles €32 pp low season, €36 pp high season.

PUBLIC TRANSPORT
Rail: Keleti pu. 1 km, Bus 7, 7A, 78, **Bus:** Népliget Station, 5 km, **Metro:** Astoria or Blaha L. tér 300 metres, 3 minutes' walk

DIRECTIONS
From anywhere in town take metro 3 (blue line) to Ferenciek tere and then take bus 7 (not red 7), 7A or 78 east (away from the river) 2 stops to Vas utca. Walk on to the crosswalk and turn down Nyár utca. The hostel is directly ahead on the left. Alternatively take tram 4 or 6 around the city ring road (körút) and get off at Blaha Lujza tér. From here you can walk 3 blocks East (or take bus black 7, 7A or 78 one stop and walk back one block) then turn right onto Nyár utca. The hostel is directly ahead on the left.

YOUTH STATION HOSTEL

Via Livorno no.5 00162 Rome
ITALY

This is Rome's only lodgings for backpackers with private bathrooms and air conditioning in all the rooms! We are young too, and we know all too well that one of the inconveniences of major European capitals is the fact that they are not suited to everyone's budget. This is why we have created a high-level structure that offers hospitality at economic costs, ready to satisfy every request and meet every budget. This is the Youth Station Hostel in Rome, a completely new and original type of hotel designed for travellers and backpackers of every age and every country. What we set out to do was focus the proper attention on entertainment, relaxation, cleanliness and security, creating a gathering place which, up to now, simply did not exist. We will be waiting for you!!!

www.youthstation.it

CONTACT Tel: +39 06 4429 2471, Fax +39 06 4429 2604,
Email: info@youthstation.it
OPENING SEASON All year
OPENING HOURS 24 hours
NUMBER OF BEDS 76: 1x4, 9x8
BOOKING REQUIREMENTS Booking is advised by phone, fax, or email. Credit card required for guarantee.
PRICE PER NIGHT From €12pp

PUBLIC TRANSPORT
From Ciampino Airport shuttle bus goes to A line metro station Anagnina. Catch metro to Termini, then B line in Rebibbia direction, alighting after 3 stops at Bologna. **From Fiumicino Airport** get train in direction of Fara Sabina (every 15 minutes) alight at Tiburtina station, then catch the B line metro in Laurentina direction, alighting after 1 stop at Bologna. **From hostel to city centre** Buses 61 and 62 go to city centre from piazza Bologna. Returning at night catch bus 40N (passing by Piramide and the Colosseum) or 6N from Termini.

DIRECTIONS
The closest Metro station is Bologna. Once you get out of the Metro Station you're in piazza Bologna. Proceed down via Livorno to no. 5.

TWO DUCKS HOSTEL ROME

Via Gaeta 25
00185 Rome
ITALY

Two Ducks is located in a safe and quiet zone, in the heart of the city within walking distance from the main railway Termini Station, which houses the most important bus and tube stations. The Hostel is equipped with very spacious rooms with common bathrooms, hot showers, refrigerator etc. The English speaking staff will be happy to suggest to you the best way to enjoy the city, discovering the monuments and antiquities of Rome. Two Ducks Hostel plans tours and Pub Crawl around the city. The price includes full breakfast, a dish of pasta every evening, blankets and sheets, city maps, luggage storage, etc.

www.twoduckshostel.com

CONTACT Vincenzo or Adriana, Tel: + 39 06 47 82 38 62., Email: info@twoduckshostel.com
OPENING SEASON All Year
OPENING HOURS 24 Hours
NUMBER OF BEDS 22
BOOKING REQUIREMENTS Not essential during the low season (Nov to Feb). Book online at www.twoduckshostel.com
PRICE PER NIGHT From €15pp

PUBLIC TRANSPORT
Two Ducks Hostel is a few minutes' walk from the Termini Railway Station. Easy access to tube, bus stops, and taxi station.

DIRECTIONS
From Termini Railway Station: exit from platform 1 (with the train tracks behind you, that's to your right). Head left on Via Marsala. After two blocks turn to right on Via Gaeta, just a few more steps and there you are in…Two Ducks Hostel!

See page 317 for advert

VICTORIA HOSTEL IN ROME

via Cavour
No 201
00184 Rome
ITALY

Victoria Hostel, located in the heart of the ancient town, is part of the Cristina Hotels group. Recently renewed, the Victoria Hostel is close to the Colosseum (a couple of minutes' walk), as well as Roma's main sights and shopping streets.

Victoria hostel offers clean and comfortable multiple bed rooms (max 8 people), breakfast (included in the price), self-catering kitchen and friendly international staff. You can get other information on our website or directly by phone or email.

www.cristinahouse.com

CONTACT Cristina, Tel: +39 06 44 70 4586,
Email: info@cristinahouse.com
OPENING SEASON All Year
OPENING HOURS 24 Hours - check in till 5pm.
NUMBER OF BEDS 14
BOOKING REQUIREMENTS Not essential during the low season (Nov to Feb). Book online at www.cristinahouse.com
PRICE PER NIGHT From €15pp

PUBLIC TRANSPORT
From the subway: take the b-line to Laurentina, just 1 stop and get off at Cavour station. The hostel is close by! **By bus**, at Piazza Dei Cinquecento take number 75, 3 stops and get off at the hostel! **From the airport Roma Fiumicino** take the train to Roma Termini railway station, get off and follow the directions.

DIRECTIONS
From Roma Termini railway station: take main exit and reach Piazza Dei Cinquecento "The Station Square", turn left and walk up Cavour Street to number 201, ring the bell marked Victoria and come upstairs.

FREEDOM TRAVELLER HOSTEL IN ROME

Via Gaeta, 25 - 00185 - Rome
ITALY

Freedom Traveller Hostel is the hostel among many hostels in Rome, that always worked very hard to offer you the most for your money. In the last year we've become the only hostel in Rome that offers our guests the Biggest Breakfast and from 1st of November to 30th of March a free pasta dinner every evening. Our Hostel is located in a safe and central location, we're 5 minutes walking distance from Termini Station. The Freedom Traveller Hostel offers you professional English speaking staff, always ready to help. The Freedom Traveller Hostel in Rome, is proud to have been included in "Let's Go Western Europe".

www.freedom-traveller.it/

CONTACT Johnny Tel + 39 06 47 82 38 62,
Email: info@freedom-traveller.it,
OPENING SEASON All Year
OPENING HOURS 24 Hours
NUMBER OF BEDS 96
BOOKING REQUIREMENTS Not essential during the low season (Nov to Feb). Book online at www.freedom-traveller.it/
PRICE PER NIGHT From €15pp

PUBLIC TRANSPORT
From Termini Railway Station, exit via platform 1 and head left on Via Marsala. At the stop light, Via Marsala changes name to Via Volturno; keep going straight on. Via Gaeta will be your first right after the light. Termini is the main station where you can find all the tubes and buses to go wherever you want.

DIRECTIONS
By car; exit at Tiburtina. Keep going straight on until you reach Viale Regina Elena, turn right. Go straight until you reach Viale dell'Università and turn left. Follow this street until it ends at Viale Castro Pretorio. Turn right on Viale Castro Pretorio. Turn onto Via S. Martino della Battaglia. At the intersection of Via S. M. della Battaglia e Via Volturno, turn right. Via Gaeta is the next right.

P AM

HOSTELS ALESSANDRO

Palace
Via Vicenza, 42
00185 Roma

Downtown
Via C.Cattaneo, 23
00185 Roma

ITALY

All roads lead to Rome and when in Rome let Alessandro's show you the best way to enjoy the Eternal City's offerings. Renowned as the best hostels in Rome with an international environment and English speaking staff, Alessandro PALACE & DOWNTOWN have been a backpacker's Mecca for over 10 years for travellers from all over the world. Clean & friendly, we offer a variety of services and Italian hospitality, providing the perfect base for travellers to explore Rome.

The hostels are centrally situated in a safe and convenient area 5 minutes' walking distance from Termini Train Station. Enjoy the Pizza Party in the rockin' atmosphere of the Alessandro's Palace bar, grab a beer and chat with fellow travellers before sampling the Roman nightlife. 24 -hr reception, bar, no curfew, free hot drinks, satellite TV, free maps, free storage, air conditioning - pizza party 3 times a week.

www.hostelsAlessandro.com

CONTACT Tel: +(39) 06 44 6 1 958, Fax: +(39) 06 493 805 34
E-mail: info@hostelsalessandro.com
OPENING SEASON All year
OPENING HOURS All day
NUMBER OF BEDS 260
BOOKING REQUIREMENTS Direct booking by website,fax,email.
PRICE PER NIGHT From €17pp. Private/family rooms from €20.

PUBLIC TRANSPORT
The hostels are a 3 minute walk from Termini train station. Easy access to Metro, bus stops and taxi station.

DIRECTIONS Palace; Exit station track 1 onto Via Marsala. Take a left on Via Marsala then first right onto Via Vicenza. At number 42 ring bell to open front door, reception is on ground floor.
Downtown; Exit station track 22 Via G Giolitti, take a left on Via Giolitti, second right onto Via C Cattaneo, No. 23 (by thc church with the garden). Ring us and come up 2nd floor, North Americans 3rd floor.

P AM

BELLAROMA HOSTEL

Via E.
Accinni 63 -
00195
Rome
ITALY

BellaRoma Hostel is a brand new backpackers heaven founded by the people behind Hotel Sandy and Pensione Ottaviano. We have used our years of experience (since 1956) to open a new hostel in a quiet, safe residential area, still close to the city centre and its many sights. It is easy to reach with public transport.

BellaRoma Hostel offer free DSL internet access, satellite TV, free bed linen and blankets, cooking facilities, hot showers, lockers, a refrigerator in each room, no curfew and just around the corner you will find a 24-hour supermarket and bakery. Our friendly, English-speaking staff will provide you with maps, arrange walking/bus tours, pub crawls and all the information you need to have a great stay in the eternal city. Ideal for those between 13 and 40 years.

www.bellaromahostel.com

CONTACT Reception, (+39) 0639 754150 Fax (+39) 0639740809, Email: info@bellaromahostel.com
OPENING SEASON All Year
OPENING HOURS 24 Hours
NUMBER OF BEDS 50
BOOKING REQUIREMENTS Booking in advance is advised at least two weeks prior to arrival. Credit card details required.
PRICE PER NIGHT From €10pp

PUBLIC TRANSPORT
From Termini Station exit from platform 24 to via Giolitti, catch bus No 70. Alight at terminus, Piazzale Cladio and follow instructions below.

DIRECTIONS
From St Peters follow Viale Leone IV until you reach Piazzale Clodio. Look for the Mitsubishi shop. We are beside it, via E. Accinni, 63.

PENSIONE OTTAVIANO HOSTEL

Via Ottaviano, 6
00192 Rome
ITALY

The Pensione Ottaviano is the longest running hostel in Rome today. Established in 1956, we have seen generations of backpackers. Since the hostel opened it has been recommended in all the main guide books of the world and we suppose there is a reason for it!

The hostel is located in a nice quiet area, one inch from St Peter's Square, from our windows there is a view of the Dome. Pensione Ottaviano is a clean, budget-wise place to crash, close to the main sights. There are several transport options, underground, buses etc.

Our international atmosphere and English speaking, friendly and energetic staff help make us "a backpackers' heaven". We help our guests enjoy their days in Rome with all the necessary information. You will find rooms with refrigerators, a lounge with satellite TV, individual lockers, book exchange and much more.

www.ottavianohostel.com

CONTACT Slim Tel: (+39) 063 973 7253 or 0639738138
Email info@pensioneottaviano.com
OPENING SEASON All year
OPENING HOURS 24 hours
NUMBER OF BEDS 100
BOOKING REQUIREMENTS Booking advised by phone or email
PRICE PER NIGHT From €12 per person

PUBLIC TRANSPORT
From Airport Fiumicino take the train to Termini station (½ hour).

DIRECTIONS
From Termini take metro line A (Direction Battistini) to Ottaviano. Exit station at via Ottaviano we are No.6 on the 2nd floor.

SANDY HOSTEL

Via Cavour, 136
00184 - Rome
ITALY

Established in 1990, Sandy Hostel has grown up to be one of the most popular and well-known places to stay for young backpackers. Since the hostel opened it has been recommended in all the main guide books of the world. The hostel is located in a nice quiet area close to the Colosseum and Roman Forum.

We know what travelling on a budget demands, close by are a variety of shops, supermarkets, grocery stores, laundromat, information stands and other essential services.

In our international atmosphere, with English speaking, friendly and energetic staff, always willing to help, you will find, book exchange, individual lockers, guide books, maps, a secure luggage store and much more besides. Walking tours can be arranged.

www.sandyhostel.com

CONTACT Slim Tel:(+39) 064 884585 or 0648906772
Email info@sandyhostel.com
OPENING SEASON All year
OPENING HOURS 24 hours
NUMBER OF BEDS 100
BOOKING REQUIREMENTS Booking advised by phone or email
PRICE PER NIGHT From €12 per person

PUBLIC TRANSPORT
From Fiumicino Leonardo Davinci Airport take train to termini station (½ hour).

DIRECTIONS
Exit Termini on Piazza Dei Cinquecento and immediately turn left into Via Cavour. Hostel Sandy is on the left. Take metro line B to Cavour.

  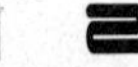       

M & J PLACE HOSTEL

Via Solferino 9
00185 Roma
ITALY

Greetings from Roma! The staff from 'M&J Place Hostel' would like to introduce you to our hostel. It is located by Rome's main train station 'Termini' and near to all main attractions (Colosseum, Trevi Fountain and others) in the heart of Rome.

The hostel has 150 beds with rooms to accommodate from 2 to 8 people. Most of the rooms have a private bath and/or balcony. The following facilities are included in our price: breakfast, use of internet, use of kitchen, TV room, common room, use of lockers, maps, sheets, bag storage, hot showers, and information. We have available: a bar, guide books, telephone cards etc. There is a discount when using the nearby supermarkets, pubs, restaurants and launderettes.

www.mejplacehostel.com
www.hostelinrome.com

CONTACT Gallo, Mario and Luigi, Tel: +39 06446 2802,
Email: mejplacehostel@hotmail.com
OPENING SEASON All year
OPENING HOURS All day
NUMBER OF BEDS 150
BOOKING REQUIREMENTS Booking advised by phone or email or online reservation through the website.
PRICE PER NIGHT From €15

PUBLIC TRANSPORT
The main train station, bus station and metro station are just a 2 minute walk away.

DIRECTIONS
Exit near platform 1 from Termini (main) train station. Turn left on Via Marsala, walk for 150m. At the traffic lights turn right on Via Solferino. Look for the No9 (first door on the street!) We are on the first floor.

YELLOW HOSTEL

44 Via Palestro
00185 Rome
ITALY

Proud to be the most unique hostel in Italy and to have been awarded the '8th best hostel in the world' winner of the 'top 10 hostel award 2004' by Hostel World.

Yellow Hostel is located in the centre of Rome, close to the main train station, (Termini) and all important monuments. Included in the price: FREE INTERNET ACCESS, bed linen, blankets, hot showers, lockers, cooking facilities, fridges, bar, air conditioned lounge with TV and DVD, laundry facilities, no curfew and no lockout. We organise great walking tours to all the fantastic sights, food, wine and cheese tours and the best pub crawl and nightclub tours. Our friendly, English-speaking staff are happy to help you in any way they can. We have lots of information on what to do, where to go and where to eat and drink. We have mixed dormitories and a funky, air conditoned, common room/lounge, and 24-hour reception. Check-in is 1.00pm. Check out is 10.00am but you can leave your baggage with us for the day free of charge. There is a pay car park nearby

www.yellowhostel.com

CONTACT Fabio. Tel: +39 06 4938 2682. Fax: +39 06 4470 28 74
Email:- info@yellowhostel.com
OPENING SEASON All year
OPENING HOURS 24 hours
NUMBER OF BEDS 125
BOOKING REQUIREMENTS Only on our secure web-site through credit card
PRICE PER NIGHT From €15 pp

PUBLIC TRANSPORT
Train station (Termini) only 3 minutes' walk. Exit Via Marsala, cross road, walk down Via Marghera for four blocks, turn left at Via Palestro we are No 44, on right hand side.

DIRECTIONS
By road from "anulare" ring road, exit at Tiburtina, follow sign to Termini Station. Take San Martino Della Battaglia to Via Palestro.

HOSTEL PENSIONE MANCINI

Via Mancini 33
80139 Napoli
ITALY

Hostel Mancini is affordable, clean and safe. The hostel is ideally located being only a short walk from Napoli Central Station which offers transport to the city centre (5 mins) to see the most important places of interest, like Duomo, Royal Palace, Archaeological Museum and so on. There are also trains to Herculaneum, Mont Vesuvio, Pompei and Sorrento nearby. It is just a ten minute walk to the ferries/hydrofoils for Capri, Ischia, Procida and Sicilia, we offer cheap day trip tickets.

The hostel is run by the family 'Alfredo, Margherita and Lello' who between them can speak Italian, English, Spanish, Polish and French. There is a helpful tourist information desk with free maps of the City and surroundings to help you plan your visit. The hostel offers a 24-hour reception, free luggage storage and all the dorms have lockers, private showers and TV. Internet available. **No curfew**. No lockout. Come and feel at home!

www.hostelpensionemancini.com

CONTACT Alfredo, Tel: +39 081 553 6731, Fax: +39 081 554 6675
email: info@hostelpensionemancini.com
OPENING SEASON All year
OPENING HOURS 24 hours Reception (no curfew)
NUMBER OF BEDS 20: 2 x 5 : 4 x doubles (can be triples)
BOOKING REQUIREMENTS Please book by telephone or fax or email with credit card number.
PRICE PER NIGHT (including breakfast) Dorm: €18. Dbl.room €45.

PUBLIC TRANSPORT
Within walking distance from Napoli central train station. 15 minutes by bus from the airport and only 15 minutes' walk from the ferries.

DIRECTIONS
Coming out of Napoli train station cross the Garibaldi Square. Behind the Garibaldi Monument cross into Via Mancini. The hostel is the last building on the left hand side, just buzz!

HOSTEL OF THE SUN

via Melisurgo 15
Naples
Italy

Hostel of the sun is the most central hostel in Naples. We are located just in front of the ferry port to Capri, Ischia and Sicily, and in front of the terminal for buses to Pompei, Ercolaneum and the Amalfi Coast. Hostel of the Sun is also very close to the most famous and historic places in Naples.

Our friendly and international staff are ready to help you with anything you need, especially recommendations on where to get the best Napolitan pizza.

www.hostelnapoli.com

CONTACT Coda Luca, Tel and Fax + 39 08142 06393,
Email: info@hostelnapoli.com
OPENING SEASON All Year
OPENING HOURS 24 Hours
NUMBER OF BEDS 35 : 3x6; 5x2; 2x3.
Under 16s in private rooms only.
BOOKING REQUIREMENTS Advisable.
PRICE PER NIGHT Per person: Dorms €18; Doubles €25; Triples €28

PUBLIC TRANSPORT
From the central train station: exit the station, cross the square and take the R2 bus. Get off at the 2nd stop in via de Pretis. Via Melisurgo is just by this stop. From the airport : take the bus called Alibus from outside the arrival terminal to Piazza Municipio, the last stop. The hostel is just 2 minutes' walk from here.

DIRECTIONS
We are located just in front of the ferry port to Capri, Ischia and Sicily, and in front of the terminal for buses to Pompei, Ercolaneum and the Amalfi Coast.

LAUSANNE GUESTHOUSE & BACKPACKER

Chemin Des Epinettes 4
1007 Lausanne
SWITZERLAND

Lausanne is in the very heart of the Lake Geneva Region. Our Guesthouse is in the heart of Lausanne. Our lucky location only 2 minutes' walking time from main train station. Our peaceful garden and barbecue, our breathtaking views on the Alps, on Lake Geneva and our extremely low price policy contribute to your best souvenir of Switzerland.

Respectfully restored in 2001 our town house built in 1894 complies with the strictest and newest ecological regulations and preserves all the 'charm' of this lovely old European establishment. All our bedrooms face Lake Geneva and the Alps, six of our ten double rooms have private bathrooms, we have a further fifteen four-bedded dormitory rooms. The hostel is equipped for the disabled, it also has high speed internet stations. You can rent an electric bike!! (hilly Lausanne).

www.lausanne-guesthouse.ch

CONTACT Anne-Marie or Laura, Tel: +41 21 601 8000. Fax: + 41 21 601 8001. E-mail: info@lausanne-guesthouse.ch
OPENING SEASON January to December
OPENING HOURS Reception 07.30-12.00 / 15.00 -22.00
NUMBER OF BEDS 80: 15 x 4 : 10 x 2.
BOOKING REQUIREMENTS Book by email, internet, phone or fax
PRICE PER NIGHT €21 dorm without sheets. €25 with sheets

PUBLIC TRANSPORT
Local train and bus stations.

DIRECTIONS
Two minutes' walk from main train station. Exit the station, when facing the Place de la Gare take the next left down, walk through the railroad tunnel, take the first right.

 See page 320 for advert

RIVIERA LODGE

Montreux - Vevey
Place du Marche 5
1800 Vevey
SWITZERLAND

Welcome to Riviera Lodge, an historical 19th-century town house, situated on the lake side, in the heart of the old town of Vevey. Only 50 minutes from Geneva airport, 10 minutes from Lausanne and Montreux, Vevey is the ideal base to discover the "Swiss Riviera" which offers the best of nature and urban life.
Cruise the Lake of Geneva on a steam boat to the world famous Chateau de Chillon. **Reach** the surrounding hill tops with funicular or cogwheel trains, and enjoy a breathtaking view over the Lake of Geneva and the Alps. **Discover** the ancestral winemaker villages and practise some local wine tasting. **Ski resorts** are reachable in less than one hour by car or public transport. Get for **free** the **"tourist info pass"** with more than CHF 250 reduction on different activities and excursions. The Riviera Lodge offers accommodation in rooms for 2,4,6 and 8 people. There are toilets and showers on each floor, a fully equipped kitchen, breakfast buffet (CHF 8), laundry facilities, TV/video, internet access and a panoramic roof terrace with views of the surrounding lake and the vineyards.

www.rivieralodge.ch

CONTACT Francois Commend, Tel: +41 21 923 8040 fax: +41 21 923 8041 Email: info@rivieralodge.ch
OPENING SEASON All year
OPENING HOURS 08:00-12:00 and 16:00 - 20:00
NUMBER OF BEDS 60
BOOKING REQUIREMENTS Tel, fax or email in advance please.
PRICE PER NIGHT From €19 (CHF26) to €28 (CHF40) per person.

PUBLIC TRANSPORT
Bus/train every 15 mins Montreux/Lausanne. 50 mins by train from Geneva Airport

DIRECTION
From highway exit at Vevey, following signs to centre of town and "place du marche". From the train station walk about 2 minutes in direction of the lake and you will join the market place. Riviera Lodge is on the right side.

BACKPACKERS VILLA INTERLAKEN

Alpenstrasse 16
3800 Interlaken
SWITZERLAND

Backpackers Villa Sonnenhof is centrally located in a villa with a park, just ten minutes' walk from either the West or Ost train stations in the town of Interlaken. Our staff have plenty of experience and adventure activities can be arranged like river rafting, canyoning, bungee jumping, paragliding, skiing and snowboarding.

The hostel has a friendly atmosphere. All rooms are clean and most come with Jungfrau-view balconies. There is no curfew or lockout and membership is not required. Facilities include free hot showers on every floor - just what you need after all those activities, fully equipped kitchen, laundry service, table soccer, billiards, internet access or you can get away from it and refresh in the meditation room. Visit our website, you can book online.

www.villa.ch

CONTACT Tel: +41 33 826 71 71, Fax: +41 33 826 71 72,
Email: backpackers@villa.ch
OPENING SEASON All year except November (closed)
OPENING HOURS Reception 7.30-11.00am and 4.00-9.00pm
NUMBER OF BEDS; 80:- 3 x 2 2 x 3 4 x 4 2 x 5 7 x 6
BOOKING REQUIREMENTS Please book using your credit card as guarantee, by telephone or web page.
PRICE PER NIGHT dorm CHF29-38 (€19-€25) **double** CHF44-53 (€29-€35) **triple** CHF39-48 (€26-€32) **quad** CHF 34-43 (€23-€29) Prices per person include sheets, breakfast and taxes.

PUBLIC TRANSPORT
Walking distance from Interlaken West or Ost train stations or take bus No2 to stop; Sekundarschulhaus.

DIRECTIONS
In the centre of Interlaken at Höhematte (large greenfield). Follow the brown signs from the stations - just 10 minutes' walk.

swiss Backpackers

DOWNTOWN LODGE

Dorfzentrum
3818 Grindelwald
SWITZERLAND

Downtown lodge is situated in the heart of Grindelwald centre, with a breathtaking view of the mountains and glaciers. Cable cars, trains, shops and bars are just around the corner.

Downtown Lodge provides clean and comfortable dorms and double rooms, a great breakfast buffet, self-catering kitchen, TV, laundry facilities, games room with pool, billiards and table football, free entrance to the swimming pool nearby and .. and .. everything that a backpacker's heart wishes.

For groups there are three lodges with own dormitories, fully equipped kitchen and lounge room.

www.downtown-lodge.ch

CONTACT Edi Portman, Tel: (0041) 33 853 08 25,
Email: downtown-lodge@jungfrau.ch
OPENING SEASON All Year
OPENING HOURS Reception open 7.30 till 12 and 4 till 8. Late check- in till 12 pm.
NUMBER OF BEDS 92: 2x2, 4x4, 6x6, 3x8
BOOKING REQUIREMENTS Book on our web page, by email, fax or phone
PRICE PER NIGHT CHF 35 (approx €23.50) Price includes sheets, breakfast buffet and taxes.

PUBLIC TRANSPORT
Grindelwald train station is 5 minutes' walk from hostel.

DIRECTIONS
From the train station follow the main street to the city centre. After 5 minutes you will see the hotel sign on the right in front of the 'minigolf' place.

GIMMELWALD MOUNTAIN HOSTEL

3826 Gimmelwald
SWITZERLAND

The Hostel is a beautiful old renovated building with a lot of charm, where we aim to give you a happy holiday. The hostel is in the centre of the skiing area in a small village where 110 people live all year round. Come up and check it, you will love it.

Gimmelwald lies on a sunny mountain-side in the heart of the marvellous winter sports and hiking paradise of the Schilthorn area. This small mountain village is an ideal starting point for hikes in the romantic countryside with its towering rock faces, cascading waterfalls, mountain forests, meadows ablaze with flowers and a wonderful variety of fauna.

www.mountainhostel.com

CONTACT Petra or Walter. Tel/Fax: 0041 033 855 17 04.
Email: mountainhostel@tcnet.ch
OPENING SEASON All year, 365 days.
OPENING HOURS 8.30am to 23.30pm
NUMBER OF BEDS 50
BOOKING REQUIREMENTS Book by email or phone
PRICE PER NIGHT CHF20

PUBLIC TRANSPORT Interlaken Ost change train to Lauterbrunnen. In Lauterbrunnen take bus to Stechelberg, from here take cable car to Gimmelwald. Interlaken to Gimmelwald 1 hour cost: CHF25 round trip.

DIRECTIONS
Ask for Mountain Hostel.

swiss Backpackers

MATTERHORN HOSTEL

Schlumattstrasse 32
3920 Zermatt
SWITZERLAND

This friendly hostel is centrally situated in the heart of Zermatt at the foot of the famous Matterhorn mountain, from which it takes its name. It makes an excellent base for a skiing holiday in the winter months and is close to the ski lifts. Matterhorn Hostel is a traditional Swiss chalet-style building which provides basic, comfortable and cosy accommodation. There is an international atmosphere and the staff are young and helpful.

The hostel is clean, comfortable and safe with a bar, restaurant and a pay phone. Showers are free and lockers are provided in all rooms. A TV and internet terminal are available for guests to use. Matterhorn Hostel can sleep 56 people and rooms have either 2, 4, 5, 6 or 8 beds. There is no lockout and no curfew. Breakfast, lunch and dinner are available on request. Have fun, feel at home and meet travellers from all over the world!

www.matterhornhostel.com

CONTACT Ruh Patrick, Tel: +41 27 968 1919,
Email: info@matterhornhostel.com
OPENING SEASON All year
OPENING HOURS All day, reception is open from 7.30am - 11am and from 4pm to 10pm
NUMBER OF BEDS 56
BOOKING REQUIREMENTS Book by fax or email.
PRICE PER NIGHT From €19 (CHF 29)

PUBLIC TRANSPORT
There is a train station in Zermatt.

DIRECTIONS
From the train station, walk up the main street. Turn left by the church and cross a large bridge. After the bridge, go to the right and the hostel is on the right hand side after about 200 metres.

CITY BACKPACKER HOTEL BIBER

Niederdorfstrasse 5
8001 Zurich
SWITZERLAND

The City Backpacker is a friendly hostel situated in the heart of Zurich's picturesque Old Town. Most of the tourist sites and many places of interest are within walking distance including a lake, museum, bars, disco, nightlife and parks.

All the things that a backpacker needs are available at the hostel. We have a self-catering kitchen, showers and washing machine. There is also a nice terrace and common room with internet station and a book-exchange. We have a luggage store and offer discounts on Swiss army knives.

For information and reservations just phone, fax, write or send an email. Check it out and see you soon ......**book online at :-**

www.city-backpacker.ch

CONTACT Receptionist, Tel: +41 44 251 90 15
Fax: +41 44 251 90 24 : Email: sleep@city-backpacker.ch
OPENING SEASON All year
OPENING HOURS Check in 0800 to 1200 and 1500 to 2200 hrs. No curfew once you have checked in.
NUMBER OF BEDS 65:- 6 x 6 : 4 x 4 : 5 x 2 : 3 x 1
BOOKING REQUIREMENTS Booking by phone, fax or email is advisable in summer months.
PRICE PER NIGHT CHF 31.

PUBLIC TRANSPORT
Zurich is well connected to mainland Europe by rail and coach services. The hostel is in the Old Town and only 10 minutes' walk from the main railway station.

DIRECTIONS
From the main railway station cross the river Limmat and take a right into the old town. Follow Niederdorfstrasse until No. 5. (Niederdorfstrasse is the main walking street in the Old Town).

HOSTAL LIS II

Olavide No. 5
41001
Seville
SPAIN

Hostal Lis II is situated in the centre of Sevilla in a pedestrianised street, near the finest monuments and main commercial centre. The hostel is in an old Sevillana building converted to current use in 1992. It offers comfortable rooms at the best prices. Internet connection and laundry service. Buses and taxis are available at any hour and public telephones and the post office are nearby.

Seville is an energetic city with impressive relics from Moorish and Medieval eras. There are two major festivals each year, the Semana Santa just before Easter, and the April Feria, in the last week of April. Hostal Lis II will guarantee your comfort and offers tranquillity in the centre of the city. It is near "La Campana" the official start route of the Semana Santa parade. Our staff are happy to tell you about Seville and to make your stay enjoyable.

CONTACT Juan Antonio Delgado, Tel: 00 34 954560228
Email: lisdos@lisdos.net
OPENING SEASON All Year
OPENING HOURS 24 Hours
NUMBER OF BEDS 19
BOOKING REQUIREMENTS The first night must be paid for in advance.
PRICE PER NIGHT Single €25, Double €38, Triple €62, Quad €76

PUBLIC TRANSPORT
From airport take bus to Puerta Jerez. From there walk to Plaza Magdalene and proceed to Olavide. From train station take bus no. 32 to Plaza Encarnation. From there walk to Plaza Campana and on to C/. San Eloy. Hostal Lis II is 2nd on left.

DIRECTIONS
Arriving from S.E. Follow signs to Centre. From Plaza Magdalena go down C/. O'Donnell and take first turning on left.

HOSTAL DEL PILAR

Calle Mesconcillo No.4
off Calle Peral, Old Town
Marbella 29600
SPAIN

Hostal Del Pilar has been British run since 1983. It has a bar with pool table and an attractive roof terrace. During the winter months there is a log fire in the bar area. Hearty English breakfasts and various snacks are available.

The Hostal is centrally situated in Marbella's picturesque old town, close to many affordable restaurants and bars. Hostal Del Pilar has proved extremely popular with backpackers due to its social scene and being an ideal place to meet new people and have fun.

www.marbella-marbella.com

CONTACT Tel: +34 952 829936
Email: hostel@hostel-marbella.com
OPENING SEASON All year
OPENING HOURS 10.30am to 12.00 midnight
NUMBER OF BEDS 30
BOOKING REQUIREMENTS 2-3 days notice please
PRICE PER NIGHT From €15pp

PUBLIC TRANSPORT
Train station and Airport Malaga, direct buses to Marbella Bus Station.

DIRECTIONS
From Bus Station; bus number 2 or 7 to The New Market, Avenida Mercado. The Hostal is opposite the Market down the steps, around the corner on left, 2nd entrance opposite the English Tavern in Calle Peral.

PUIG CAMPANA MOUNTAIN CLIMBING REFUGIO

The Travellers Friend
Font Del Moli 36
03509 Finestrat, Alicante
SPAIN

The Climbing Refugio is a collection of self-contained studios and apartments at the base of the Puig Campana Mountain, only minutes from the start of the climbing and walking routes. The Refugio is newly built in rustic Spanish style using reclaimed materials and kept meticulously clean. It has panoramic views of the mountains and the sea, and a BBQ area set amongst lemon and orange groves. The picturesque village of Finestrat with its many fine bars, restaurants and shops is only a short walk away and it is only a five minute drive from the coastal resort of Benidorm and La Cala.

The Single Studio sleeps 1 or 2 people in single beds. The Studio sleeps 2 or 3 people in a double bed and a single bed. The One Bedroom Apartment sleeps 2 to 4 in a double bed and a double sofa bed. The Two Bedroom Apartment sleeps 4 to 6 people with a comfortable double bed room, and a bedroom with bunkbeds.

www.thetravellersfriend.com

CONTACT Martin Herglotz, Tel: +34 647258901,
Email: martinherglotz@hotmail.com
OPENING SEASON All Year
OPENING HOURS 24 Hours
NUMBER OF BEDS 21: 2 x 6/7, 1x4, 1x3, 1x2
BOOKING REQUIREMENTS Phone with credit card, 20% deposit
PRICE PER NIGHT Price per week (or any part of) Single Studio £90-£150, Studio £150-£190, 1 bed Apart. £190-250, 2 bed Apart. £250-£390

PUBLIC TRANSPORT
Minibus collection from Alicante airport (we also organise flights).

DIRECTIONS
From Alicante take A7-A332 north towards Valencia or Barcelona. At Benidorm follow signs to Finestrat.

P

AUBERGE DE JEUNESSE CAHORS

20 rue Frederic Suisse
46000 Cahors
FRANCE

The youth hostel of Cahors occupies a medieval building which was once an ancient convent. The building has an ambiance of the middle ages which accords well with the medieval town around it. Cahors, with its ancient streets and some of the finest medieval architecture in France has rich picking for the tourists. These monuments include the Valentre bridge which has spanned the river 'Le Lot' for over 500 years, the Ramparts, the Barbican and Roman remains. This area of France is known for its good food and wine and Cahors is famous for truffles, and a dark wine originally produced by the Romans. There is a traditional Saturday morning market.

The youth hostel is in the middle of the town, close to the GR 36 and 65, and only 500m from the station. The hostel has various rooms of 2 to 10 beds. There is a restaurant which serves meals and automatic hot and cold drinks machines. The hostels has a television room, a reading room and a laundry room. There is also a bike shelter for those using this perfect form of transport to explore the surrounding rural landscape with its sleepy villages.

CONTACT Tel: +33 5 65 35 64 71, Fax: + 33 5 65 35 95 92
Email: fjt46@wanadoo.fr
OPENING SEASON All Year
OPENING HOURS 24 Hours
NUMBER OF BEDS 56 : 2 x 10; 2 x 8; 2 x 6; 2 x 3; 1 x 2
BOOKING REQUIREMENTS Please phone in advance.
PRICE PER NIGHT €9.50 per person

PUBLIC TRANSPORT
The hostel is 5 minutes' walk from the train station.

DIRECTIONS
From the train station take rue Joachim Nurat, turning right onto rue de la Chartreuse after 300m. Take 2nd left is rue Frederic Suisse, on which the hostel is situated.

BED & BREAKFAST

42 rue Poissonnière
75002 Paris
FRANCE

Our cheerful hideaway lies in the very heart of Paris. Thanks to it's convenient location between Les Halles, the Marais, the upscale opera district and the Picasso Museum, it is the ideal base from which to explore the unique atmosphere of Paris and its stunning attractions. In the evening enjoy the nightlife and many restaurants or take in a movie at Europe's largest cinema palace, Le Rex, just across the street. We have no curfew.

Bed and Breakfast is comfortable and respectable and its owner, Michael, who is fluent in English, Spanish, Hebrew and Arabic welcomes all ages, groups and families. The hostel offers four, six and eight bed rooms all with satellite TV, stereo and heaters. There are full toilet facilities and hot showers are also available if you need to freshen up after a busy day of sightseeing. Sheets, blankets, towels and a copious breakfast are included in the price.

CONTACT Tel: + 33 14 02 68 308, Fax: + 33 14 02 68 791
OPENING SEASON All year
OPENING HOURS All day
NUMBER OF BEDS 50
BOOKING REQUIREMENTS Recommended by phone or fax - best to phone in advance to arrange arrival time.
PRICE PER NIGHT €15 per person (including breakfast and bedding) No credit cards.

PUBLIC TRANSPORT
The nearest train stations, Gare du Nord and Gare de l'Est, are 10 minutes from the hostel. From airport or rail stations take the Metro line 8 or 9 to Bonne Nouvelle stop.

DIRECTIONS
From Bonne Nouvelle Metro station, take exit marked Boulevard Poissonniere. Walk to Rex cinema, (you can see Rex sign from the metro exit). At Rex cinema turn left to Rue Poissonniere.

ALOHA HOSTEL

1 rue Borronée
75015
Paris
FRANCE

Aloha Hostel is centrally located, within easy walking distance of Paris' most famous sights : the Eiffel Tower, the Arc de Triumph, the Champs Elysees, the Musee Rodin, the Musee des Armees and the lively Boulevard Montparnasse. With a Metro station only a stone's throw away from our door the rest of Paris can easily be discovered.

At Aloha we have newly renovated 4-6 bedred rooms with traditional Parisian decor. Private double rooms are also available. A free breakfast is served each morning and to prepare other meals we provide our guests with a fully equipped kitchen. A variety of supermarkets, laundromats, bakeries and a post office are all found nearby. At night you can have cheap drinks, music and special events (like film nights) in a cool cosmopolitan atmosphere.

www.aloha.fr

CONTACT Tel: + 33 1 42 73 03 03 , Email: friends@aloha.fr
OPENING SEASON All Year
OPENING HOURS 8am to 2 pm
NUMBER OF BEDS 120
BOOKING REQUIREMENTS Booking is essential
PRICE PER NIGHT €16 in winter, € 22 in summer

PUBLIC TRANSPORT
From Charles de Gaulle airport take RER line B train to Paris and get off at Denfert Rochereau. Here take metro line 6 in direction of Charles de Gaulle Etoile until Pasteur. Here change to line 12, direction Mairie d'Issy and get off at Volontaires. From Volontaires take a right and first left, and rue Borronée is on your left.

DIRECTIONS
You could take Metro line 4 in Porte d'Orleans direction changing at gare Montparnasse to line 12 in Mairie d'Issy direction. Get off at Volontaires. Leaving the metro station turn right and first left and rue Borronée is on your left.

P H AM

PASSAGE

Dweersstraat 26
8000 Brugge / Bruges
BELGIUM

Passage, an 18th-century house situated in the heart of medieval Bruges, offers accommodation in 2 x 7-bedded rooms, 2 x 6-bedded rooms, and 6 x 4-bedded rooms. For more privacy family rooms and double rooms are also available in the small luxury house next door.

With it's hardwood floors and high ceilings, a stay at Passage will give you the impression of travelling through time. The cosy bar has a great art-deco style and the restaurant offers a wide variety of world-famous Belgian beers and traditional Belgian cuisine. There's even a section for vegetarians.

Recommended by Let's Go, Rough Guide, Lonely Planet, Berkeley Guide, Frommers, and Le Guide du Routard, Passage is the place to be... for its character, personality, wonderful cosmopolitan atmosphere and typical Belgian cuisine. We are also Bruges' most central hostel.

www.passagebruges.com

CONTACT Vandedorpe Sabine. Tel +32 50 340232.
Fax + 32 50 340140. Email info@passagebruges.com
OPENING SEASON All year
OPENING HOURS Reception open 8.30am till approximately midnight. Night access is available by using a code.
NUMBER OF BEDS 50 + 24 in building next door.
BOOKING REQUIREMENTS Booking is recommended, by fax, email or telephone.
PRICE PER NIGHT From €12 per person Youth Hostel. Doubles €40 for two persons in hotel, breakfast included.

PUBLIC TRANSPORT
Bruges is well connected by train and coach services.

DIRECTIONS
The hostel is downtown just 10 minutes' walk from the train station. From the station follow Mainstreet and take the first street on the left. We are just opposite Parking Zilverpand.

P H

BEST WESTERN NEW HOTEL DE LIVES

Ch. DeLiege 1178
B-5101 Namur
(Lives-sur-Meuse)
BELGIUM

New Hotel de Lives is nicely situated on the banks of the River Meuse and only 6km away from the train station and the centre of Namur. The hotel is easily accessible from the motorway.

The main building has 10 private rooms + 10 new rooms in the hotel annex fully equipped with colour TV, and bath or shower.

In the morning we offer you a large buffet breakfast and in the evening you can relax in our comfortable pub and try our different local beers. Restaurant open from 1200-1700 and 1800-2200.

Our multi-language staff will help you and will give you a personal welcome. Pick-up service on request.

www.newhoteldelives.com.

CONTACT Francis. Tel: + 32 81 58 05 13.
E-mail: info@newhoteldelives.com
OPENING SEASON All year
OPENING HOURS All day
NUMBER OF BEDS 20 rooms
BOOKING REQUIREMENTS Book by phone, fax, email, or post. Credit cards accepted.
PRICE PER NIGHT €59 to €130 per room including buffet breakfast.

PUBLIC TRANSPORT
Take the No 12 Bus from Namur Station. Bus stops at hotel.

DIRECTIONS
Namur is at the cross roads between two major highways E411/E421, 3km away from the Brussels/Luxembourg motorway E411 exit No 15 (**Loyers** (Namure sud) direction **Andenne** (N90). The hotel is situated on the river bank.

GREEK YOUTH HOSTEL ORGANISATION

75 Damareos Str.
Athens 11633
Tel: +30210 751 9530/Fax 0616
Email: skokin@hol.gr
Email: y-hostels@otenet.gr

We welcome you to Greece and are happy to offer you accommodation with the famous traditional Greek hospitality in the following places:-

ATHENS

Athens Youth Hostel
75 Damareos Str
Athens 11633
+30 210 7519530.Fax:7510616
Email: skokin@hol.gr
Email: y-hostels@otenet.gr
Manager Yiannis Triandafillou

MACEDONIA

Thessaloniki Youth Hostel
44 Alexandre Svolou Str
Tel: +30 2310 225946
Fax: +30 2310 262208
Manager Fedon Siskos

PELOPONNESE

Patra Youth Hostel
62 Heroon Politechniou Str
Patra, Peloponnese,GR
Tel: +30 2610 427278/222707
Fax: +302 610 452152
Manager Theodoros Vazouras

Olympia Youth Hostel
18 Praxitelous - Kondili Str
Tel:+ 30 26240 22580 Fax 23125
Manager Dimitrios Lolos

CRETE

Heraklio Youth Hostel
5 Vironos Str
Tel:+30 2810 286281.Fax 222947
Manager Ioannis Koukoulakis

Rethimno Youth Hostel
45 Tobazi Str
Tel: +30 28310 22848
Email: yh_rethymno@yahoo.com
Manager Emmanuel Kalogerakis

Plakias Youth Hostel
Province Agiou Vassiliou
Nomos Rethimnou
Tel: +30 28320 32118/31560
Fax +30 28320 31939
Manager Frederikos Kalogerakis

CYCLADES

Thira Youth Hostel
Fira, Santorini
Tel: +30 22860 22387
Tel: +30 22860 23864
Manager Georgios Koustoulidis

Perissa Youth Hostel
Perissa, Santorini
Tel: +30 22860 82182/81943
Manager Panagiotis Fiorentis

Oia Youth Hostel
Oia, Santorini
Tel/Fax +30 22860 71465
Manager Markos Karvounis
Open May to October

Australian Capital Territory

Canberra

Nomads City Walk Hotel
Ph 1800 600 124 (Australia only)
Fax +61 (0)2 6257 0116

Victoria

Melbourne

Nomads Market Inn
Ph +61 (0)3 9690 2220
Fax +61 (0)3 9690 2544

Nomads Chapel Street Backpackers
Ph +61 (0)3 9533 6855
Fax +61 (0)3 9533 6866

Nomads Pint-on-Punt —Windsor
Ph +61 (0)3 9510 4273
Fax +61 (0)3 9529 5518

Nomads Hotel Claremont
Ph +61 (0)3 9826 8000
Fax +61 (0)3 9827 8652

All Nations St Kilda
Ph +61 (0)3 9534 0300
Fax +61 (0)3 9534 0308

Echuca

Nomads Oasis Backpackers
Ph +61 (0)3 5480 7866
Fax +61 (0)3 5480 7867

Mildura

Nomads Juicy Grape International Backpackers
Ph +61 (0)3 5024 2112
Fax +61 (0)3 5024 2112

South Australia

Adelaide

Nomads Raglans Central Backpackers
Ph (08) 8231 4602
Fax (08) 8410 0921

Nomads Adelaide Travellers Inn Backpackers
Ph (08) 8224 0753
Fax (08) 8224 0753

Kingston

Nomads Kingston on Murray
Ph (08) 8583 0211
Fax (08) 8583 0206

Wilpena Pound (Flinders Ranges)

Wilpena Pound Resort
Ph (08) 8648 0004
Fax (08) 8648 0028

Western Australia

Perth

Nomads Billabong Resort
Ph (08) 9328 7720
Fax (08) 9328 7721

Nomads Underground Backpackers
Ph (08) 9228 3755
Fax (08) 9228 3744

Fremantle

Nomads Sundancer Backpackers Resort
Ph (08) 9336 6080
Fax (08) 9335 6088

www.nomadsworld.com

Broome

Nomads Kimberley Klub
Ph (08) 9192 3233
Fax (08) 9192 3530

Mackerel Island

Club Thevenard
Ph (08) 9184 6444

Northern Territory

Darwin

Nomads the Cavenagh
Ph (08) 8941 6383
Fax (08) 8941 4541

Melaleuca on Mitchell
Ph (08) 8941 7800

Kakadu National Park

Aurora Kakadu
Ph 1800 818 845 (Australia only)
Fax (08) 8979 0147

Alice Springs

Nomads Toddy's Backpackers
Ph (08) 8952 1322
Fax (08) 8952 1767

Nomads Heavitree Gap Outback Lodge
Ph (08) 8950 4444
Fax (08) 8952 9394

Ayers Rock

Outback Pioneer Lodge
Ph (08) 9339 1040
Fax (08) 9332 4555

Kings Canyon

Kings Canyon Resort
Ph (08) 8956 7660
Fax (08) 8956 7410

Tasmania

Hobart

Central City Backpackers
Ph +61 (0)3 6224 2404

Launceston

The Devils Playground
Ph +61 (0)3 6343 3119

Huon Valley

Nomads Huon Valley Backpackers
Ph +61 (0)3 6295 1551

Queensland

Surfers Paradise

Nomads Islander Backpackers Resort
Ph +61 (0)7 5538 8000
Fax +61 (0)7 5592 2762

Brisbane

Prince Consort Hotel
Ph +61 (0)7 3257 2252
Fax +61 (0)7 3252 4130

Tinbilly Travellers
Ph +61 (0)7 3238 5888

Hervey Bay

Beaches Backpackers
Ph +61 (0)7 4124 1322
Fax +61 (0)7 4124 1366

Nomads Happy Wanderer Village
Ph +61 (0)7 4125 1103
Fax +61 (0)7 4125 3895

Bundaberg

Nomads Bundaberg Workers and Diving Hostel
Ph +61 (0)7 4151 6097
Fax +61 (0)7 4151 7277

Airlie Beach

Bush Village Resort
Ph +61 (0)7 4946 6177
Fax +61 (0)7 4946 7227

Townsville

Civic Guest House
Ph +61 (0)7 4771 5381

Magnetic Island

Nomads Maggies Beach House
Ph +61 (0)7 4778 5144
Fax +61 (0)7 4778 5194

Cairns

Nomads Serpent Hostel & Bar
Ph +61 (0)7 4040 7777
Fax +61 (0)7 4031 8401

Port Douglas

Dougies Nomads Backpackers
Ph +61 (0)7 4099 6200
Fax +61 (0)7 4099 6047

New Zealand

Auckland

The Fat Camel Hostel & Bar
Ph +64 9 307 0181

Rotorua

Treks Backpackers
Ph +64 7 349 4088

Christchurch

New Excelsior Backpackers
Ph +64 3 366 7570

Fiji

Nadi

Nomads Skylodge
Ph +679 672 2200

Malolo Island

The Resort Walu Beach
Ph +679 665 1777

Momi Bay

Seashell Cove Resort
Ph +679 670 6100

ST. CLAIR HOTEL

577 Richards Street
Vancouver,
British Columbia V6B2Z5
CANADA

Located right downtown close to Chinatown and Gastown. You may walk to restaurants, nightclubs, buses (local for Vancouver Island), skytrain, north Vancouver Ferry, Stadium and Ice Hockey Arena.

This heritage listed building was built in 1911 by Henry Pybus, captain of the Canadian Pacific steamship "Empress of Japan" which took the blue ribbon while setting the Trans-Pacific crossing record 1887. The hotel originally accommodated railway and ocean going travellers returning to both Pacific and Atlantic.

A nautical theme is retained, 34 private rooms, 12 per floor, showers on each floor, no dorms, all linen provided, parking facilities in same block. City bus from airport one block at "The Hudson Bay Department Store".

www.sourceenterprises.bc.ca

CONTACT Manager Tel: +604 684-3713. Toll free (USACanada) 1-800-982-0220. Email: sourceentvan@telus.net
OPENING SEASON All year round
OPENING HOURS 24 hours. Check in 8-30am/10-30pm, no curfew.
NUMBER OF BEDS 77: 3x1 : 24x2 : 6x3 : 2x4
BOOKING REQUIREMENTS Book ahead if possible
PRICE PER NIGHT C$27 single room, C$39 double room, C$45 triple room. Weekly single C$140, weekly double C$210. All private

PUBLIC TRANSPORT
Buses operate from local Airport, Greyhound and rail station.

DIRECTIONS
From train station or Greyhound take Sky Train to Granville Station, at The Hudson Bay Department Store. From Airport take bus #424 change at airport station, board 98"B" line to Granville Station (skytrain stop). Walk to Dunsmuire, turn right, first left into Richards Street.

THUNDER BAY INTERNATIONAL HOSTEL

RR 13, 1594, Lakeshore Drive,
Thunder Bay, Ontario P7B 5E4
CANADA

Thunder Bay Hostel is located on an ancient delta of the Mackenzie River. The grounds are forested with pines and spruces on a rocky outcrop. There are several beaver dams within a km radius of the hostel, bears at the local dump (2 km) and other wild animals: such as raccoon, skunk, porcupine, deer, lynx, coyote and wolf in the area.

The main attractions close by are Mackenzie Point, Mackenzie River (swimming), Lake Superior (swimming, cross-country skiing in season) and Silver Harbour Park (rock climbing). This is the closest hostel to Ouimet Canyon and Sleeping Giant Provincial Park.

US visitors should change money at a bank before coming to hostel. No Visa, Mastercard,Iinterac. ATM available at Mackenzie Inn, I km.

Headquarters for Backpackers Hostels Canada

www.backpackers.ca

CONTACT Lloyd, Willa, or manager. Tel: (807) 983-2042, Fax: (807) 983-2914, Email: info@thuderbayhostel.com
OPENING SEASON All year
OPENING HOURS 24 hours (be reasonable)
NUMBER OF BEDS approx. 40
BOOKING REQUIREMENTS No booking necessary
PRICE PER NIGHT C$20.00

PUBLIC TRANSPORT
Hostel is 18km east of Thunder Bay Ikm south of 11-17 highway, (Lakeshore Drive parallels for 20 km) at Mackenzie Station Rd and Lakeshore Drive, Ikm east of intersection with 11-17 hwy. Sign on main highway in both directions

DIRECTIONS
The Greyhound bus will drop you off at the highway and pick you up at Mackenzie Station Road, Ikm from the hostel upon request. Cyclists should use Lakeshore Drive (there are no hills).

BACKPACKERS HOSTELS CANADA
AUBERGES BACKPACKERS CANADA
2005

Over 100 Backpackers Hostels to serve you across Canada.

Our motto is: clean, safe, friendly hospitable facilities across the country. All ages welcome

Information www.backpackers.ca

Want to start or invest in a new Canadian hostel? Let us know.
info@backpackers.ca

Headquarters: BHC/ABC, Longhouse Village, RR 13, Thunder Bay, ON P7B 5E4 Canada
(807) 983-2042 (807) 983-2914

CONTACTS UK AND IRELAND

Mountaineering Council of Scotland. National representative body for Scottish hill walking and climbing clubs with over 130 club huts across the UK. www.mountaineering-scotland.org.uk. See page 288.

IBHS Independent Backpackers Hostels of Scotland, For a free leaflet to approximately 100 hostels in Scotland. see page **249**

SUSTRANS National cycle network. see pages **70,71**

CTC - the UK's national cyclists' organisation campaigning for on and off-road cyclists in the UK. Membership from £12 per year. CTC Cotterell House, 69 Meadrow, Godalming, Surrey GU7 3HS.
Tel. 0870 873 0060 Email cycling@ctc.org.uk www.ctc.org.uk

The Ramblers' Association Walk Britain 2005 is indispensable for walkers in Britain. In addition to its extensive accommodation guide for walkers it also tells you your rights and responsibilities in the countryside, public transport information, details of over 60 long distance paths, walking holiday providers and listings of countryside organisations, local authorities and Ramblers' publications. Members receive a free copy of Walk 2005 plus four magazines each year as well as supporting Britain's biggest charity working to promote walking and improve conditions for all walkers, no matter what their age, ability and background. Contact The Ramblers' Association, 2nd Floor, 87-90 Albert Embankment, London SE1 7TW Tel 020 7339 8500. www.ramblers.org.uk. email: ramblers@london.ramblers.org.uk

LDWA Long Distance Walkers Association: For those who enjoy long distance walking. Membership benefits include reduced entry fees to our renowned challenge events, a thriving programme of group social walks and activities and our magazine Strider, produced three times a year and packed with articles, information and expert advice. In addition the Long Distance Walkers Handbook and companion Chart details over 600 long distance paths in the UK. For details of membership contact:- LDWA, 63 Yockley Close, The Maultway, Camberley, Surrey, GU15 1QQ or visit www.ldwa.org.uk. For the handbook and chart contact, Merchandising Officer, 2 Sandy Lane, Beeston, Nottingham, NG9 3GS. The handbook is also available from all good booksellers, ISBN 0 7136609 6 1, price £12.99. For details of long distance routes contact Les Maple, 21 Upcroft, Windsor, Berks, SL4 3NH. see page **252**

The Backpackers Club, UK based club for the lightweight camper information on camping in the UK and abroad. For details contact:- Peter and Carol Shiner, 117 Swinford Road, Selly Oak, Birmingham B29 5SH. e-mail pc@shiner117.freeserve.co.uk

IHO, Independent Hostel Owners of Ireland. see page **292**

IHH, Independent Holiday Hostels of Ireland. A co-operative society of over 100 tourist board approved hostels throughout Ireland. No membership required / all ages welcome / open all day. Welcoming, comfortable, reasonably-priced accommodation offering private rooms, dorms, family rooms and en-suite. The IHH Guide is a colourful, easy-to-use hostel guide - a handy reference tool when touring Ireland. For a copy, call IHH at +353 (0)1 836 4700 or email IHH at info@hostels-ireland.com IHH website: www.hostels-ireland.com

Irish HostellingOnline see page **292**

CONTACTS WORLDWIDE

New Zealand BBH Backpackers Accommodation Guide. A 108 page guide listing 350+ hostels with BPP% customer satisfaction ratings. Available free and post free from BBH NZ, 208 Kilmore St, Christchurch, NZ. BBH now has a NZ$40 BBH Club Card that guarantees preferential member prices at BBH hostels and includes $20 of economical phone calls. **www.bbh.co.nz.** email ihginfo@backpack.co.nz. See page **355**

VIP Backpackers Resorts International, Riverbank House, 1 Putney Bridge Approach, London, SW6 3JD, Telephone/Fax 020 77364200, email: UKoffice@vipbackpackers.com For more information about hostels and membership check out www.vipbackpackers.com

NOMADS WORLD Email info@nomadsworld. see pages **356-359**

Backpackers Hostels Canada/Auberge Backpackers Canada. A network of 117 hostels, see page **362**

Gomio.com, run by Europe's independent hostels, aims to provide the budget traveller with everything they need to explore Europe, including country and city guides, a backpacking community through the forums, travel tips and links, and online hostel bookings.